INFANT
CULTURE

INFANT CULTURE

Jane Flannery Jackson
and
Joseph H. Jackson

Thomas Y. Crowell, Publishers
Established 1834   New York

FIRST EDITION

Designed by Janice Stern

Library of Congress Cataloging in Publication Data

Jackson, Jane Flannery.
  Infant culture.
  Bibliography: p.
  Includes index.
  1. Infants. 2. Infant psychology. I. Jackson, Joseph Hollister, joint author. II. Title.
HQ774.J33 1978   155.4'22   78-4351
ISBN 0-690-01670-0

---

78 79 80 81 82 10 9 8 7 6 5 4 3 2 1

. . . I had not the smallest conception that there was so much in a five-month baby.

Charles Darwin

To T. A. J.

whose infant culture we were
privileged to study in depth

CONTENTS

Foreword

The authors of *Infant Culture* have provided an invaluable service to those unfamiliar with the voluminous recent research that depicts infants as having far more affective, cognitive, and communicative abilities than naïve observers usually presume. *Infant Culture* is quite remarkable in accomplishing the aim of cogently and clearly presenting selected research findings "to parents, to those who deal with babies professionally, and to readers with a dash of curiosity about their beginnings." In addition, the book may be tremendously helpful to students who are beginning to explore the research literature on infants.

Infant Culture describes many of the recent keystone research endeavors with infants carried out by developmental psychologists, particularly in the area of social development and communication, and provides complete and, to our knowledge, accurate documentation. In areas where there is research on adults or animals that the Jacksons deem similar, interesting, and relevant to the infancy findings, they report it and note its connection to the infancy research. Description of the infant experiments is exceptional in that it usually includes the numbers and special characteristics of the infants studied, the methodology employed, some conflicting research findings, and, at times, alternative explanations for the findings. Yet the book is not a tedious compilation of research results. For, in this preliminary sketch of investigators' attempts to paint a portrait of infants, the Jacksons have captured the dynamism of much of current infant research.

T. Berry Brazelton, M.D., Chief
Nancy Kozak, Psychologist

Child Development Unit
Children's Hospital Medical Center
Boston, Massachusetts

Preface

In books still loading library stacks, newborn babies are called "unconscious," "decerebrate," or "cerebrally insufficient," "incomplete, helpless creatures," who are "cognitively confused." Babies, it has been asserted, not only learn more slowly than the monkey, but are outstripped by the cat, the dog, and even the lowly rat. Opossums and kangaroos are still fetuses at birth, but it is not they but human infants who have been declared to be less capable of fending for themselves than any other newborn organism. The newborn's mental structure has been presumed so fuzzy that accurate measurement of his or her capacities has been ruled out. Most discouraging of all, perhaps, is the claim that nothing that occurs in the first year of life is soundly predictive of what an infant will become—leaving parents at the end of a very long limb indeed.

From the past decade or two of intense scientific preoccupation with the newborn period and early infancy, a new concept of the infant is taking shape, one totally at variance with the traditional picture. Through their investigators, infants have at last begun to answer their detractors. But the facts now known about infants in their first year are not easily come by. The findings of an army of investigators now studying the infant lie hidden in hundreds of volumes containing literally thousands of research reports and symposia detailing almost every aspect of infant behavior. Even professionals cannot always cope with this flood of information, and so it is to be expected that little of this exciting new knowledge has filtered down to the large public, who, in one way or another, take care of or are simply interested in babies.

Infant Culture is our attempt to select from a plethora of discoveries those that are the most interesting and the most significant to parents, to those who deal with babies professionally, and to readers with a dash of curiosity about their beginnings. In our endeavor to present a faithful and coherent account of infant capabilities through the first year, we have consulted with scientific authorities on infant research, and several have reviewed our manuscript. But in the final analysis the total perspective of infancy that emerges from these pages, as well as any errors that it may contain, is our responsibility. However, we owe special and grateful acknowledgment to T. Berry Brazelton, M.D., Chief of the Child Development Unit, The Children's Hospital Medical Center, Boston, and to his research assistant, Ms. Nancy Kozak, whose comments on our manuscript were extremely helpful and who have so graciously provided a foreword for it. For their assistance in a variety of ways, we also wish to thank Hugh Rawson, Thomas Y. Crowell Company's editor, and Ms. Miriam K. House.

Readers should know that we use the masculine pronoun to refer to an infant in the abstract reluctantly, in the absence of an acceptable (to us) alternative. Thus, whenever possible, we have used the genderless "they."

"What is the best way to bring up a baby?" is a question that concerns many people, whether they are intimately involved in caring for babies, only interact with them occasionally, or are simply concerned that children be given the best possible start. Burton White, of the Laboratory of Human Development at Harvard, provides an eminently sensible answer to this question: "The best way to rear an infant is to be knowledgeable about his rapidly changing abilities and interests and to arrange his environment and schedule so as to provide sequences of experience that are suitably matched to those developing characteristics, starting immediately at birth."[1]

The new knowledge being generated about infants is as yet far too incomplete to serve as a guide to raising a baby. Nor does each and every discovery about infants have the instant application to child-rearing practices that some demand. Many studies of infant behavior are, in fact, undertaken with altogether different goals in mind. But if the ideal environment for infants is the one most in tune with their needs and capacities as they develop, acquaintance with the rich substance of infant research will bring us several giant steps toward that ideal.

Jane Flannery Jackson
Joseph H. Jackson

Niantic, Connecticut

CHAPTER 1
The Infant Reassessed

. . . Is it any wonder that there has been recently an almost frantic interest in what the laboratories of the behaviorist psychologists have to say about *infant culture?*   John Watson, *Psychological Care of Infant and Child*

Judy Bartnoff, newly named, rests quietly in her bassinet, practicing breathing through her nose. She has no need to work on swallowing, since she mastered that skill some months ago. She is just 12 hours old, and no food has yet appeared. But suddenly there is this stick, with a wisp of cotton on the end, waving under her nose. Down go the corners of that small triangle, her mouth, and her upper lip peaks at its center. Out shoots a minute pink tongue and, without further ado, Judy, as yet unschooled in the social graces, emphatically spits. If she had not recently been born, anyone would swear that Judy, having just inhaled the odor of rotten eggs, is disgusted.

Is Judy's universe to consist of nothing but a bad smell? Not at all, because here is another stick, with yet another wisp of cotton, waving back and forth. But this time the luscious scent of ripe bananas is in the air. Things are looking up! Judy relaxes; the triangle widens and is transformed into a curve. Is she perhaps smiling? Her lips smack, as though with relish.

The experimenter standing beside the bassinet and wielding the sticks is the Israeli neurophysiologist Jacob Steiner.[1,2] Some time ago, he made videotapes of infants' responses to various tastes. So he is not particularly surprised when Judy makes different faces as good and bad odors successively emanate from the cotton. Nor is he at all inclined to describe Judy's changes of expression as "accidental movements of facial muscles in response to internal stimuli." More commonly known as the "gas-pain" theory, this has been the explanation offered to generations of mothers who dared to suggest that their infants' facial expressions communicated something.

It has been the conventional wisdom that the state of the newborn infant is a kind of mindless oblivion, akin to the Buddhist vision of Nirvana, in which virtually nothing goes on and to which little penetrates. Thus, it would not occur to anyone that a 12-hour-old infant could not only distinguish the scent of ripe bananas from the odor of rotten eggs but express liking for the one and distaste for the other. In our familiar world, newborns have gas pains, not likes and dislikes. They cry when they are hungry—or wet—and what else is there to say? Especially when this view of the infant has borne the stamp of scientific approval.

The past decade of infant research, covering almost every aspect of infant behavior, has turned this tidy world upside down. From the work of Steiner and hundreds of other investigators, a new portrait of the infant is emerging that bears small resemblance to the "little stranger" dangling from the stork's beak in a diaper hammock.

Take, for example, the baby's presumed helplessness. "A baby is so helpless," people are given to saying. The very thought can make us misty-eyed! But the truth is that this compassion is misplaced. We have failed to make a distinction between two very different states: dependence and helplessness. True, the human infant is dependent on caregivers for a longer period than the young of any other species. But dependence on others is part of the human condition and persists throughout life, peaking during infancy and again in extreme old age. To be helpless, on the other hand, means to be "incapable of action" and to "lack protection and support." For an infant, as for any living thing, such conditions would be incompatible with life.

A newborn's "helplessness" is no more real than that of a vessel foundering in mid-ocean but with a competent "sparks" on board and a wireless in working order. Just as a ship's SOS is universally understood as a call for assistance, so is an infant's cry. No, infants cannot change their own diapers, keep themselves warm, or forage for meals on their own—no more than a captain can rescue his own ship—but they can direct others to perform these tasks for them. Looked at in this way, the crying of infants becomes a sign not of helplessness but of their ability to promote their own survival.

Skeptical as we are about infants' talents, we readily admit their expertise in communicating distress. But having consigned infants to psychological apartheid, we have overlooked their sensitivity to anything more subtle than the discomfort of an empty stomach or a wet diaper.

Steiner's much broader view of infant sensitivities developed in a roundabout manner. The research that culminated in the waving of scented sticks under Judy Bartnoff's nose had taken many twists and turns. It all began with an experiment that had nothing at all to do with infants. Steiner has a special interest in how the human senses function, and the goal of this particular experiment was to find out how people react to the four basic tastes—salt, sour, sweet, and bitter. The subjects were a large group of men and women of various ages and from a wide variety of backgrounds, including a sprinkling of psychotic patients from mental hospitals.

As the study went on, Steiner began to notice something odd: identical expressions flashed over the faces of all the subjects, normal and psychotic, in response to each of the tastes. A "down-in-the-mouth" look and protrusion of the tongue followed bitter tastes. Sweet tastes elicited a relaxed, smiling expression. Sour tastes caused pursing of the lips and swallowing. The expressions appeared almost instantly, often before comments were made about the tastes. Participants' reports that they could not control these reactions confirmed Steiner's initial impression that these expressions were automatic in character.

How was Steiner to account for the uniformity of these expressions in such a large and diverse group of people?

We learn many things by imitation, in a "monkey sees, monkey does" fashion, and facial expressions seem made to order for mimicry. Perhaps as small children we observe the faces people make when sucking on a lemon, for example, "decide" that this is the correct expression to assume when eating something sour, and incorporate it into our own behavior. Steiner considered this possibility. But he was forced to conclude that expressions so identical that they might all have been printed from the same negative were probably not learned. Rather, this kind of facsimile behavior is typical of the inborn responses called "fixed-action patterns" that appear consistently throughout a given species. Among other things, these patterns serve a protective function—the human gesture of shaking the hand when something "crawly" is felt on it is an example. Or they may communicate something of importance to survival, such as the inedibility of certain foods.

But how was Steiner to determine whether or not the "gustofacial response," as he now called it, was innate? Only by turning to infants. And to rule out the possibility of learning, the infants' reactions had to be observed before their first feeding.

Steiner set up a simple experiment that met these requirements and provided the evidence he needed. It involved putting drops of dilute sugar (sweet), quinine (bitter), and citric acid (sour) on the tongues of 75 newborn, as yet unfed, infants in a hospital nursery and observing their reactions. The results were much as Steiner had expected. In the majority of the infants, the gustofacial responses to each taste were identical, not only with each other, but also with those observed in adults. Since these infants had had no experience with tastes—with the tastes of this world, at any rate—the inference of the inborn character of these responses was solidly established.

Steiner's enthusiasm over the clear outcome of this experiment led him one bold step further: Do infants have similar unlearned reactions to foods? Can they signal their caregivers that certain foods are "good" or "bad"?

Devising an experiment to answer this question took considerable ingenuity because of the strict limitations on what a newborn infant can be fed. However, except for saltiness, sweetness, sourness, and bitterness, the sensations loosely called tastes are actually "smells"— which accounts for the inability to taste when a severe head cold blocks the nasal passages. Taking advantage of this fact, and enlisting the aid of some chemist collaborators, Steiner came up with a series of "tastants"—chemicals that gave off foodlike odors, some pleasant and some unpleasant. They were dropped on cotton-tipped sticks and waved under the noses of Judy Bartnoff and other 12-hour-old infants. The babies' responses left no doubt at all that in their first hours of life they can evaluate food odors and make their reactions known to their caregivers. Their expressions of aversion to the smell of rotten eggs and the fishy aroma of shrimp were as unanimous as their beatific looks of satisfaction on smelling fruit, butter, and vanilla. And so past assumptions that acceptance or rejection of certain foods must be either learned or capricious have proved to be unfounded.

The meaning of certain infant signals, such as facial expressions, has been obscured by a fog of prejudice about infants' capabilities. But another infant capacity, their power to make themselves the center of attention, has, until recently, been ignored merely because, like the purloined letter, it was too obvious to notice.

Infants of any species have enormous appeal for people of all ages, a fact well known to anyone whose pet has had a litter. And the newborn human infant's ability to command the rapt attention of other human beings is evident in the steady procession of visitors that follows the arrival of a new baby home from the hospital. Why do they come? It appears for the sole purpose of making an inventory of the baby's physical charms: "His eyes are like saucers!" "Her hands are so tiny," "Look at his fat little legs!" And the inevitable "Can I hold her for just a minute?"

What lies behind the capacity of infants to rivet attention on their physical persons? Some recent speculations and observations contain the seeds of an answer.

Most attractions can be accounted for by looking into the needs they satisfy: An empty stomach entices us to the dinner table, and the lure of breathing stems from our need for oxygen. Attraction, then, can be thought of as a need-fulfillment device that assures our unflagging interest in and pursuit of the things necessary for survival. But how can this conceivably be applied to the attractiveness of infants? People may say such things as "I could gobble you right up!" as they hug and kiss a baby, but fortunately, this is only a metaphorical expression of their attraction and delight. Here, according to current theory, is a need-fulfillment mechanism operating in reverse, in that the attraction serves the interests, not of the attracted, but of the attractor, namely, the infant. And further, it is the infant's physical characteristics that constitute the attraction.

For one thing, the infants of any species are small and roly-poly caricatures of their elders. The head of a human infant is proportionately larger than that of an adult. It makes up a fourth of total height as opposed to the seventh it will eventually become. Infants' legs make up only a third of their height as compared with half in adulthood. Babies' faces and eyes thus seem large and their legs exceedingly short. Babies also have noticeably flattened faces and chubby cheeks. These are the features emphasized in Disney cartoon characters to project the image of "cuteness." Ethologically minded psychologists have proposed that infants' facial features trigger immediate attention-giving behavior in older persons.[3] Ethologists hold that each species, including the human, has a set of inherited fixed-action behavior patterns designed to ensure its survival, and that these patterns are "released" by certain specific "sign stimuli." Thus, in their view, the human infant's facial features are sign stimuli for caregiving.

In a recent ethological study at the State University of New York at Stony Brook, 692 introductory psychology students were shown a series of full-face drawings of infants and were asked to rate their preferences for the faces on a 7-point scale ranging from extremely unattractive to extremely attractive.[4] One series of drawings varied the vertical position of facial features (eyes, nose, mouth, and ears) from very low with hardly any chin and much forehead to very high with little forehead and a deep chin. Other series showed varying size of iris, varying width of eyes, varying height of eyes, and eye width and height varying together.

Statistical analysis of the ratings showed that the students preferred a baby face with a moderately small chin, relatively high forehead, and eyes wide and high, with a medium-sized iris. This finding was significant in two senses of the word. In ordinary usage, "significant" means "important" or "noteworthy." "Statistically significant" means "likely to occur *by chance* 5 or fewer times out of 100." Statistical tests applied to the judgments of the ideal infant face indicated they would occur by chance no more than 1 time in 1000.

The researchers concluded that infantile facial features act as "releasing" stimuli to elicit adult approach and caring behavior and to inhibit aggressions toward the infant. But what about the infant who lacks these ideal features? The investigators suggested that such a deficiency might account in part for the battered child syndrome and the scapegoating of one child that occurs in some families.

The possibility remained that the students' judgments may have been derived from exposure to the ideal infant faces as depicted in advertisements and the like. The investigators ruled out this possibility on the grounds that exposure or nonexposure to real infants (determined by a questionnaire filled out by the students) had no effect on the ratings.

Attraction to infants develops with age, a recent study at Temple University has shown.[5] Boys and girls in grades 2, 4, 6, 8, 10, and 12 and male and female graduate students were shown pairs of photographs of human infants and adults, and animal infants and adults, and asked which photograph of each infant-adult pair they preferred. Overall, human infants and animal infants were judged nearly equally attractive, and females preferred infants, both animal and human, more than did males. However, both boys and girls from grades 2 though 6 preferred adults over infants, with the girls' preference for adults significantly greater than that of the boys. Then, with increasing maturity, came a striking shift in preference. As a group, children in grades 8 through 12, and graduate students as well, preferred infants significantly more than adults. But while the shift was established in girls between grades 6 and 8, it was far more gradual in the boys, whose preference for infants was not statistically significant until grade 12.

Thus, attraction to infants seems to be related to the onset of puberty, which occurs about two years later in boys than in girls, suggesting that biological factors may be at work. However, as the investigators pointed out, as adolescents become aware of their capacity to reproduce, they begin to see themselves in a new social role, as future parents, and this, too, may stimulate an interest in babies.

Some inkling of the influence of social pressures on judgments of the attractiveness of infants has come from a recent investigation at Florida State University.[6] Groups of all-female and all-male college students, most of whom were under 21 and unmarried, were shown slides of subhuman primate adults and infants and asked to rate their immediate emotional appeal on a scale running from not at all attractive to somewhat unattractive, neither attractive nor unattractive, somewhat attractive, to very attractive. Half the students were asked to express these judgments publicly by holding up a card with their rating that could be seen by the others in the group. The rest made their judgments in private, noting their reactions on rating sheets.

The overall scores for all groups, public and private, showed that both sexes were more attracted to infants than to adults. The women were significantly more attracted than were the men, but the investigators had not found this sex difference in a prior study using students at Pennsylvania State University. Men reported less attraction to infants in the all-male public groups than when making their judgments in private. Women, on the other hand, reported greater attraction to infants when their judgments were made in the presence of other women than when made in private. In both cases, then, a desire to conform to traditional male-female role expectations appeared to be influential.

Although the investigators did not claim that their findings ruled out biologically determined sex differences in the response to infants, they expressed their reservations about the importance of such differences. If, they said, small differences in the subjects (students differing only in the university they attended) and minor changes in the social context (public versus private judgments) affect the response, any innate sex difference in attraction to infants means very little.

What besides the physical features apparent in photographs may tend to attract our attention to babies and make us eager caregivers? Surely, their cries must be included, along with their appealingly clumsy brandishing of arms and legs and their clinging to whatever is at hand. All kinds of infant mammals from elephant seals to woodchucks, elk, reindeer, cats, dogs, and many primates, including humans, secure maternal attention by their cries.[7] In addition, when babies are awake and alert, it is hard to predict what they will do next. Perhaps this lack of predictability satisfies some inborn human need for relief from the boredom of the familiar. Furthermore, babies pose no threat to our security or self-esteem. They will hardly judge us. And so we can lower our customary social defenses, approach them without anxiety, and give to them forthcomingly.

Finally, the swift changes that characterize an infant's development never lose their power to fascinate and amaze. As one mother put it: "It was incredible the way Maggie changed! At first she seemed so ordinary—just like every other baby. But within a month, I saw that she had her own ways about her. She turned into a remarkably independent little baby, very insistent on what she wants, and so different from her brother. She became a person in just a few weeks' time!"

Whether it is just babies' distinctive shape and features, their communicative signals and movements, their unpredictability and spontaneous growth, or all of these rolled into individually charming bits of humanity, babies do attract. And, to the extent of their understanding and ability, people associated with infants inevitably find themselves drawn into answering their signals and providing for their needs. Given attraction, attachment soon follows. And, with further intimacy, attachment develops into affection. The currently popular technical term for this is "bonding." Its perennial expression is love.

Deep beneath the compulsion to respond to infants, is there perhaps an urge to extend human life? Is there a need to assure at least one kind of immortality through offspring? Beyond our own individual drive toward survival, is there a drive to propagate our own genes or those of our species into the future? These are speculative questions with moral overtones that in some eyes make them inappropriate for scientific investigation. Yet if social control of population growth ultimately becomes necessary for human survival—a not unlikely prospect—some knowledge about such profound human needs will become essential for any rational and workable plan.

Whatever the deepest sources of our attraction, we are all drawn, more or less as the case may be, by various features of infants. But this is only the beginning of our interactions with them. Beyond this, each of us responds to babies in terms of a fixed constellation of attitudes, emotions, and convictions. As we grow up, we develop a set of what might be called commonsense notions about the kind of creatures babies are and how they should be handled. Furthermore, we tend to hold dogmatic beliefs about how a proper baby should and should not behave—a sort of infant "ten commandments," with "Thou shalt not cry," or "Thou shalt sleep through the night," probably heading the list! Drawing on our stock of infant lore, we confidently make evaluative statements about particular infants. We call them "fussy," "cranky," and "spoiled," or "angels," with "sunny dispositions," who are "no trouble at all."

This inner network of intermingled ideas, attitudes, emotions, and standards about infants in each of us springs from many sources: our own experiences as infants, the way we and our siblings were regarded and treated by our parents, the reactions of our peers, and the patterns of behavior toward infants in the culture to which we belong. In addition, to the degree of our interest in the subject of infants, we have been influenced by a long line of philosophers, scientists, and pediatricians, from Plato to Rousseau to John Watson,

Jean Piaget, Benjamin Spock, Lee Salk, and Burton White, who have advised from their varying perspectives on how best to rear our children.

Countless books have been written about the care of infants and ways of fashioning them into admirable adults. But until the past decade or so, scientists as a group have shown little interest in applying the laboratory techniques of experimental psychology to the study of infants. This is not only because such experiments are extremely hard to devise, but also because scientists, like the rest of us, have looked on the infant as little more than a "squirming bit of flesh" and thus unlikely to reveal much of scientific value. G. Stanley Hall, a pioneer in the scientific study of child development at the turn of the century, expressed the consensus that was to prevail for decades.[8] Surveying the infant, Hall saw only a "squinty, crossed-eyed, potbellied, and bowlegged creature" with a "monotonous and dismal" cry and "red-shriveled, parboiled skin" and promptly lost interest in infant research. Another renowned psychologist of the same era, William James, more kindly but no less disparaging, depicted the infant's psychological state as bordering on pandemonium. The infant, he said, is "assailed by eyes, ears, nose, skin, and entrails at once" and feels that "all is one great blooming, buzzing confusion."[9] And until very recently, James's assessment of the infant state of mind was generally accepted as accurate.

A single example of a remarkably sophisticated infant perceptual ability reported in 1977 by a trio of developmental psychologists working in Paris will suffice to demonstrate how far off the mark James was.[10] These investigators, two French and one Australian, interested in determining whether or not infants perceive sound rhythms, designed the following experiment: Babies 2 or 3 months of age were settled comfortably in reclining infant seats facing a 15-inch distant white screen on which the simple outline of a black square appeared. When they gazed directly at the square, they heard a taped rhythmic series of sounds, or "pips," from a loudspeaker behind the square. The rhythmic pips, which had been extracted from an electronic-organ chord, continued as long as the babies looked at the square, stopping when they looked away. Two different rhythms were thus presented to the babies in each of three experiments.

Although it is known that infants enjoy looking at a black square on a white background, it is also known that they soon tire of it, or, as psychologists say, become habituated to it. The experimenters could therefore safely assume that continued gazing at the square signified an interest in the rhythmic sound that such gazing produced. The babies' length of fixation on the square served as a measure of their attention to the rhythm. And if attention to a particular rhythm, measured in this way, waned with repetition but was renewed when a different rhythm was presented, the perception of a difference between the two rhythms could be established.

In the first experiment, the infants first heard a fast, regular rhythm, in which the pips were separated by a pause of two-tenths (0.2) of a second (2-2-2-2). After habituation to this rhythm and thus loss of interest in the square, the babies heard a fast, irregular rhythm (1-2-3-2) (pip–0.1 [sec] –pip–0.2 –pip–0.3 –pip–0.2), and their interest in the square revived, indicating perception of the difference. In the second experiment, they distinguished a slow, regular rhythm (3-9-3-9) (habituation rhythm) from a slow, irregular rhythm (3-6-3-12) (novel rhythm). However, in both these experiments, rather than perceiving a difference in rhythm, the infants might simply have noticed that some of the pauses between pips in the novel rhythm were of a different length than the pauses in the habituation rhythm. The crucial test came in the third experiment, when pauses of the same lengths were used for both rhythms, but were rearranged (1-3-6 versus 1-6-3). A highly significant difference in fixation time followed the presentation of the second rhythm, demonstrating that the infants were distinguishing between the rhythmic pattern made by these separate sounds. The chances were only 5 in 1000 that the difference in fixation times was not related to the infants' perception of rhythm.

No differences between the discriminative capacity of 2- and 3-month-old infants were observed in any of these experiments. This suggests that the skill of grouping isolated sounds into rhythmic patterns is acquired very early in life and explains in part why infants enjoy rhythmic games such as pat-a-cake and are soothed by a lullaby when they are fussy. Language comprehension, the researchers pointed out, requires a similar capacity in that meaning is derived from perceiving a sequence of individual sounds as a whole. Thus, an important prerequisite for understanding speech is present very early in life, long before we would presume such a skill has any possible utility.

The investigations so far described are only a few among hundreds that have been designed and carried out in recent years. These studies, covering almost every conceivable aspect of infant (and caregiver) behavior, have been so numerous that an account of only the most significant can be given here. Scientists have been exploring the behavior of infants at (and even before) birth, their many fixed-action patterns, including facial expressions, their acute sensory and perceptual capacities, and their ability to learn from experience. Many unexpected things have come to light in all these areas. New knowledge is accumulating about infant emotions and temperaments, the ways in which they begin to explore their new worlds and acquire a large repertoire of skills, their communications with others as they advance from gestures to words to mastery of the language of their culture. What is being discovered is sometimes equally in conflict with scientific tradition and with folk wisdom. At other times, it clarifies or amplifies what is already established.

Some practical souls may question the value of all this research. Why should hundreds of scientists around the world be spending millions of dollars just to study babies? Don't we already know everything about them we need to know? We must be sure that they get the proper food, are kept clean and warm, have enough sleep, and are given tender, loving care. This stripped-down, bare-bones approach overlooks countless infant needs that should be filled and talents that should be nurtured. For example, do babies have a sense of humor? If so, when and how does it appear, and how does it develop through the first year? Just as understanding infants' facial expressions of pleasure and disgust tells us something about the origins and expression of our adult values, so a grasp of infant humor and how it can be elicited and encouraged reveals a great deal about the resources for laughter and wit in us now. With enlightenment about the capacities of infants and the significance of some of the things they do, we enjoy them more, simply because it makes them more interesting. And we learn something about ourselves, for we, too, were once infants.

CHAPTER 2
Enter Infant

By the end of the second month of gestation, the human embryo has become a fetus, and although it is then just an inch in length and weighs only three-fourths of an ounce, it can now be distinguished from its nonhuman primate cousins. By the close of its third month, the fetus's body has grown nearly two inches, but it could still be mailed first class at the minimum rate, for it has gained only a quarter of an ounce. Yet it has, to put it mildly, come a long way from the primitive cluster of undifferentiated cells that represented its totality just a short time ago. Its almost microscopic hands and fingers are well formed, and its thumb is already opposable to its forefinger, badge of membership in the human species. Intricate sets of neuromuscular connections have been formed, and the external genitals already proclaim its sex. And by or before its ninetieth day of existence, discernible expressions are fleetingly seen to cross its face.

All these developments have taken place in an ecological setting that in several respects is much like that of an astronaut's spacecraft.[1] Physiological thermostats ensure the fetus's even temperature much as air conditioning keeps the temperature of a spacecraft constant. Totally immersed in the fluid of the amniotic sac, floating gently in it, the fetus is almost weightless, for the fetal specific gravity is nearly equal to that of the fluid, maintaining equal pressure all around the fetus. So, like the astronaut returning to earth from orbit, the infant at birth will have to adjust to the pull of gravity. And as the astronaut's survival is dependent on the food and oxygen he brings into space, so is the fetus sustained only by the oxygen and nutrients that flow through its lifeline, the umbilical cord.

Despite the restraints imposed by the amniotic sac, the fetus begins to flex its muscles long before birth.[2] The mother first becomes aware that the fetus has "quickened" sometime during the fourth month, although quickening can sometimes be detected by stethoscope a month earlier. Later, the mother is able to distinguish movements of the fetal arms and legs from movements of the fetal head or trunk. Sometimes the fetus will seem to respond to a tap on the mother's abdomen or to jump at loud noises or sharp vibrations in what appears to be a startle reaction. And, toward the end of term, the mother may feel the rhythmic rise and fall of the fetal chest.

Rhythmic movements of the fetal chest akin to breathing were noted as early as 1798. The idea did not take hold, however, as it also failed to do when a German investigator, Frédérick Ahlfeld, reported in 1888, 90 years later, that he had seen fetal chest movements that seemed to involve the same muscles as those used in postnatal respiration. He proceeded to record these movements as they were transmitted through the maternal abdominal wall, finding that they occurred from 38 to 76 times per minute. When he finally published his records in 1905, claiming that the human fetus makes spontaneous respiratory efforts, his claim was firmly rejected by two very influential obstetricians of the day, who saw no proof in Ahlfeld's report that the respiratory muscles were actually involved. The weight of their authority was so overwhelming that the subject remained virtually closed for the next half-century or so.

In 1971, two researchers at the University of Oxford reported that by means of sophisticated detectors they had recorded traces of chest-wall movements in fetal lambs delivered toward the end of gestation.[3] The chest movements were easy to distinguish from the lambs' far more rapid heartbeat. Variations in the pressure of amniotic fluid in the fetal tracheas (windpipes) were recorded simultaneously. Increases in this pressure were found to be associated with the chest-wall movements, indicating that the rise and fall of the lambs' chests was drawing fluid into their windpipes.

The researchers then tried their method on seven women whose pregnancies were at 36 to 42 weeks of gestation, at or close to term. And in only one of the fetuses, a fetus that was small for its gestational age, did they fail to detect chest-wall movements. Remarkably close to Ahlfeld's measurements, these movements occurred at a rate of 40 to 70 per minute.

In the next phase of their investigation, the Oxford researchers, with four pregnant women as subjects, made simultaneous recordings of fetal chest-wall and maternal abdominal movements.[4] At the same time, they visually observed the correlated movements of the mothers' abdomens that Ahlfeld had described back in 1905. Having learned from this experience the art of detecting the visible sign of fetal breathing, they embarked on a larger study, using 100 women from 36 to 42 weeks pregnant as their subjects and observing the women's abdominal movement for five minutes.

Fetal breathing movements were seen in 34 of the 100 women. The mothers sometimes felt these movements and could often distinguish them from their own pulses. The movements were easier to see in women who had previously borne a child, and the later in the pregnancy, the easier they were to detect, since the abdomens of such women are usually stretched thinner than in first or early pregnancy.

It was found that the position of the fetal parts determined where on the maternal abdomen the rise and fall of the fetal chests would be detectable. In some mothers, fetal "breathing" produced abdominal movements below the navel. In others, the chest movements were transmitted, apparently, through a fetal limb, to a spot about the size of a 50-cent piece above the mother's navel.

Failure to observe maternal abdominal movements does not necessarily mean that the fetus is not engaging in respiratory activity. When the fetuses of 34 women in the study were examined by a detector, chest movements were found in all.

As noted, the chest-wall movements of fetal lambs produced changes in the pressure of the fluid in the windpipe. However, this does not imply that the fetus is actually breathing the amniotic fluid in and out of the lungs. The lungs do not expand until birth, and the density and viscosity (stickiness) of the fluid in fetal lungs is so great that changes in tracheal pressure do not affect it. When contrast material—the material used for x-rays—is injected into the amniotic fluid around lamb fetuses, it gradually appears on x-rays not of the lungs but of the gastrointestinal tract. Thus, fetuses can successfully swallow amniotic fluid, but their breathing movements are not sufficient to carry it into the lungs.[5] Fetal chest-wall movements therefore cannot be thought of as breathing in any real sense. Rather, the fetus appears to be exercising and strengthening the respiratory muscles that must be ready to function at the moment of birth. These warming-up exercises may also establish the rhythmic action of the centers in the brain that will automatically control respiration throughout life.

As opposed to the rhythmic "breathing" of the fetus close to term, reflex inspiration and expiration in response to a stimulus has been seen in fetuses of only 11 weeks' gestation. (A reflex is an involuntary reaction to stimulation—the "knee jerk" is a well-known example.) This was reported by Tryphena Humphrey of the University of Alabama in Birmingham, who, together with Davenport Hooker of the University of Pittsburgh, made detailed studies of the reflex behavior of fetuses surgically removed at various stages in early pregnancy.[6] The first fetal reflex, an avoidance reaction, occurs about five weeks after conception. When stimulated by a hair around the mouth, the fetus bends its head and trunk away. The arms extend, the feet separate, and the rump sometimes rotates away from the stimulus, behavior that Humphrey described as "a little hula wiggle, obviously a very primitive reaction."[7]

A little later, by 7 to 8 weeks, the fetal mouth also opens with vigorous stimulation.[6] During this period, rather than turning away, the fetus occasionally begins to turn toward the side of the face that has been stimulated. Then by 8 to 9 weeks, instead of turning its head and body to the side, the fetus begins to extend and straighten its head and trunk, thus avoiding the stimulus in another manner. And by about 9 to 10 weeks, the fetal reflexes manifest still further development. With stimulation around the fetal lips, the head bends forward *toward* the stimulus. If the mouth is open, it closes; the larynx is raised, and swallowing occurs as the larynx is subsequently lowered. When the fetal head becomes capable of rotation, the fetus then rotates its head away from the stimulus; later, with further development, the head is rotated toward it. Then, by about 13 weeks of gestation, the mouth will often open when the lips are stimulated— and then close on the stimulator.

A rudimentary fetal grasping reflex is first seen at 8 to 9 weeks of gestation. When the fetal palm is stimulated, the fingers are flexed, closing incompletely, without motion of the thumb. The hand—and sometimes the forearm—is flexed, and several or all four fingers close and then open so rapidly that only on film can it be seen that the fist really does not close. By 10 to 11 weeks, the thumb also begins to participate in this reflex action, moving across the palm. By 14 to 15 weeks, the fetus may close its fingers on the stimulator and weakly maintain its hold. This is accompanied by distinct thumb action. At 18 weeks, the grasp is held, but is still weak. By 23 weeks, the grasp has become stronger, and the thumb is typically placed at the side of the fist or caught under the fingers. By 27 weeks, the fetus can nearly support its full weight for a brief interval.

Most newborns respond to scratching of the fleshy mound at the base of the thumb by contracting the mentalis muscle of the chin and the muscle around the lips, so that they become pursed and the mouth opens somewhat, as if preparing to suck. This odd reaction is called the palmomental reflex, and it has been elicited in fetuses at 14 weeks of gestation. Another peculiar newborn head-mouth response, the Babkin reflex, occurs with stimulation of both palms. The mouth is opened, the head bends forward, and the eyes sometimes close. The head may rotate to a midline position, and the forearm may be flexed. The tongue may be pushed forward and then withdrawn while the mouth is open. In fetuses, a Babkin-like reflex has been observed on stimulation of the palm at 14 weeks' gestation age, with mouth opening, raising of the tongue, and turning of the head toward the midline. Called the most primitive of reflexes, the Babkin response is most easily elicited in premature infants, and it disappears within a few months after birth. However, the palmomental reflex lingers on in some children and can be elicited in adults with electrical stimulation of various areas of the body surface, including the soles of the feet. The function of these two reflexes is very obscure, but it has been suggested that the mouth opening, at least, may be important for the formation of the palate, which if defective may seriously interfere with the infant's respiration.

By the time the fetus is 11 weeks old, the facial muscles and nerves involved in the expression of emotion are functioning.[7] It is at this point that a stimulator drawn over a fetal cheek and eyelid will produce not only a contraction of the eyelid muscle that looks like a squint but also a sneerlike raising of the upper lip. The stimulation of the fetal back from below upward results in a complex response that is uncannily like the reaction to tickling. The fetal shoulder shrugs, the mouth opens, and there is a sharp breathing movement like a gasp. It has been proposed that laughing may originate in the gasping component of this response. And by 14 weeks' gestation, the muscles in the brow contract in a scowl-like reaction. Although Humphrey emphasized the reflex nature of these expressions and quite naturally assumed that no emotion was present, she nevertheless reported that at this stage of development the fetus sometimes looks "distressed" and sometimes "pleased with itself."

Much painstaking effort has gone into the unearthing of the very few facts now known about fetal behavior. The inaccessibility of the fetus makes this hiatus in our knowledge almost inevitable. Yet the little we know should cause us to question past assumptions that at birth the infant is rudely thrust into the world unprepared to cope with its exigencies—unprepared even for that most crucial task, breathing.

As soon as the infant emerges from the birth canal, mild stimulation, such as gentle tapping of the back or the soles of the feet, will usually suffice to initiate respiration and, with it, a typically lusty cry. This newborn cry, the first sound uttered by a human being, has been the subject of endless, mostly fanciful speculation.[2] It has been interpreted as a lament over the harshness of a strange new world, as wrath at the inability to move, as woe on entering a sinful place far from the Garden of Eden, as helplessness in the face of an alien environment, as distress from the travail of birth, or simply as fear of the unknown. All these interpretations involve two assumptions: first, that the infant is born with a full complement of adult emotions, and second, that birth is a traumatic experience.

To Sigmund Freud, birth was simply the first of a long series of traumas, the prototypical anxiety-producing event:

> We believe we know the early impression which the emotion of fear repeats. We think it is birth itself which combines that complex of painful feelings . . . of physical sensations, which has become the prototype for the effect of danger to life, and is ever after repeated within us as a condition of fear. . . . We shall also recognize how significant it is that this first condition of fear appeared during the first separation from the mother.[8]

Although Freud often referred to the birth trauma as a "primal source" of anxiety, he did not consider it the sole or even the dominant source. This was left to Otto Rank, a disciple who eventually broke with Freud mainly on this point.[9] Rank held that although this primal anxiety might be repressed by the infant, it would reappear with such conflict-producing experiences as weaning and toilet training, which again would raise the specter of separation from the mother, reviving the primal anxiety that accompanied the first such separation at birth.

Freud described birth as a fierce struggle in which a frightened infant teeters on the verge of suffocation, but this description seems actually restrained when compared to the horrors depicted by the contemporary French obstetrician Frederick Leboyer, advocate of "birth without violence":

> Newborn babies don't talk? Let's wait a moment before making up our minds. What more proof do we need? That tragic expression, those tight-shut eyes, those twitching eyebrows. . . . That howling mouth, that squirming head trying desperately to find refuge. . . . Those hands stretching out to us, imploring, begging, then retreating to shield the face—that gesture of dread. Those furiously kicking feet, those arms that suddenly pull downward to protect the stomach. The flesh that is one great shudder. This baby is not speaking? Every inch of the body is crying out: "Don't touch me!" And at the same time pleading: "Don't leave me! Help me!" Has there ever been a more heartrending appeal? . . . Hell is what the infant must suffer through to arrive here among us.[10]

However, the newborn that appears in *Birth,* a film made by Leboyer, has a beatific smile. This infant was delivered by the Leboyer method, which requires, first, that the delivery room be darkened and sounds kept at a minimum, in contrast to the noise and bright lights of the usual delivery room. Immediately after delivery, the baby is laid on the mother's abdomen, tenderly massaged for a few minutes before the umbilical cord is cut, and then gently bathed in a tub of warm water to recreate the intrauterine environment. All procedures are directed toward making the transition at birth as gradual and gentle as possible.

Leboyer believes that infants delivered in this manner tend to be less excitable, nervous, and fearful than those delivered in the traditional way. Thus, in his view, the "shock" of birth, if not cushioned, can have long-lasting effects.

Is birth the traumatic hell conceived by Leboyer, or is it merely a strenuous event? René Spitz, a child psychoanalyst of the Freudian school, reported in 1965 that he had analyzed a number of films of infant deliveries and had seen no indication that birth was traumatic.[11] He noted that right after delivery the infant "shows brief respiratory distress and the manifestations of negatively tinged excitation . . . this subsides literally within *seconds* and gives way to complete quiescence." Thus, despite his Freudian bias, Spitz, on the evidence, rejected the concept of the birth trauma.

What feelings, if any, lie behind the infant's "negatively tinged excitation" at the moment of birth is impossible to determine. But when the umbilical cord is cut and the infant's organ systems must abruptly begin to function entirely on their own, it seems reasonable to assume that the infant undergoes considerable stress. Birth is a supreme challenge to an infant's physiological system. It is for this reason that within the first minute after delivery, and again at the end of five minutes, most infants today are given a test developed in 1952 by Dr. Virginia Apgar, an American anesthesiologist.[12]

The Apgar test provides an immediate evaluation of the newborn's basic physical and behavioral status. A numerical value of 0, 1, or 2 is assigned to each of five indicators of this status: heart rate, respiratory effort, muscle tone, skin color, and reflex irritability. For a score of 2, the newborn's heart rate must be over 100 beats per minute. Regular breathing with a lusty cry at birth also merits a score of 2. Poor muscle tone (0 score) is exemplified by a hand hanging limply from the wrist, good muscle tone (scored 2), by a hand held out with fingers spread. Skin color is indicative of cardiovascular status. A pink infant receives a score of 2, an entirely blue infant a score of 0. Reflex irritability refers to the infant's responsiveness when stimulated, for example, by a glass tube thrust into a nostril to clear the nasal passage. Coughing or sneezing scores 2, and grimacing scores 1. The total Apgar score is obtained by adding the numerical values assigned to each indicator. The higher the total score, the sounder the infant.

Apgar scores for many thousands of newborns have been gathered and analyzed statistically.[13] For analysis, they are usually classified as low (0 to 3), medium (4 to 6), and high (7 to 10). Newborns scoring 10 are in top-notch condition, and the status of those whose total scores range from 7 to 9 is considered adequate or good. Infants with scores in the medium range are in guarded condition and will have to be watched intensively, particularly during their first few days. Scores from 0 to 3 reflect a critical state and alert the delivery-room staff that emergency measures are required to save the infant's life.

Of all newborns given the Apgar test, 80 percent have high scores and 14 percent score in the medium range. Only 6 percent of infants fall into the low-scoring group whose lives hang in the balance during the first minutes after birth. Infant mortality is highest in the first two days after birth and, on the average, infants dying within this period have significantly lower Apgar scores than those who die within 3 to 28 days after birth, which is indicative of the high reliability of the test.

Apgar scores are often used in infant research studies, either to assess the normality of the infant subjects or as a measure of the effects of environmental factors on the infant's behavior at birth. In a recent study of firstborn infants of 85 middle-class mothers, for example, significant information was obtained about the relationships between Apgar scores and the use of pain-relieving drugs during labor.[14] The infants were delivered by private obstetricians in various hospitals in suburban Washington. During their eighth month, the mothers' attitudes toward their pregnancy were explored by means of a detailed questionnaire, since the effect of the mother's emotional state on the infant's behavior after birth was also to be studied. The mothers were asked if they had wanted the baby; if they had fears about themselves or the baby; if they were aware of any maternal feelings; if they were dependent on others; if they were irritable and tense during pregnancy; and if they sometimes felt depressed and withdrawn. After the infants were born, all without mishap, records of the pain-relieving drugs used during labor, the 5-minute Apgar scores, the results of behavioral assessments when the infants were 2 days old, and the questionnaire data were collected and analyzed. All the infants were full-term and judged normal at birth. Except for one infant with a 5-minute Apgar score of 7, their scores ranged from 8 to 10.

Significant correlations were found between the emotional state of the mothers during late pregnancy and the number of times that pain-relieving drugs were administered during labor. Thus, on the average, mothers who reported fears, feelings of tension and irritability, and a tendency to become depressed and withdrawn had to be given higher doses of pain-relieving drugs during labor than mothers who did not report these reactions.

A relationship between lower than normal Apgar scores and the use of pain-relieving drugs had been well established some years before this investigation was undertaken, but the lower scores had usually been observed only when excessive amounts of such drugs had been administered to the mother. Although only normal amounts of drugs were given during labor to mothers in this study, nevertheless the Apgar scores, high as they were, still reflected the depressant effects of the medication. The degree of depression, however, depended on the time during labor that the drugs had been maximally effective and the time of last administration of a drug. The later the drug had been given and the later it had been maximally effective, the lower the Apgar score. The same relationship held when the results of the behavioral assessment at 2 days of age were analyzed. Infants of mothers in the early-administration, early-maximal-effectiveness group spent a greater proportion of their time in quiet sleep than did infants in the late group. They also reacted more strongly to unpleasant stimulation, recovering more quickly from it. All these measures reflected their greater stability. Apparently, when drugs are administered early in labor, their effect on the child is minimal, since they are more likely to be metabolized and disappear than are drugs administered later.

Thus, judging by this study, maternal anxiety and other negative feelings affect the behavior of the newborn only indirectly in that mothers poorly adjusted to their pregnancy require more pain-relieving drugs than do those who take it in their stride. Although the immediate effects of these drugs were apparent in the Apgar scores, the investigators cautioned against linking an infant's behavioral difficulties after the newborn period with the use of drugs during labor. They pointed out that the anxious mother, who most requires these drugs, may also be ineffective in interacting with her baby. Thus, the "permanent disposition" of the mother, rather than drug use in labor, may be at the root of the infant's problems.

Immediately after the first gasp and cry accompanying the onset of respiration, the just-born infant may be "bright-eyed and bushy-tailed," alert and active for up to a half hour or more before he goes to sleep. The quiescence described by Spitz is by no means characteristic of all babies. A second period of activity follows about the fourth or fifth hour after birth.[15] The baby's head and eyes are involved in much of his early activity, giving the impression that the newborn is about to take off on a scouting expedition to "spy out" the new territory. His head moves from side to side, and his eyes open and close, permitting brief glimpses of rapid, jerky eye movements. He makes faces, and the twitching of his nostrils suggests that he is sampling the odors of his new domain. His mouth is frequently in motion: He purses his lips, sucks, chews, swallows, smacks, sticks out his tongue, roots with head rotating from side to side, and chews his fingers. (He may even have small lesions on his wrists as a result of vigorous prenatal sucking.)[16] He cries on occasion, but not for long, and the crying starts suddenly and stops as abruptly.

During the first hours, the newborn may shiver and shake, since his temperature-regulating mechanism is not yet operating at full capacity. Tremors and jerks of limbs, tongue, and diaphragm are seen frequently. He brandishes his arms and legs, as if reveling in his newfound freedom. He startles, both spontaneously and in response to sounds.

These, then, are the spontaneous activities of newborn infants as they recover from the stressful experiences of birth and adjust to the extrauterine world. Within two or three days, when the newborn has settled down, it will be feasible to evaluate his behavioral development by testing his responses to various kinds of stimulation.

The Neonatal Behavioral Assessment Scale is a test that may be given one or preferably more times through the infant's first month (the newborn period) and as early as the third day.[17] The test focuses particularly on the capabilities bearing on an infant's future social interactions and relationships, but also assesses the infant's responsiveness to stimulation and ability to control his responses in his own interest.[17] The scale was constructed by T. Berry Brazelton, a pediatrician and developmental psychologist affiliated with the Harvard Medical School, with the help of numerous collaborators, and involves the observation of some 30 different newborn responses. A description of some of the principal responses covered by the scale reveals the numerous capabilities of normal newborns, many of which are relevant even to their earliest interactions with others.

The assessment takes 20 to 30 minutes and begins with the newborn asleep in his crib, covered and dressed, about midway between two feedings. The newborn's state, that is, his "state of consciousness," is observed and recorded throughout the assessment, for it has an effect on his responses. Using standard criteria to determine state, the examiner describes the infant as in deep or light sleep, drowsy, awake and alert, awake and active, or crying. During the assessment period, the examiner notes the frequency and smoothness with which the baby moves from one state to another, the typical pattern and direction of the state changes, and which state (or states) predominates.

While the infant is in light or deep sleep, the ability to "shut out" disturbing stimuli that are presented up to 10 times is tested. A flashlight is shone briefly onto the baby's closed eyes, a rattle is shaken, and a bell jangled. Some infants are unable to protect themselves against these disturbing stimuli and continue to blink, startle, or give some other aversive response right through the repetitions. But the responses of most infants will diminish after a few such stimulations and then cease entirely. Also while drowsy or asleep, the infant is stimulated on the heel of his foot with a pin pushed through a cork to expose a sixteenth of an inch of its point. If both feet are withdrawn and the entire body responds, and if this reaction continues to occur, some immaturity of the nervous system or neurological damage is indicated. The response of infants with a more mature nervous system will be limited to the stimulated foot, will gradually decrease and then disappear, and the infant will become alert.

The newborn's defensive reactions to an aversive stimulus are measured in another test when he is in a drowsy, active, or alert state. As the infant lies face up in his crib, a small cloth is placed over the eyes and held there with light pressure of the examiner's hand. An imperturbable baby will show no response or only quieting or mouthing. Others will turn their heads from side to side and stretch their necks up and down in an effort to dislodge the cloth. Some will go further, waving their arms and making swipes with their hands toward the cloth, sometimes successfully removing it.

Newborns may become upset, fuss and fret, and reach a peak of excitement and cry in reaction to aversive stimulation. Others may even cry simply on being undressed, on being pulled up to a sitting position, or on being placed in a prone position. The examiner notes how rapidly, how often, and to what extremes the infant builds up to a peak of excitement and crying during the testing and how irritable or imperturbable he seems to be. Some infants never cry irritably during the testing, others respond with crying to a number of the testing situations, and some seem very sensitive and irritable. These reactions give a broad measure of irritability, which can have a major effect on the baby's interactions with people, perhaps one of the most significant in shaping their treatment of their infant.

Orientation responses to various inanimate and social stimuli are assessed when the infant is awake and alert. A bright red ball may be used to test his visual attention to inanimate objects. Newborns usually focus on such objects and follow them with their eyes as they are moved back and forth. They may attend to such stimuli only briefly, following them with somewhat jerky eye movements, or more smoothly and continuously, following the object over a considerable arc. On the other hand, the infant may not focus on or follow the stimulus at all. Thus, infants demonstrate varying degrees of the capacity to orient toward and attend to stimuli, a capacity that bears on the infants' alertness to events going on around them.

To assess the infant's reactions to social stimuli, the examiner bends over the infant and moves his face slowly back and forth and up and down until the baby stops following it. Then the examiner moves to the side, out of the infant's sight, and talks softly and continuously to him. Finally, he leans over the baby and talks to him, combining visual and auditory stimulation. Most babies, even those as young as 3 days of age, follow these proceedings with great interest, focusing on the examiner's face, following him with their eyes, and orienting toward his voice. The attention of some babies may be riveted on these social stimuli and they may "lock onto" them for a long time.

If and when the newborn becomes upset and cries during the testing, the examiner determines the amount of intervention that is necessary to console the baby. Some babies will quiet down at the mere sight of the examiner's face, or to his face and soothing voice. Others calm to a hand on the belly, or on restraint of one or both arms. But further intervention is often required, and the infant must be picked up, held, and rocked. A finger or pacifier in the mouth, combined with holding, may be required to console some babies. A few newborns will not be consoled by any kind of intervention and will simply "cry themselves out."

When an infant is placed prone in the crib with his face against the sheet, or when his palm or cheek is stroked, he will often respond by bringing his hand to his mouth. The manner of this response, which may appear in any of an infant's states, varies considerably. Some infants merely swipe toward the mouth with their hands but without actual contact. Others manage to insert a hand in the mouth briefly, and still others manage to keep it there and then suck on their fingers or fist. The hand-to-mouth response may also be initiated by the baby himself and used as a self-comforting device when he is upset and fussing. This and other self-quieting responses, such as fixation on a visual or auditory stimulus, are noted during testing and are considered a measure of the extent to which the infant is capable of self-control.

The pristine behavior that is thus assessed by the Brazelton scale will be immediately evident in the infant's first interactions with the parents. The reactions his or her behavior engenders in them will in turn be fed back to the infant, and the shaping of their relationship will have begun.

CHAPTER 3
Opening Moves

Newborn infants make ideal research subjects. In copious supply in the hospital nurseries where they are held captive for some three to five days after birth, they can be investigated right on the premises, with their parents footing the bill for maintenance. Merely by storing a few pieces of research equipment close to the hospital nursery and obtaining the informed consent of the parents and the hospital, investigators can study large numbers of newborns in depth with a minimum of fuss and expense. Meanwhile, the infant participants in the studies are carefully protected from harm through safeguards mandated by hospital, university, and granting-agency committees on human infant experimentation.

The first task of any investigator undertaking an experimental study of newborn behavior is to ascertain the infant subject's "level of consciousness" or "level of arousal," commonly referred to as "state." This is not an easy matter, for in the newborn period the infant's state goes through such rapid and subtle changes that at any given moment, correct assessment of it requires concentration on minute details of the infant's behavior.

In some of the early infant studies, particularly those concerned with infants' responsiveness to various kinds of stimulation, failure to recognize the subtleties of newborn states caused endless confusion. Newborns in one study would promptly respond to a particular stimulus while awake and alert, but in others, infants presumably in the same state would not respond to it at all.[1] Conflicting results of this sort became so commonplace that serious doubts arose about the feasibility of experimental infant studies. Eventually, the difficulty was traced to lack of comparability between infant states from one study to another: If infants were awake in one study but only appeared to be awake in another and were actually drowsy, their responses would, of course, be different. Recognition of this fact led to demands for objective standards for judging infant states, and to concentrated study of these states, which still continues today.

Infant-state studies demand the patience of Job, since they entail painstaking observations of fleeting events over long periods followed by the exhaustive analysis of the records of those events in order to chart the sequences of the various states. Infant-state subjects are usually observed at certain times daily, such as after midmorning and midafternoon feedings. The observations often begin when the infant is 1 to 3 days old. Later, the infant may be watched at home in once-weekly sessions over two to three months. The infants selected for these studies are mainly those whose deliveries were normal, who were not subjected to any known adverse prenatal influences, and who had high Apgar scores at birth, ranging from 8 to 10. When their purpose is to study the inner-initiated behavior that unfolds spontaneously, researchers must scrupulously avoid stimulating the babies in any way. In other studies, carefully controlled stimulation may be administered to the infants to note its effects on their state.[2]

In a typical infant-state study, the infant, having just been fed, is brought from the newborn nursery to an infant laboratory set up in the hospital. There, he is placed in a transparent Plexiglas crib, which is warmed to the proper temperature for a newborn. The room is quiet and the lighting subdued to keep external stimulation at the lowest level possible. Watching the infant intently, the investigator records his behavior at 10-second intervals over varying intervals of time, often covering all the successive states that usually appear between feedings. Investigators who are focusing on the physiological indicators of state, such as the infant's bodily movements in the crib, heart and respiration rates, and electrical activity of the muscles and brain, make instrumental recordings of these events.[3]

In the state of quiet sleep, the baby's eyes are closed, breathing is slow and regular, and the body is relaxed, except for occasional brief startles or rhythmic mouthing. In active sleep, on the other hand, breathing is irregular and faster, and the infant may twitch and writhe, with facial movements such as grimaces, frowns, mouthing, smiles, and sucking. Although the eyes are usually closed, movements of the eyeballs can be seen beneath the lids. This rapid eye movement

(REM) helps to distinguish active from quiet sleep, in which no rapid eye movements (NREM) are apparent.

In the state of drowsiness between sleep and awake states, the infant's eyes may open and close, but appear glassy or dazed when open. The body or limbs may move haphazardly, then relax, followed by jerks as the eyes fly open, reminiscent of people dozing in a waiting room and awakening with a start. Breathing is fairly regular but faster and more shallow than in sleep. Infants may pass in either direction in this transitional state between sleeping and waking.

At least three awake infant states are usually distinguished. In quiet awake, the infant's eyes are usually open and have a bright, shiny look, although they may close on occasion. He lies peacefully still, with only rare general movements. Breathing is quite regular, although less so than in quiet sleep. The infant may occasionally grimace, grunt, or vocalize quietly in other ways. But in the active awake state, the infant's body, arms, and legs are frequently in motion. Breathing is quite irregular, and the infant may orient toward and fix his attention briefly on various sights and sounds. He vocalizes a lot in this state and may begin to fuss or fret, crying briefly. But in the crying awake state, the infant has fretted himself into a turmoil, with thrashing body, brandishing limbs, grimacing face, and puckered mouth. His bursts of crying become more continuous, with manifest excitement, unhappiness, and protest.

On the average, newborns sleep from 17 to 20 hours a day, dividing their sleeping time between active (REM) and quiet (NREM) sleep. They may be found in a drowsy, transitional state for perhaps an hour or two a day. And they are usually awake from 4 to 7 hours a day, spending more time in the active awake state (2 to 3 hours) than in the quiet awake state (1 to 2 hours) or in crying (1 to 2 hours).[4] Thus, newborns are awake, ready to nurse or just look about at the host of fascinating things and persons around them, for a greater proportion of the day than it appears. This is when they need the most attention from their caregivers and sometimes announce this need quite vehemently.

After a feeding, newborns held quietly in the arms or put to bed occasionally stay alert for a few minutes, keeping their eyes open, but the more common response to a full stomach and the exertion of sucking is almost instant slumber. And so, after flinging out an arm once or twice and crimping his lips briefly, the baby signals by the firm closing of his eyelids that he is going to sleep. Neonates almost always go directly into active (REM) sleep, indicated by the fluttering motions of their eyes beneath the lids, for a period of 15 to 25 minutes. Then they pass into quiet (NREM) sleep for about the same length of time, then back to active sleep, and so on, alternating between the two states of sleep. By the age of a month, infants go directly into active sleep only two-thirds of the time, entering quiet sleep at least once (as do adults) a third of the time, for the proportion of time spent in active sleep has already diminished.[5] By 6 months of age, only a third of an infant's sleeping time will be spent in active sleep, and the proportion of active sleep will continue to diminish thereafter, to about 20 percent by 3 to 5 years of age and to 13 to 15 percent in old age.

Traditionally, sleep has been viewed as the means by which brain deficits are restored by passage through a period of inactivity. But the discovery that there are at least two kinds of sleep has discounted the belief that sleep has only one function, for only NREM sleep qualifies as a genuine rest period.[6] REM sleep predominates in newborns, but infants born before the 38 weeks of gestation spend an even greater proportion of their time in REM sleep—two-thirds of it at 35 weeks' gestation—and it has been suggested that all fetal sleep may be of the REM variety.

It is tempting to conclude that REM sleep is "primitive," but observations of REM sleep in animals imply the opposite: The higher the animal on the evolutionary scale and the more developed its brain, the greater is the proportion of REM sleep. REM sleep has been found in cats, apes, rats, and sheep—in fact among all mammals in which it has been looked for. On the other hand, birds, whose brains are notoriously small, devote less than 1 percent of their sleeping time to REM sleep and it does not appear to occur in reptiles at all. Rather than being a primitive manifestation, REM sleep may have developed only with the evolution of more complex brains.

In both infants and adults, the presence of REM sleep can be detected not only by the visible fluttering under the lids but also by the typical spikes that appear on simultaneous brain wave recordings.[6] The function of REM sleep is still a matter of speculation, despite the past two decades of intensive study of human sleep. Its function in newborn infants is particularly baffling. It is known that human beings require at least a minimum of REM sleep and will try to make up for it when they have had less than this minimum. Subjects in sleep experiments, if deprived of REM sleep for a night or two by being awakened whenever it begins, will have more REM sleep than usual during succeeding nights. If deprived of REM sleep for several nights, they tend to become restless and irritable. And when awakened from REM sleep, they often report that they have been dreaming.

For some time after the correlation between dreaming and rapid eye movements in sleep was discovered, it was believed that the sleeper's eyes were following the events in the dream. Rapid eye movements recorded before a sleeper was awakened often corresponded with those required to observe the events described by the dreamer. Thus, the eye-movement record of one subject who dreamed of walking up a stairway with five or six steps and then over to a group of people at the top showed five vertical, upward eye movements followed by several horizontal ones. But it has subsequently been shown that in some instances eye movements are unrelated to the events of a dream, and further, that dreams are sometimes reported by subjects awakened from NREM sleep.[7] Thus, eye movements are not essential for dreaming. The current view, based on more recent studies, is that the frequency, not the direction, of eye movements is related to dreams, and not to their content, but to their vividness, intensity, and "emotionality."

Since the visual experience of newborns is limited—in part because they sleep for such long periods—it is unlikely that they are able to produce the succession of visual images that makes up a dream. However, REM sleep has been observed in the congenitally blind and thus is not precluded by lack of visual experience. What, then, accounts for the intensive oculomotor activity observed in sleeping infants?

The brains of human fetuses and infants pass through two periods of very rapid growth.[8] The first occurs between 15 and 20 weeks after conception, when the immature nerve cells of the brain begin to multiply very rapidly. The second, which is even more rapid and lasts from about 25 weeks' gestation through the first year of life, involves both proliferation of the structural cells in the brain that surround and support the nerve cells and the development of myelin (fatty) sheaths on the larger nerves, which speeds up the conduction of nerve impulses. There is considerable evidence to indicate that in the nervous sytem, structural growth, particularly myelinization, may be preceded by functional stimulation.[6]

The visual system is probably the only sensory system for which no stimulation (except pressure) is provided in the fetal environment, for the fetal retina is not exposed to light. Yet the visual tracts in the cerebral cortex show substantial myelinization at birth, and it has been proposed that fetal REM sleep may provide the stimulation of the visual system that is lacking during gestation. This hypothesis might explain, at least in part, why the proportion of REM sleep is so high at birth and begins to decrease in a few weeks.

A relationship between visual stimulation and REM sleep after birth was demonstrated in an experiment with 22 newborns averaging 30 hours of age by James Boismier of the University of Nebraska Psychiatric Institute.[9] About 20 minutes before a scheduled feeding, the infants were observed in their cribs after a piece of cardboard (patterned or unpatterned) was placed in a curved, "Quonset-hut" arrangement about 8 inches above the infant's head and his states were recorded. The infant was then fed by a nurse. After feeding, the infant's states were again observed and recorded until the end of the first REM-sleep period. Each of four groups of infants was exposed to one of four "stimulus conditions": a gray cardboard surface, a checkerboard pattern of 3-inch squares, or a similar pattern of half-inch squares was presented continuously; or 3-inch and half-inch checkerboard squares were presented alternately.

Boismier was testing a hypothesis based on previous work with colleagues that the quiet-awake state, or "alert inactivity" as he called it, has the following relationship to the REM sleep state: the greater the amount of alert inactivity, the less the amount of REM sleep. The four stimuli were expected to produce varying durations of the alert activity state. Thus, the unstimulating blank gray surface was expected to produce the minimum amount of alert inactivity, the checkerboard patterns a moderate amount, and the alternately presented checkerboard patterns the greatest amount.

Comparison of the average duration of alert inactivity in the four stimulus conditions substantiated these predictions. The progressive decreases in the length of REM sleep that paralleled the increases in the duration of alert inactivity confirmed the hypothesis that the two states are inversely related. Thus, the infant's need for REM sleep appears to be regulated, at least in part, by the amount of visual stimulation his environment provides.

The series of states through which infants pass so effortlessly (and at least during sleep, automatically) reveals the fundamental architecture of their early days.[2, 10] Within these states, however, particularly in sleep states, newborns engage in a variety of distinctive spontaneous activities that fill in the details of the overall design of their behavior. As noted, these spontaneous activities include twitches or jerks of face and limbs, general startle reactions involving much of the body, sighs or sobbing inspirations, mouthing and sucking, grimaces, smiles and frowns; and in male infants, penile erections may be observed.

Startles are a prominent feature of newborn behavior, occurring perhaps every two or three minutes. They are seen particularly in quiet sleep. In startles, the whole body quivers, the arms are extended outward and upward, and the head and trunk are bent forward.[11] Startles can be distinguished from the Moro, or embracing, reflex pattern, in which the infant raises his legs, extends his arms, and then brings them forward together in a grasping motion. These two reflexes used to be considered one and the same by most investigators, but a British study, reported in 1972, demonstrated unequivocally that they differ significantly.[12] The Moro reflex can be initiated by letting the baby's head drop slightly, or by shaking the crib or pulling a blanket out from under the infant. Thus, it is response to loss of support more than an internally caused action. The Moro reflex diminishes and disappears within a month or two, as opposed to the startle, which persists. Startles may be spontaneous reactions or may be caused by sudden external stimuli, such as sudden loud sounds.

Some years ago one investigator called attention to a "clear and consistent trend" in her data indicating that newborn males tend to startle more than females, and that mouthing and smiling tend to occur more often in females than in male newborns.[13] However, in the language of research a "trend" is only suggestive and proves nothing. Undeterred, the researcher proceeded to speculate about this indication of a sex difference: Perhaps the greater tendency to startle might reflect the boys' greater muscular vigor and activity, while more mouthing and smiling might manifest a female tendency to concentrate more on the oral cavity—and eventually on language. Whether or not such speculations were prompted by a sexist bias, they were soon cast into doubt by another, similar study of newborns in which the female infants startled as much as the males.[14]

All the spontaneous movements that occur in newborn sleep tend to taper off in frequency and strength after the first month or two. Some are believed to be incorporated gradually into the awake infant's responses to external stimuli. It has been proposed that during the first weeks and months of life, the nerve impulses that give rise to newborn sleep behavior may be assisting in the maturation and differentiation of the central nervous system, particularly of the brain, which grows like a weed during this period. Muscular twitches, sighing, and sobbing gradually disappear during the first month. Within another month the spontaneous startles of the whole body during sleep have been reduced to occasional twitches. Rhythmical mouthing persists perhaps for six months, but long before that, smiling and frowning have begun to be associated with external events.

Penile erection is one newborn reflex that will, quite obviously, persist for years to come, and its ultimate incorporation into awake behavior has been well established. But why "that mighty inch," as Freud called it, is so active in the newborn period, when it has no apparent function, is more speculative.

In 1940, an investigator at Yale University carried out a study of infant erections that has yet to be surpassed for thoroughness.[15] His subjects, nine infants ranging in age from 3 to 20 weeks, were placed in a semicircle of cribs around him as he observed and recorded their erections, urinations, and bowel movements over periods of 6 to 8 hours a day for 10 days. In both sleep and waking states, the erections occurred at a rate of one to two per hour, a rate that was confirmed in a study reported in 1969.[13]

The 1940 observations showed not only that erections are common in infants, but also that they often occur in a series, with one directly following another. Some lasted a mere half minute, others up to an hour or longer, with great differences in frequency and duration from infant to infant. During erections, the infants were restless, and stretched, fretted, screamed, or squealed, and frantically sucked their thumbs, manifesting varying degrees of disturbance. Pleasurable feelings were not evident. Erections were most frequent in the first three hours after feeding, and there was a close association between erection, defecation, and voiding, all of which occurred most frequently after feeding. This association, as well as the frequent subsidence of erections after voiding, led the investigator to conclude that pressure on the bladder, either from the feces in the colon or rectum or from a large volume of urine, is the most probable cause of erections in infants.

In a later study it was shown that in newborns erections are about twice as frequent during REM sleep as during NREM sleep.[13] This may be the beginning of the intimate association between erections in adult males and REM sleep, a period in which 95 percent of their erections in sleep are observed to occur.

Circumcision of male newborns during the first few days after birth is a common practice in the United States. Almost as commonly, the possible psychological effects on the infant are disregarded. However, some evidence strongly suggests that circumcision does in fact have an impact on newborn behavior. It has been found, for example, that after circumcision, NREM sleep is prolonged and the number of NREM periods increases.[16] Immediately after the operation, infants tend to be awake for long periods, during which they fuss and cry, which may account for the subsequent increase in quiet sleep. It has also been proposed that the different methods used to remove the foreskin have differential effects on behavior.

In the United Kingdom and Europe, very few newborns are circumcised, because the procedure is considered unnecessary and potentially dangerous.[16] On the other hand, probably more than four-fifths of male newborns are circumcised in the United States—the procedure has become so routine that it is difficult to obtain exact figures. If, as the evidence suggests, circumcision causes behavioral changes in newborns, specifically in their states, American and European studies might well come up with different results, which should be particularly evident in investigations of inborn sex differences. This has proved to be the case. American investigators, whose male infant subjects are usually circumcised, have reported male-female differences in newborns' sensitivity to skin stimuli and to stimulation by light, as well as in taste preferences, while British and Dutch investigators have not found these gender differences. However, except in the taste studies, the American investigators obtained their data by different methods, which may have contributed to the lack of agreement. Moreover, researchers often exclude infants from their studies who fret or cry too much, as well as those too sleepy to be alert. This might exclude many male infants reacting to circumcision and diminish its distortion of the results.

In any event, some infant researchers have expressed concern that when circumcised male newborns participate in studies of sex differences, any differences found would be attributed to sex when they were actually results of the effects of circumcision.[16] They are also concerned that the immediate as well as the long-term effects of circumcision have not been sufficiently explored. In addition to the need for more extensive studies of the problem, these investigators have called for the labeling of male infant subjects as circumcised or uncircumcised in research reports. Reports that provide this information are now beginning to appear.

In addition to their repertoire of discrete movements, newborns also come equipped with a set of "fixed-action patterns," so called because in normal infants they always consist of the same sequence of movements, like the gustofacial responses discovered by Steiner.[17] Some of these patterns such as rooting, sucking, swallowing, and aversive reactions are essential to the infant's immediate survival. Others, such as orienting, cuddling, clinging, grasping, and crying release caregiver attention and assistance.

The pristine form of the rooting reflex in which the newborn, when touched around the mouth, moves his head from side to side or to the side stimulated is seen only briefly, for the infant soon begins to orient toward the sight, smell, or touch of the nipple and the primitive searching movements no longer occur. In a similar development, newborns at first suck with lips closed on the nipple, and suction is produced by the partial vacuum this creates in the mouth. Then they shift to using the tongue to press the nipple to the roof of the mouth and squeeze out the milk. Fixed-action sucking and rooting patterns are thus modified as the newborn acquires experience with the way things work.

Inborn patterns of clinging and grasping help infants hold onto and maintain contact with their caregivers. A cuddling response is also seen in most newborns. When picked up and held, they mold their bodies and legs into the cavity of the arms. Cuddling not only serves to maintain the contact of infant and caregiver, but also helps to keep the infant secure and warm in the caregiver's arms, and contributes to the development of attachment. But cuddling is not strictly speaking a fixed-action pattern, since it is not universal. A few newborns will actively resist being held, stiffening, pushing themselves away, or threshing about. Some do not attempt to cuddle, but simply lie passively in the caregiver's arms like a sack of meal.

Far less appealing than the cuddling response but far more essential to the infant's survival is the fixed-action pattern of crying. Nothing, perhaps, is quite so attention-getting as the piercing cry of a healthy newborn infant—or so effective in galvanizing an adult into instant action, which is its obvious function.

Infant crying has one curious aspect: It seems to be as "catching" as a yawn. The crying of one baby in a pediatrician's waiting room is likely to have a Chinese-firecracker effect, with one infant after another joining the chorus. Is the distress of one newborn baby somehow communicated to others?

Researchers who have studied this "crying circuit" have found that infants as young as 1 or 2 days of age cry significantly more often on hearing the taped cries of another infant than when they hear no cries or a synthetic "infant cry" simulated by a computer.[18] An additional finding in several of these experiments was that female infants were more apt than males to cry "empathetically." However, the tape of a newborn girl crying was used in all these studies, and girls may be particularly empathetic to female crying. Therefore, until further studies are made using tapes of crying by both sexes, stereotypical views of women as naturally more empathetic than men can be neither confirmed nor disproved via this route.

The "group crying" of newborns may well be an innate survival mechanism, since the crying of several infants is unquestionably a greater stimulant to action than the crying of one. An alternative explanation derives from the fact that infants hear their own cries, and since these cries are associated with distress in one form or another, the infants might learn to link the sound of crying with unpleasant feelings and thus tend to experience these feelings when they hear the cries of others. Whether the group response is innate or learned cannot be settled until it is studied within a few hours after birth. But whatever its function or origin, the existence of "social crying" has been well established.

Perhaps no one has sketched a more accurate picture of the crying infant than Charles Darwin in his *Expression of the Emotions in Man and Animals,* published more than a century ago:

Infants, when suffering even slight pain, moderate hunger, or discomfort, utter violent and prolonged screams. Whilst thus screaming their eyes are firmly closed, so that the skin around them is wrinkled, and the forehead contracted in a frown. The mouth is widely opened with the lips contracted in a peculiar manner, which causes it to assume a squarish form; the gums or teeth being more or less exposed. The breath is inhaled almost spasmodically.[19]

Darwin was interested in the expression of infant emotions, not in suppressing them, but the question of the so-called pacification of infants has a venerable scientific history, as the well-known developmental psychologist Yvonne Brackbill has pointed out.[20] During the 1880s, for example, one scientist reported that infants listening to a sound moved much less than usual. In 1913, another noted that infants' respiration and pulse rates were more regular when they were listening to an apparently enjoyable sound. During the 1930s, a group of investigators at the University of Iowa found that moderately high intensities of sound, light, and even restraint by swaddling (an age-old custom) had a quieting effect on newborns.

Then in the early 1960s, the American pediatrician Lee Salk reported that continuous exposure to the sound of a heartbeat for four days not only reduced the amount of newborn crying but also served to increase infant food intake and weight.[21] In a later experiment, Salk compared the times taken by 2-year-old children to fall asleep when listening to lullabies, the ticking of a metronome, and a heartbeat and found that the heartbeat put them to sleep twice as fast as the other sounds. From his series of experiments, he formulated the hypothesis that the infants had been "imprinted" with the sound of their mothers' heartbeats during gestation.

However intriguing the Salk hypothesis, it was not borne out in several later experiments. In one of these, reported by Yvonne Brackbill and her colleagues, groups of newborns averaging 48 hours of age heard either no sounds or rhythmic sounds in the form of metronome ticks, unfamiliar lullabies in a foreign tongue, or a tape recording of a heart beating at the same rate as the metronome.[20] The sounds as a whole yielded significantly less crying, less muscular activity, and greater regularity of heart rate and respiration than the no-sound condition. However, the heartbeats did not have a significantly greater quieting effect than the other sounds.

Although a more recent test of Salk's hypothesis also failed to confirm it, it turned up some new and interesting information about the effects of maternal heartbeats on infants.[22] One- and 2-day-old newborns were divided into two groups: those whose mothers had normal heart rates a month or two prior to delivery and those whose mothers had rapid heart rates at that time. When crying, the newborns were exposed to tape recordings of normal or rapid heartbeats or to blank tapes with no sound. The infants who heard heartbeats quieted and fell asleep significantly faster than did those who heard no sounds, whether or not the heart rates matched those of their mothers. However, the quieting effect of continuous rhythmic sound stimulation was again demonstrated. A corollary finding of the study was that babies of mothers with normal heart rates in late pregnancy were more "soothable" than those whose mothers' heart rates were rapid, quieting significantly faster and more consistently, whatever the reason for this might be.

Adults prepare for sleep by shutting the bedroom door, turning off the radio, lying down quite motionless, and covering themselves with blankets that provide a constant temperature. In other words, to reduce their state of arousal and get to sleep, they find it necessary to exclude as much external stimulation as possible. In infants, however, the conditions that lead to sleep are reversed.[5] Nearly any continuous, moderately intense stimulus will tend to reduce their level of arousal and induce sleep. Loud sounds, strong lights, temperatures above normal, the continuing tactile stimulus of tight swaddling from neck to toes in strips of flannel, or even constant swinging or jiggling have been found to reduce infant arousal. In addition, the arousal is further diminished by increases in intensity of the stimulation, as well as by the addition of a second stimulus, different from the first. Thus, the combination of strong light and a loud, continuing noise level is more effective than either alone. It is not recommended, however, that parents quiet babies by such intense stimulation under normal circumstances. Constant high-intensity stimulation of infants is not desirable. Further, babies may go to sleep simply to shut out this stimulation. Devoting their energy to shutting it out, they may not gain the full benefits of sleep. But, as will be noted, continuous stimulation is useful in special situations.

Brackbill has investigated the cumulative effect of continuous auditory, visual, tactile, and temperature stimulation presented in succession to infants averaging 1 month of age.[23] The sounds were tape-recorded heartbeats amplified to a loudness level equivalent to that of heavy traffic. The light stimuli were fluorescent and incandescent lamps suspended 4 feet above the infants' cribs, yielding a total light intensity of 400 watts (equal to four 100-watt bulbs). An increase in the average temperature of the room from the normal 50 degrees to 60 degrees provided the temperature-sense stimulus. Tactile stimulation consisted of tight swaddling of the infants. Observers noted the infants' states, and instruments recorded their heart and breathing rates and movements in the crib. Experimental sessions began directly after feeding, with the infants in a quiet awake state. Each infant was observed under five stimulus conditions: no stimulation and continuous stimulation of one, two, three, and four senses.

As the number of senses stimulated increased, progressive decreases occurred in the duration of the crying awake state, as well as in heart and breathing rates and infants' movements in the crib. And there were concomitant increases in the duration of quiet sleep. The duration of quiet awake, drowsy, and REM sleep states was not greatly changed.

Brackbill noted that the effect of continuous stimulations does not appear to be dependent on the presence of a cerebral cortex, a conclusion derived from a study of an "anencephalic" infant she and two colleagues had made.[24] This 90-day-old infant had been born with a brainstem and cerebellum but no cerebral cortex and was totally blind although sensitive to sounds and touch. The only state identifiable in the infant was REM sleep, and so state changes could not be observed. But when he was exposed to continuous sound stimulation or continuous tactile stimulation (by swaddling), quieting was evident in the infant's decreased heart and respiration rates.

The pacifying effects of continuous stimulation have been amply demonstrated, but Brackbill suggested that it be used only to quiet normal infants when they are very cranky, colicky, or ill. She recommended it particularly for abnormal infants, such as those born very prematurely, who are sometimes so hyperactive and have such severe tremors and spasms that they become debilitated and may even die if not quieted.

Continuous stimulation, then, has a place in the quieting of infants in unusual or emergency situations. Mothers and other caregivers, however, already have at their disposal a considerable array of techniques for dealing with a crying or cranky infant. What methods do they prefer, and how successful are they? These questions were answered in a study done by Silvia Bell and Mary D. Salter Ainsworth at Johns Hopkins University.[25]

Bell and Ainsworth observed 26 infant-mother pairs at home for four-hour periods during the infant's first year. For the purpose of the study, crying was defined as any instance of vocal distress, from unhappy noises to fussing sounds to full-blown cries. The mothers' responses to their infants' cries were tallied as follows: picks up, holds, vocalizes, interacts, feeds, approaches, touches, offers a pacifier or toy, removes something disturbing, enters the room, and "other."

New mothers will be happy to learn that the duration of infants' crying spells decreased from an average of 7.7 minutes per hour in the first three months to an average of 4.4 minutes per hour (a mere 7 percent of the time) in the last three months. However, the frequency of crying spells remained at about four per hour throughout the year. Thus, year-old infants cry as often as newborns but not for so long.

Nearly half the crying spells were ignored by the mothers during the first three months, but this proportion dropped to 37 percent by the fourth quarter. The degree of responsiveness shown by individual mothers remained relatively stable, however. Those who responded infrequently in the first quarter of the year tended to ignore their infants' cries in subsequent quarters. Similarly, mothers responsive in the first three months tended to be responsive during the rest of the year.

Throughout the year, the most successful intervention by far was picking up and holding the baby—and it was also the method the mothers used most frequently. The next most effective cry-stopper was feeding, followed by giving the baby a pacifier or toy (in the first three months). More effective toward the end of the year, but less so when the infants were younger, were talking to the baby, entering the room, and coming close to or touching the baby. The newborns were most soothed when actually held, but infants in the last quarter of their first year were soothed simply by having their mothers nearby and attentive. And it was found that the single most effective factor in stopping a baby from crying was the promptness of the mothers' response.

Recent editions of the U.S. Children's Bureau's *Infant Care* advise mothers to follow their natural impulse and respond to their baby's crying. But for over twenty years *Infant Care* warned mothers that picking up a baby between feedings was to be avoided at all costs.[26] To do so, it said, would teach the baby that "crying will get him what he wants, sufficient to make a spoiled, fussy baby, and a household tyrant whose continual demands make a slave of the mother." However, in the Bell and Ainsworth study, "spoiled" infants, that is, the infants who cried and fussed a lot after the first few months, were the infants whose mothers had *failed* to respond to their cries or who had responded only after considerable delay. And it has been found in other studies that infants whose mothers respond promptly to their signals are more independent, tend not to be distressed when their mothers leave the room briefly, and need little physical contact with the mother by the end of the first year.

Most mothers respond without delay when the baby cries. But are they able to tell what the baby is crying about? Many believe that they can, and some developmental psychologists have held that mothers can learn to distinguish various meanings in their baby's cries after a few weeks. This question has been controversial, however, and the results of studies designed to answer it have been conflicting.

A more definitive answer was obtained in a study reported in 1974, but the range of cry-stimulating situations used was narrow, the number of mothers and infants observed was small, and the investigators considered their findings tentative.[27]

Tape recordings were made of the cries of eight healthy infants 3 to 5 months old in response to pain (after snapping of a rubber band against the sole of the infant's foot), startle (after a loud noise was produced behind the infant's head by slamming two wooden blocks together), and hunger (after feeding was stopped a few seconds after it began). The recorded cries (with no indication of the stimulus situation) were assembled in random order on a tape and played to the infants' mothers and to 10 other mothers of infants of comparable ages. Each mother was asked to indicate whether or not it was her baby crying and whether the cause of the crying was pain, startle, or hunger.

Although the mothers recognized the cries of their own infants with little difficulty, they failed miserably in their attempts to identify the reasons for the cries, either of their own or others' infants. Hunger was a favored explanation, but real hunger cries were often misinterpreted. This result led the investigators to conclude that the function of the cry in the normal situation is merely to alert the mother, and that "any of her suppositions concerning the situation that evoked the crying behaviour must be based upon additional environmental cues."

It is hardly surprising that mothers are familiar with the unique characteristics of their own infants' cries. But infants 20 to 30 days old would not be expected to distinguish their own mothers' voices from the voices of strangers. However, it has been shown that infants of these ages who have learned that sucking produces a voice, either the mother's or a stranger's, will suck faster and longer to produce the mother's voice.[28] Thus, infants recognize the characteristics of their mothers' voices before they have reached the age of 1 month.

Perhaps the infant's recognition of the mother's voice contributes to its soothing effect, but, as shown in the Bell and Ainsworth study, the mother's voice is far less effective in quieting infants than simply picking them up and holding them. And when mothers pick up and hold their babies for soothing purposes, they inadvertently provide them with visual experiences as well.

When crying infants are picked up and put to the mother's shoulder, they will also often open their eyes, look bright and alert, and scan their surroundings. However, Anneliese Korner and Evelyn Thoman, working with infants 2 to 3 days old at Stanford University, found that the degree of visual alertness that results from this kind of intervention depends on the way infants are picked up and the way they are held.[29]

Each infant in the Korner and Thoman experiment was picked up or held (or both) in three different ways: He was put to the shoulder with his head supported and his face above shoulder level; lifted horizontally and cradled in the investigator's arms; and held close while lying on a table. Three other kinds of intervention were also used: raising the infant to an upright position in an infant chair, moving him to and fro in the chair, and talking to him in a high-pitched (female) voice. To determine whether these interventions were more effective when the infant was roused from sleep (REM) or was crying, 40 of the infants were tested while crying, 24 while sleeping.

The main objective of the study was to measure the relative effect on visual alertness of (1) contact and (2) stimulation of the "vestibular system," with or without the upright position. The vestibular system of the inner ear contains the receptors for the sense of balance, which are stimulated by movement. And stimulation of this system also affects eye movements.

Highly statistically significant differences were found in the degree of visual alertness produced by these various interventions in crying infants. Contact alone (holding the baby as he lay on a table) had no more effect than the high-pitched voice (no contact). But vestibular stimulation (lifting the baby or moving him in any way) had a powerful effect. The combination of contact, vestibular stimulation, and the upright position produced the most visual alertness; 76 percent of the infants who were picked up and put to the shoulder with the head supported and face above the shoulder level scanned their surroundings. The infants who were roused from sleep for these investigations showed little or no response.

The yield of visual alertness from the movement, handling, and picking up of newborns suggests that infants who are deprived of this stimulation have limited visual experience. If this is the case, low-birth-weight infants, who are often also born before term, may be at a particular disadvantage. Ordinarily they are kept in the hospital until they have reached a weight of 5 to 5½ pounds, which may take two to three weeks or longer, depending on their birth weight. Further, they are rarely handled and are kept in Isolettes that shield them from infection but also shield them from stimulation. Developmental psychologists are concerned that this isolated existence may have adverse effects on development and have tried out various methods of providing the stimulation these infants lack.

In one such experiment, low-birth-weight infants were given a program of extra stimulation during their stay in the premature nursery (an average of 6 weeks), and their mothers were encouraged to continue the program through the infant's first year.[30] In the hospital, mobiles were suspended over the infants' cribs within a few hours after birth. As soon as they were strong enough—usually within a week after birth—the newborns were removed from their Isolettes eight times a day for feeding and play periods. They were rocked, talked to, fondled, and patted while they were held close in the nursing position and were burped at the shoulder. When the infants went home, their mothers were supplied with infant chairs, tops, rattles, wall posters, picture books, and so on, to use in stimulating their babies at the appropriate stage of development. A control group of low-birth-weight infants received only the conventional isolated, germ-free care, and no special guidance or equipment was provided for use at home.

Standard tests of development given to the two groups of babies at 1 week showed the control infants to be slightly ahead of the experimental group. By 4 weeks of age, however, the stimulated infants had forged significantly ahead of the control infants. And by the end of the first year, their behavioral status was equal to that of year-old full-term infants. Similar studies have indicated that guidance provided for mothers at home is not necessarily taken advantage of. Nevertheless, the beneficial effects of early stimulation were apparent.

A briefer investigation with more limited objectives has clearly delineated some of the beneficial effects of early extra physical stimulation on premature newborns.[31] A dozen premature babies were studied while still in the hospital. Half the infants received the routine isolated nursery care and were handled only for changing, feeding, and physical examinations. The experimental group were given extra tactile and and kinesthetic stimulation during 15-minute periods for four consecutive hours daily from their second through their eleventh days of life. During these periods, their bodies were rubbed all over and their arms and legs gently flexed back and forth by the experimenter, who tried to keep out of the infants' direct line of vision insofar as possible, so that the effect of social stimulation would not distort the findings.

By 12 days of age, the stimulated newborns had gained 10 percent more weight than had the control newborns, not because they had more feedings than the control infants, but because they took more with each feeding. Their nurses described them as eager nursers, retaining their food well, and as more alert than the control infants, who often spat up, took their formula poorly, and seemed lethargic. These findings underline the adverse effects of the conventional treatment of premature newborns. But they also demonstrate that even such a simple maneuver as vigorous physical stimulation can ameliorate a major disadvantage of being born prematurely.

The extent to which infant capabilities are open to early stimulation and will be accelerated by it was also shown in an investigation of the effect of early "walking" exercises of infants.[32] Walking is a very complex pattern of behavior of which infants are not normally capable until they are, on the average, 12 to 14 months old. However, any normal newborn infant whose feet are let down on a flat surface and who is supported under the arms will make full-fledged walking movements. This capability is lost by about 8 weeks of age and does not normally reappear until infants are ready to pull themselves up to a standing position and begin to take their first steps by themselves. One group of parents in the study exercised their infants' "walking reflex" from the first through the eighth week of life. Another group of parents exercised their infants by pumping their legs while the infants remained flat on their backs. Control infants were not exercised at all.

Infants who had received walking exercises for four three-minute periods a day responded with increasingly more competent walking during the eight weeks. And by 10 months of age, they were walking by themselves. Those whose legs were only pumped walked at 11.4 months, and those who received no exercise program walked at 11.7 months. Clearly, the early walking exercises had appreciably accelerated their walking alone. But not only that—their walking exercises had produced spatial, visual, and kinesthetic experiences that helped them to learn faster and perhaps even to feel a greater sense of competence in dealing with the world.

CHAPTER 4
First Impressions

Viewed symbolically, the cutting of the umbilical cord transforms the infant from a maternal parasite to a vulnerable loner in an alien world of which his mother is now only a remote, infinitesimal part. And, unlike a plant, which remains rooted motionless in the earth that will provide its support from seed to maturity, the infant must, willy-nilly, now make it on his own. Or so it may appear. But to depict infants as rootless and alone in a world they "never made," as bereft as Linus without his security blanket, makes for good drama but poor biology. By and large nature is not a free-enterprise operation. Rather than having to fend for themselves, infants from the moment of birth are sustained by a biological welfare system whose sole purpose is to promote their survival and growth. The elements of this system are their automatically functioning life-support mechanisms, their capacity to interact with and adapt to an infinite variety of environmental events and conditions, and sensory receptors that convey the requisite information about these events and conditions. Today, investigations of the sensory world of infants have begun to reveal that the sensory part of this sustaining system begins to operate far earlier and with far greater efficiency than had been assumed.

Infant science is such a new discipline that most discoveries about infant sensory capacities appear in reports that still smell strongly of printer's ink. But occasionally, on dustier shelves of the archives, a striking foreshadowing on this or that discovery turns up.[1] Thus, a century and a half ago, J. C. G. Jörg, then director of the obstetric hospital in Leipzig, Germany, and a keen observer with an encyclopedic knowledge of babies, said of the taste reactions of the newborn infant: "He takes sweet fluids with the expressions and sounds of well-being, everything else with the expression of disgust. Particularly, salty, spicy, and bitter things absolutely displease the baby." In a publication of the same year, 1826, the French physiologist F. Magendie independently expressed an identical opinion. Sweet-tasting substances, Jörg and Magendie had noted, made infants lick their lips and begin to suck, with facial expressions reflecting pleasure. Salty, bitter, and spicy substances made infants grimace, shut their eyes, protrude their lips and tongue, and even drool and spit. Their descriptions of infant reactions to sweet and bitter tastes are remarkably consistent with those reported by Jacob Steiner in the 1970s, although, unlike Jörg and Magendie, Steiner has not yet observed any distinguishable reactions to salty tastes in either infants or adults. In effect, then, Steiner merely confirmed what had been recorded long ago in the notebooks of Jörg and Magendie. But by today's standards, their records, consisting of some random observations made probably under varied conditions and without control of extraneous factors that might affect the infants' behavior, would be viewed with great skepticism.

Early infant studies consisted almost entirely of diaries or notebooks in which scientists recorded observations of their own or others' infants over a period of several years, often in minute detail. Among the most notable of these infant biographers was the celebrated British naturalist Charles Darwin, whose descriptions of the expression of emotions in infants laid the foundation for the research being done in this area today. In this century, the French-Swiss psychologist Jean Piaget derived the successive stages in the development of intelligence from meticulously detailed records of the behavior of his three children. In the hands of two such gifted scientists, the biographical method can be remarkably productive.

Without technical assistance, however, not even a visual observer of genius caliber would have detected certain astonishing feats of sensory discrimination performed by 1- to 3-day-old newborns in a recent study of infant taste reactions at Yale–New Haven Hospital carried out by Geoffrey Nowlis and William Kessen of Yale University.[2]

The task of the infants participating in this experiment was to ingest solutions containing varying concentrations of a substance they liked immensely, namely, sugar. The question at issue was whether or not their responses would indicate awareness of the differences in sweetness. To ensure that the infants would be hungry, the tests were usually made three to five hours after their previous feeding. After fresh diapering in the nursery, they were taken individually to an experimental room in the newborn special care unit. There, a seated experimenter held the baby in one arm and offered him a bottle containing a small amount of sugar solution of measured strength. Several grades of sweetness were used, most of the infants receiving sugar solutions of four different concentrations. They were allowed to suck on a special rubber nipple either until they had consumed all of the solution or until they had stopped sucking for two minutes, presumably having taken all they wanted. The special nipple was a fine piece of engineering design, measuring the intake or "pull-in" pressure from the sucking reflex at the front of the infant's tongue, any rejective or "push-out" pressure from the reflex at the back of the tongue, and the strength of suction or "vacuum" in the infant's mouth as he consumed the solution. In one series of these tests, sugar solutions of four different concentrations were presented to 10 infants and their sucking for each measured and recorded.

By all the measurements, these infants showed that, in their judgment, "sweeter was better." Their average "pulling-in" tongue pressures increased directly with the sweetness of the sugar solutions, consistently moving higher from the weakest to the strongest solutions. In other words, as the sugar concentration doubled, the sucking tongue pressures doubled. The "pulling-in" tongue motions were precisely graded to the sweetness of the sugar solutions time after time. Comparison of this newborn ability to distinguish the strength of sugar solutions by taste with the taste discrimination of adults led the researchers to two conclusions:

> First, the sensory apparatus responsible for assessing relative sweetness of sugars is essentially as competent in the newborn as it is in the adult. Second, this sensory apparatus is capable of systematically eliciting a precisely graded response in the human newborn. . . . Thus, the ability of the infant to utilize the gustatory apparatus to discriminate among ingestible substances has here been clearly demonstrated.

In another newborn taste study, infants given water to suck before and after sucking on sugar solutions of varying concentrations sucked less water after taking very sweet solutions than after those of less sweetness.[3] Oddly, to adults, plain water has a sour-bitter taste after they have been eating or drinking something sweet, a fact that the reader can easily verify by experiment. The researchers believed that the infants' diminished enthusiasm for water after they had sucked on an intensely sweet solution indicated that they, too, experienced the same unpleasant change in the taste of water that adults notice.

The experimental evidence that is accumulating suggests that infants' ability to make subtle discriminations among tastes is at least as good as that of adults. Infant taste reactions, then, are not capricious or meaningless but are based on the capacity of their taste buds to distinguish fine gradations in the flavor or substances. (Taste buds, the receptors for taste, are located in the mouth, throat, and tongue.) In fact, infants have a more plentiful supply of taste buds than do children and adults. Since the number of taste buds diminishes with age, elderly people often find to their dismay that everything tastes alike.

Apparently it is because of their delicate taste sensitivities that infants show such decided preferences for certain foods. Human infants, like cats, are notoriously finicky, accepting some foods with obvious relish and rejecting others with undisguised revulsion. But what course of action should be taken when infants reject foods that presumably are "good" or "essential"? Should they be fed only what they accept, or should "good, nutritious" food that they forcibly reject be rammed through their tightly closed lips? It is the lot of caregivers to be continuously impaled on the horns of this or some other dilemma.

If bewildered parents with a finicky infant seek the guidance of an experienced pediatrician, they are likely to be told to relax and let their baby do what comes naturally. Alternatively, they might be advised to increase the statistical probability of acceptance by giving their infant a wider variety of choices. A few pediatricians, however, made of sterner stuff, frown on such permissiveness. Prominent in this group is Professor Albrecht Peiper, who as chief of the department of pediatrics at Leipzig University warned mothers of the folly of catering to their infant's taste.[1] If foods that infants reject are removed from their diets, he said, a "one-sided diet, with all its shortcomings, results." As opposed to this abject submission to an infant's will, he strongly recommended that infants be forced to eat the "right" food. Admitting that an infant's aversion to new and different-tasting food is hard to overcome, he enjoined his fellow physicians to insist that it be done. To bolster their resolve in this endeavor, he cited the "experience in institutions," where, he said, "we usually succeed without any difficulty in getting the infant accustomed to a kind of food refused at home." Better not to dwell on how such feats were accomplished!

Peiper acknowledged that "the taste reaction is very useful," but his assumption that infants respond favorably only to sweet tastes led him to conclude that a mother who is guided by it "exposes her child to grave dangers." Had Peiper been aware that infants enjoy a variety of tastes, as demonstrated by Steiner's experiment with tastants, he might have accorded more importance to infants' preferences.

Some sporadic reports of the infant's reaction to odors began to appear during the 1930s. But for over three decades there was to be no general consensus as to what infants could or could not smell. Some investigators found no evidence of newborn olfactory reactions except to very strong odors. They reported that infants reacted to such odors by tightly closing their eyes, grimacing, and moving about restlessly—responses that recall Steiner's descriptions of newborns rejecting food odors. To particularly strong odors, such as ammonia or vinegar, newborns responded by breath holding ("Kratschmer's reflex") or by breathing irregularly, and often by sneezing. Some observers held that newborns sought the breast by smell, but others suspected that this might be aided by vision or temperature, either alone or in combination with smell. The newborn sense of smell seemed to be more difficult to stimulate and harder to measure than any other sense. Furthermore, newborns seemed to adapt very quickly and thoroughly to smells, paying no attention to them after initial fleeting reactions.

An investigation made in 1963 at Brown University helped to explain this lack of consensus.[4] Newborn infants were presented from their first through their fourth days successively with Q-Tips saturated with seven graded concentrations of asafetida, an odorant that is universally considered offensive. To monitor their responses, the infants were placed in a "stabilimeter," an apparatus that recorded fine changes in their movements. A pneumograph around the infant's abdomen kept track of changes in respiration rate. Each day, the infant was presented first with the weakest concentration of the odor, then the next strongest concentration, and so on, until a change in respiration rate or movement indicated a definite response. The olfactory threshold, or smallest concentration of asafetida that first elicited a response, was thus observed. On the first day of age, the average newborn's threshold was at 60 percent concentration, decreasing to 30 percent on the second day, 15 percent on the third day, and 12 to 13 percent on the fourth day.

Thus, major changes in sensitivity to smells occur in the first few days of life. No doubt this variability had frustrated earlier attempts to obtain reliable information about newborn olfactory capacities. It may perhaps be attributed to the gradual clearing of the mucus that often partially plugs the nose at birth.

This investigation cleared up some of the confusion about the early development of the sense of smell, but it did not stir up a resurgence of interest in the subject. Most researchers remained skeptical that infant olfaction was a fruitful area of study, and only a handful of the most persistent continued to investigate it. One significant result of this persistence was the discovery that infants can discriminate between the smells of alcohols of various chemical structures.[5] But so heavy is the hand of tradition that after the publication of this study, it was still being asserted that the infant's sense of smell is rudimentary.

The ability of infants to discriminate between various alcohols was verified in a later, more detailed study of 125 infants averaging 2.5 days of age.[6] As in the newborn threshold experiment, the infants' responses were measured by a stabilimeter and pneumograph. Five alcohols were used, containing either 3, 5, 6, 8, or 10 carbon atoms. This provided odors of increasing strength, from relatively weak to strong. If the infants were able to discriminate one alcohol from another, lower and lower concentrations should be required to elicit a response as the strength of the alcohols increased. They passed this test with flying colors, in effect "arranging" the alcohols in an ascending order by number of carbon atoms. Adults asked to discriminate between these alcohols arranged them in a similar fashion.

To what extent do infants actually use their acute sense of smell? One recent experiment explored the possibility that infants can recognize their mother's unique odor, distinguishing it from the odors of other women.[7] Smelling tests were conducted with 10 breast-fed infants at 2 days, 2 weeks, and 6 weeks of age. The stimuli used in each test were a clean, moist pad and pads that the infant's mother and another mother had kept in their bras for three hours before the test. The infants were tested close to feeding time and while sleeping.

Each pad was held close to the infant's nose for 30 seconds, and the criterion for response was arousal from sleep.

Only one of the infants tested at two days reacted to any of the pads. This infant made sucking responses both to the mother's and to the strange woman's pads. At two weeks after birth, however, arousal was general, with eight infants responding, but only three responding solely to their own mother's pad. At six weeks, their ability to discriminate between the odors had markedly improved. Of seven infants responding, six responded only to their own mother's odor and in a pattern of orienting and sucking that was strikingly different from their responses to the strange woman's odor. None of the infants ever responded to the odorless stimulus.

Maternal identification and attraction by smell is reminiscent of the olfactory signals by which animals communicate with each other for a variety of purposes, including mating. Conceivably, a human adult might be able to recognize others by smell, or distinguish his or her own odor from that of others.

Before the infant study was begun, the same investigator had done a comparable experiment with college freshmen. He asked male and female students (who are among the handiest of subjects) not to use any soap, perfume, or deodorant for 24 hours and then to wear a T undershirt for another 24 hours. These shirts were then placed in buckets with a small hole in the cover. The students were given three containers to sniff—one with their own shirt, one with a strange male's shirt, and one with a strange female's shirt—and asked to indicate their own. In a second test they were given the strange male and female shirts used in the first test and asked to specify the sex of the wearer. In both tests, 81 percent of the males and 69 percent of the females made correct choices, identifying themselves and the sex of the wearer by odor alone. A frequent comment was that the male odors seemed "musky" and the female odors "sweet."

Thus, the sense of smell may play a role in human communication that goes unrecognized because of the dominance of two other sensory systems, hearing and vision.

Vision is probably the most complicated, highly developed, and frequently used human sense. Although it does not greatly outstrip hearing in these respects, vision is regarded by most people as more essential.[8] In a 1976 Gallup Poll, when people were asked to select from a list of physical disabilities the one they dreaded the most, 76 percent chose blindness; only 4 percent chose deafness. According to this same poll, among eight diseases and afflictions, the second most feared, next to cancer, was blindness. This deep concern with the sense of sight may explain in part why, of all the senses, vision has received the most attention from scientists.

Contradictory opinions about whether or not infants see color have been bandied about for a hundred years.[1] Some claimed that infants are totally color-blind. Others, with equal vehemence, declared that even the newborn can see every color in the visible spectrum. Still others regarded the color sense as a late development, estimated variously as occurring any time from the end of the first year to the fourth to sixth year, and later in girls than in boys. It was said that children first see a given color at a certain stage of their development. Various sequences were suggested, such as blue first, then red, white, green, and brown; or yellow first, then green, blue, and red. All kinds of variations on these sequences were dreamed up, some even including black and white.

None of these theories, though often proposed as certainties, was backed by a shred of experimental evidence that would be taken seriously today. Even that meticulous observer Charles Darwin thought that his children were color-blind, when in fact they had normal color vision. Only when the study of color vision was brought into the laboratory was the proper framework provided for a systematic testing of this crazy quilt of theories.

The difficulties encountered in approaching the study of infant vision are formidable. For one thing, infants cannot report what they see. For another, visual sensations are a complex amalgam of several distinct properties. They vary in brightness (depending on intensity), in hue, or color (depending on wavelength), and in saturation, or vividness (the extent to which a color is diluted or undiluted with white). A visual sensation, for example, may be described as "red," "very bright," and "unsaturated" (pale or pastel). It has been estimated that the human eye can distinguish some 7.3 million different "colors" when the three variables of brightness, hue, and saturation are included, and can distinguish from 120 to 150 different hues alone.[9] Furthermore, brightness varies with hue—reds, for instance, are usually deemed brighter than blues or greens of the same physical intensity. And the nature of the light, natural or artificial, has a strong effect on hue.

Researchers have to keep all these variables under firm control when designing investigations of color perception, whether in infants or adults. Otherwise, there would be no assurance that the subjects were seeing and responding to color (hue) and not to some other visual property such as brightness.

The visual preference test is a technique that has often been used in the study of infant color vision. If, when presented with two colors side by side on a screen, an infant gazes at one longer than the other, apparently displaying a preference, it can be inferred that the infant is able to differentiate between those colors and therefore must be able to see color. But suppose the infant gazes as long at one color as the other, dividing the time between them. This could mean either that the infant had no preference or was unable to discriminate between the two colors. When such nonpreferential gazing occurred in a number of studies, the value of the visual preference test began to be questioned.

In 1974, an investigator at Case Western Reserve University devised a more successful variation of the visual preference test by taking advantage of a well-established characteristic of infants' visual behavior. Many studies had shown that infants as young as 10 hours old, as well as older infants, prefer to look at patterned things, such as checkerboard designs or clippings from newspapers, rather than unpatterned things, such as plain colored squares.[10] Therefore, if infants gazed preferentially at a stimulus that looks patterned only to those who have color vision, infants' ability to see colors would be demonstrated. Accordingly, this investigator made up two kinds of checkerboards.[11] One was constructed by pasting small squares of one color onto a large square of a different color. The other was constructed in the same manner, except that the pasted-on squares were the same color as the background squares. A dozen different patterned squares were made to provide a wide range of differences in color, such as blue on purple-blue and red on green. All the squares were equated for brightness and saturation on the basis of adult judgments.

The checkerboards were shown to 157 male and female infants ranging in age from 13 to 25 weeks, and the percentage of total fixation time devoted to each type of square was calculated. It seemed clear from the infants' overwhelming preference for the patterned stimuli that they were able to detect the difference in color. Not only that—but the greater the difference, as in the red-green checkerboard, the longer they gazed at the pattern.

Although a few younger infants participated in the experiment, the investigator circumspectly concluded that "infants are capable of discriminating on the basis of hue by 4 to 6 months of age." Naturally elated at the success of this experiment, he suggested that the same method could be used to investigate color discrimination in infants from birth onward, as well as for the early detection of deficiencies in color vision.

At first glance, this appears to provide a striking verification of infant color perception by means of an ingenious technique. However, a scientific "conclusion" has much in common with New England weather as described by Mark Twain: "If you don't like it, wait a minute!" Typically, early in 1975, a detailed critique of this study appeared, casting serious doubt on the investigator's conclusions.[12] The critic suggested that, to infants, the different colors in the checkerboard patterns may well have varied in brightness. They may have fixed their attention on a patterned checkerboard simply because it was of a different brightness than the unpatterned one. This possibility occurred to him because it had been adults who had judged that all the brightnesses were equal, and he felt that the lens of the infant eye probably absorbs light differently than does the adult lens. He went on to list a number of other factors in the experimental situation that might have caused variations in the brightness of different hues.

The original investigator published an instant rebuttal, citing statistical data that he believed definitively ruled out the possibility that brightness differences accounted for his findings.[13] He then reaffirmed his contention that the study's results "indicate hue discrimination on the part of the infant." And there the matter rested—but not for long.

There are few more powerful stimulants to productive scientific activity than a lively controversy, which often sets off a diligent search for a new method that will resolve it once and for all.

In a study of infant color discrimination published in 1975, the year following the color-brightness dispute, two investigators reported on a new way to control the variable of brightness.[14] Two 2-month-old female infants were shown a vertical bar of white light on a white screen placed in front of them. In a series of trials, the intensity of the light, and hence its brightness, was varied in small steps but over a wide range. When the brightness of the white bar differed substantially from that of the white screen, the infant would gaze fixedly at the bar. But when the brightness of the white bar closely approached that of the screen, the infants' staring became random, indicating that they could no longer distinguish the bar from the screen. These trials were made to determine just how sensitive the infants were to differences in brightness. And these very young infants proved to be remarkably so, for they could still distinguish the white bar when its brightness (intensity) varied by only a few percentage points from that of the screen. As the researchers pointed out, this sensitivity made it entirely possible that in the checkerboard experiment, minor differences in brightness rather than perception of differences in color could account for the infants' preferential gazing and seeming ability to distinguish colors.

These preliminaries set the stage for a test of color discrimination, in which a red bar on a white screen was presented to the infants. The bar's brightness was also varied by making small changes in its intensity, again over a wide range. Thus, the brightness of the bar was bound to come to a point at which it was the same as the brightness of the white screen. At this point, the infants, if they were unable to perceive red, should have stopped looking, as they had with the white bar. However, their attention continued to remain fixed on the red bar, no matter what its brightness.

Although this experiment did not prove that infants' color perception encompassed the whole spectrum, it did at least establish that two infants could perceive red—a small but important step toward a resolution of the controversy.

In the same year, Marc Bornstein of Yale University announced a major discovery about infant color perception.[15] In his study, 67 infants, 4 to 5 months of age, viewed pairs of colored circles projected on a screen placed in front of them. Each circle of a pair was of a different color, and the infant's preference for one over the other was measured in terms of gazing time. The colors were equated for brightness using a sensitivity scale that adjusted for lesser sensitivity toward the blue end of the spectrum (failure to make this adjustment was mentioned in the critique of the checkerboard study). In all, eight colors were shown, although no infant saw every one. Four were primary colors (blue, green, yellow, and red), and four were colors on either side of a primary color in the spectrum (red-blue, blue-green, green-yellow, and yellow-red), called "intercolors," or "boundary colors." The infants were divided into four groups, and each group saw a different set of pairs. An additional group was shown a set of single colored circles, one by one.

The color preferences of a group of adults (averaging 24 years of age) were also tested with the same circles by asking them to rate the colors from 0 (most unpleasant imaginable) to 10 (indifferent) and to 20 (most pleasant imaginable). In this way, the color preferences of infants, if such there were, could be compared with those of adults, which had been investigated in several prior studies as well.

In every group, even in infants shown single circles, differences in color were reflected by marked differences in average infant fixation time. The infants also looked significantly longer at primary than at boundary colors. Moreover, with only a few exceptions, there were significant correlations between adult likes and dislikes and infants' longer and shorter gazing times. Both the adults and infants were most "taken" with the primary colors blue and red. The boundary colors blue-red and yellow-red came next for both. Green, yellow, and green-yellow were liked least by adults and were least gazed at by infants, but here there were some differences: infants gazed longer at yellow than at green, for example; adults rated green more pleasant than yellow.

This striking agreement between the color preferences of infants and adults, if confirmed by others, may have far-reaching implications. It could mean that color preferences are to some extent innate and not entirely the result of cultural influence. Although it may or may not be relevant here, it is interesting that rhesus monkeys' favorite colors are blue and green and that they dislike red and yellow intensely.[16] (In this instance, cultural determination of color preferences can safely be ruled out!)

Bornstein regarded the parallel between adult judgment of the pleasantness of colors and infants' preferential gazing as evidence that infants attend to colors simply because they are pleasant to look at and not because they are "studying" the colors for educational purposes as some have proposed.[17] He also felt that the "pleasure hypothesis" was further supported by the infants' greater attention to primary than to boundary colors, since primary colors also tend to be more pleasing to adults than the colors that border them on either side of the spectrum.

This was a multifaceted investigation that was designed to answer a number of questions about infant color vision, all of which cannot be detailed in this necessarily brief sketch. However, the definitive answer to one question provided by this study and a subsequent study of 3-month-old infants[9] should be added here: Yes, infants *are* able to discriminate between colors. They discriminate, therefore they see.

A later investigation by Bornstein and two colleagues not only reaffirmed that infants respond selectively to colors but also revealed that they have an even more sophisticated talent: the ability to divide colors into categories, that is, into blues, greens, yellows, and reds.[18] Impressed with the similarity between infant and adult color preferences, the investigators suspected that infants, as adults do, would divide the visible spectrum into categories. They used the process of habituation to test this hypothesis.

As noted in the discussion of the rhythm experiment, infants become habituated, or accustomed, to a sensory stimulus, attending less and less to it as it is repeatedly presented to them. Thus, when infants are shown the same color many times in rapid succession, their gazing time diminishes, since they tend to shift their attention to other, more interesting things in the immediate environment. If, after habituation to one color, infants are shown another and their gazing time increases, they have indicated, in effect, that they are seeing something new. If, on the other hand, their attention does not increase, they reveal their inability to distinguish the new stimulus from the old one. It has been proposed that infants, by becoming habituated in this fashion, also demonstrate short-term memory (memory that lasts only a few seconds)—short-term because the intervals between presentations of the habituating color are so brief.

In the color-category experiment, eight groups of ten 4-month-old infants were first habituated to a color—for example, a color of a wavelength in the center of the blue wavelengths, which adults would call blue. Infants habituated to this particular blue were then shown a test color of a shorter wavelength, but normally also called blue by adults. Then they were shown another test color of a longer wavelength than the habituation stimulus but one adults normally call blue-green, that is, between the basic color categories blue and green.

Both the test colors differed from the habituation stimulus by the same number of wavelengths. Habituated to the color-center blue, the infants' attention to the blue of shorter wavelength, which adults also call blue, did not increase, indicating that they saw nothing novel about it. However, when shown the color of longer wavelength, their gazing time increased, demonstrating that they distinguished it from the habituation stimulus as an adult would do by reporting that the blue had become blue-green. Thus, infants, like adults, see the spectrum as divided into color categories of blue, green, yellow, and red, even though the spectrum itself is physically continuous and has no divisions.

Besides reconfirming infants' ability to discriminate between colors, this discovery has another important implication: Since infants put colors into categories before they have learned the language that adults use to categorize colors in the same way, color classification must be a natural ability that does not have to be acquired through language. Infants will eventually be told that "This is red" and "That is green." But all they will be learning is a new way to indicate what they already know.

Recent investigations tracing the optic nerve impulses of macaque monkeys from the retina into the brain have revealed four classes of nerve cells sensitive to red, blue, green, and yellow respectively.[19] These cells are located in the lower brain, in an area known ponderously as the "lateral geniculate body" and appear to be specialized to analyze color information. Their firing rates reach maxima when the light stimulating the retina is near the center of the wavelengths for the basic colors, blue, green, yellow, or red. And these colors, as had been mentioned, elicit the longest fixation of attention from human infants (as well as adults)—much longer than that elicited by boundary colors between these wavelengths. If the human brain also contains specialized cells of this kind, their activity may well underlie the color preferences that both infants and adults express.

As noted earlier, infants' ready habituation to a color they see over and over in rapid succession has been interpreted as short-term memory. But can infants store in their memories a color they have seen and recognize it some time later? This question was explored in a study reported from Princeton University in 1976, by the same investigator who carried out the color-category study.[20]

Fifty 4-month-old infants were habituated to greenish yellow. A three- to five-minute delay followed the habituation. For some infants, this interval was filled with nine viewings of a color that was entirely different from the habituation stimulus. Other infants engaged in face-to-face interaction with their mothers during the interval. Then, both groups of infants were again shown the greenish-yellow hue to which they had become habituated earlier. They showed by their cursory attention to this color that they were still habituated to it. Thus, they had retained a memory of the color after an interval that not only was several minutes long but also had been filled with distracting stimuli. And, as the investigator commented, they did so whether the distraction was "along the same dimension—hue—or along an entirely different dimension—mother's face and voice."

For a long time, psychological research remained adult-oriented, and since language figures so prominently in so many adult psychological processes, it was taken for granted that language is necessary to recognize and to classify colors. Children, it was assumed, learned from adults how to identify reds, yellows, greens, and blues and separate one from the other. Memory was also conceived as dependent on language. It was considered highly unlikely that memories of things could be stored in any other form but words. The infant color experiments, among others, provide abundant evidence that these assumptions were unjustified—and, since the superiority of the adult was taken for granted, chauvinistic as well.

Language has been ruled out as a necessary element in still another complex sensory ability. Although they may not be aware of it as such, people take advantage of this ability numerous times daily. It involves integrating information from two different senses, a process that psychologists call "cross-modal matching" or "intersensory equivalence." For example, we can often identify an object correctly by touch alone when previously we have only seen it. In experiments with primary-school children during the 1960s, children as young as 5 years of age correctly judged that two shapes, such as two squares, were identical when they had seen one but only felt the other.[21] How is this crossover of information from one sense to another accomplished? It has generally been accepted in the past that it is done through the mediation of language. That is, by giving the tactual and the visual shapes the same name, "square," the children were able to equate them.

However, the language theory received a body blow when two researchers found that 4-year-old children could easily perform cross-modal matching, from vision to touch, with shapes they could not name.[22] The naming of the shapes, a rectangular and a "bridge-shaped" object, was beyond the language capacities of these preschool children. Even when questioned following the experiment, none of the children could name the shapes. Nonetheless, they could correctly recognize the shape they had seen when they later experienced it only by touch.

The language theory became even less tenable when scientists at a primate research center reported that five apes (three chimpanzees and two orangutans) were also perfectly capable of cross-modal matching, from vision to touch.[23] This was determined by an experimental procedure in which the animals were rewarded with food when they correctly matched an object they were given to feel with one they had previously only been shown. They had been trained to indicate their choice by a downward pull on the matching object. Any effect of previous experience was ruled out by using objects totally alien to an ape's experience, such as drawer handles and coiled springs.

The experimenters had some difficulty in finding receptive ape subjects. Two unruly gorillas and several excitable chimps had been prospective subjects but had either flown into temper tantrums or attempted to take the experimental apparatus apart. However, five more sedate and responsive apes, lured by the reward of a choice tidbit, correctly indicated which of two different felt objects was like the one they had previously only seen.

In subsequent experiments with a similar design, chimpanzees given a series of some 40 sets of objects to match proved capable of choosing the correct matching objects about 75 percent of the time—a performance significantly better than chance.[24] Furthermore, in other tests, chimpanzees showed evidence of long-term memory by picking out the matching object after delays of from 5 to 20 seconds. And, at first sight they were able to match both color and black-and-white photographs of objects with objects they had felt, even when the photographs pictured the objects at only a fourth their actual size. By these feats of cross-modal matching, the researchers commented, the chimpanzees demonstrated "higher cognitive abilities . . . once thought to be unique to man."

If language is not essential to cross-modal matching and chimpanzees can do it, it is conceivable that human infants might also have this ability. A group of psychologists at Oxford University decided to look into this possibility.[25] Since they did not wish to give small infants food rewards for correct behavior, some other lure had to be devised to induce the infants to indicate that a visual object and a felt object matched. Aware that infants are attracted to, and readily grasp for, anything that makes a noise, the experimenters hollowed out small fiberglass "eggs" and placed a bleeper within each. Activated by a liquid mercury switch, the bleeper "bleeped" when the eggs were tilted. Two of these bleeping fiberglass eggs were used, one with a deep notch to distinguish its surface from the other both by vision and by touch.

The experimental group consisted of 60 infants averaging 8 months of age. Each infant sat on the mother's lap in front of a table on which the two eggs were placed by an experimenter and left for the infant to look at. After removing both eggs and hiding them briefly, the experimenter then brought one egg back to the infant concealed in her hand. Still hiding the egg with her hand, she placed the infant's hand on the egg, giving the infant an opportunity to feel the egg's surface. After she tilted the egg to make it bleep, the egg was removed. At no time during this phase of the procedure did either the infant or the mother see the egg. The experimenter then put both eggs back onto the table and pushed them within the infant's reach. A highly significant proportion of the infants reached for the object they had heard bleep, which was the smooth egg in some cases and the notched egg in others. In only 6 cases out of 1000 would this occur by chance, according to the researchers' computations. The infants had been able to match the feel of the egg, smooth or notched, with the visual appearance of its surface.

Infants' capacity for cross-modal matching was substantiated and extended by the feats of 26 one-year-old babies studied by a somewhat different technique at the Albert Einstein College of Medicine in New York City.[26] The strong tendency for infants of this age to prefer novel to familiar things was capitalized on by using it to demonstrate their visual recognition of things previously only touched. First, the infants became familiar for half a minute with one of a pair of differently shaped objects by having it placed either in their mouths to tongue or suck, or in their hands. Then the object was removed, and after a wait of 20 seconds the pair of objects was shown to the infant on a tray. The investigators measured the length of visual fixation on each object and noted which object the infant reached for. Significantly longer fixation times and more reaching for the novel member of the pair proved that the babies had made the cross-modal transfer from touch to vision. Also, for the first time, babies had demonstrated that they acquire information simply by mouthing objects—information which they can subsequently transfer for use by their visual sense. Mouthing things, then, gives babies another avenue through which they can increase their knowledge of the world.

The ability of infants to perform the complex task of matching visual and auditory temporal sequences was tested in a study done at Vanderbilt University.[27] Major decreases in heart rate were used as one indicator of matching. Such decreases are known to accompany attention to a stimulus. The auditory stimulus was a pure tone, the visual stimulus a flashing light, presented to infants averaging 7 months of age when they were in a quiet awake state and seated in a reclining infant chair. Two temporal sequences of tones or lights were used. In one sequence, two stimuli—either two tones or two lights— were separated by a third of a second, followed after nine-tenths of a second by a third tone or light. In the other sequence, all three stimuli were separated by nine-tenths of a second. After habituation with one temporal sequence, either visual or auditory, the infants showed much greater decreases in heart rate when presented with a different temporal sequence than when the sequence was the one to which they had become habituated. This difference held whether or not the habituation sequence was auditory and the test sequence visual, or vice versa. Thus, familiarity of the temporal sequence in one sense led to recognition of the sameness or difference of temporal sequence in the other sense.

It has not yet been established that infants under 7 months of age are capable of cross-modal matching, although it has been suggested that neonates may have this capacity.[28] As the well-known Scottish developmental psychologist T. G. R. Bower has put it, a "primitive unity of the senses" may be built into the nervous system.[29] That is to say, the nervous system might be so constructed that very early,

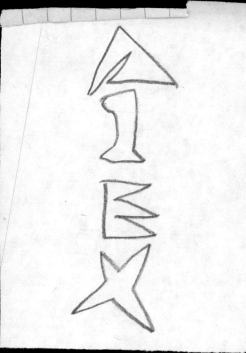

perhaps even at birth, certain kinds of information are automatically channeled from one sense to another.

The behavior of very young infants in an experiment done at the Harvard Center for Cognitive Studies might be interpreted as evidence that such crossovers occur early in development.[30] In this experiment, two investigators studied the reactions of 24 infants to the shadows of objects or to the objects themselves zooming in on them (but stopped before striking them). To isolate any learning effects, the infants selected for the study were of three successive age groups: 2 to 5 weeks, 5 to 8 weeks, and 8 to 11 weeks of age. Each baby was seated in an infant chair, supported, but not restricted, by an adult. The baby faced a boxlike apparatus in which a hanging 2-inch Styrofoam cube, carried by a belt over pulleys, either cast looming shadows on a translucent screen or, with the screen removed, appeared itself to be approaching the baby. A videotape record was made of the babies' reactions, including their vocalizations, as they faced this ingenious contraption.

When the infants perceived the looming shadow or the actual cube as coming directly toward them, on a collision path, they stiffened, moved their heads back and away from the object, brought their arms up toward their faces, and occasionally fretted and cried, in a strong avoidance-reaction pattern. However, when the shadow or object was on a miss path off toward the side, the babies simply turned their eyes and head to track it, seemingly confident that it would not strike them. The reaction patterns were so characteristic that people who watched the film without knowing what the infants were reacting to remarked that they seemed to be avoiding (or following) something.

The detection of such a collision or no-collision path required the swift perception of the object's, or the shadow's, direction of motion and relative distance, as accurate as that of an outfielder catching a high fly or an end receiving a rifled pass. It made no difference how old the infants were: the 2-week-old infants performed as well as the others. Thus, learning could have played little, if any, role in their performance.

The consummate skill of these infants in predicting the path of a moving object is astonishing, and their evident wish to avoid objects—and even shadows—on a collision course is even more so. It is highly improbable that 2-week-old babies have already experienced the consequences of a collision with flying objects—infants are normally protected against such encounters. It seems far more likely that by some sort of interchange between the visual and tactual sensory systems the infant is alerted to certain visual objects that can have harmful tactual effects. But how were the infants able to determine whether or not the object or shadow was coming close to them?

Distance perception is a complex process in which several visual cues, or variables, are involved. One such variable is the angle of convergence—formidable-sounding but really very simple: As an object, such as a pencil, is brought closer and closer to the eyes, they must be turned more and more inward to focus on it. Conversely, as the pencil is moved away from the eyes, the eyes turn gradually outward.

T. G. R. Bower, in discussing the implications of this experiment with respect to infants' ability to perceive distance, suggested that the infants may have been responding not to distance per se but to another distance variable, the expansion of an object's image on the retina of the eye as it comes nearer to the eye. The infants may have dodged the approaching object because it appeared to them to be growing larger, not because it was coming closer.

To test this hypothesis, Bower devised a modification of the collision experiment in which 1-week-old infants, seated in an infant chair, were presented with two objects.[31] One object, a foam-rubber cube 8 inches on a side, approached to only 3 inches from the infant's face. The other object, a cube 20 inches on a side, approached to only 8 inches. This arrangement ensured that both cubes would cover an equal area of the infant's retina and thus would appear to the infant to expand equally in size as they approached. The angle of convergence was the same in both cases. Nonetheless, infants responded with defensive reactions only to the cube that approached more closely, with no response at all to the other cube, despite its identical size on the retina. Bower concluded that "The full-scale response to the small, near object and no response at all to the large, distant object . . . indicates that it was in fact perceived change in distance that was being responded to."

In a more recent discussion of the question, however, Bower was not fully satisfied that this experiment had really proved infant perception of distance. He pointed out, as have others, that the expansion of the image of an approaching object on the retina could still appear to the infant to indicate motion of the object rather than distance of the object, and that the same interpretation might be made of other distance cues like convergence. All such cues may be interpreted as motion rather than distance, even by adults on occasion. Perhaps, Bower said, the infants were responding not to the object's apparent expansion but to the occlusion (hiding) of more and more of the background by the object as it moved closer to the eyes.

A classic study of distance perception in infants, however, provides some evidence that at least where stationary objects are concerned, infants do perceive distance.[32] Two Australian experimenters used the habituation technique to explore infants' reactions to changes in the distance of an object they had grown tired of looking at. Again, changes in gazing time were used to measure the infants' responses. Two groups of infants, 6 to 12 weeks and 13 to 20 weeks of age, were shown a black-crossed white cube suspended in an observation chamber. When a light came on, illuminating the cube, the length of time during which the infants' attention was fixed on the cube was measured. This procedure was followed in both the habituation and the test phases of the investigation.

In the habituation phase of the first experiment, a 2.5-inch or a 7-inch cube was suspended at a distance of either 12 or 39 inches from the infant. The habituation cube was presented 10 times for 10-second periods. Attempts at habituation to either the 7-inch or 2.5-inch cube at 39 inches were unsuccessful. At this distance the infants paid little or no attention to either cube, looking for only an average of 1 to 2 seconds. And, when shown a new cube—either a 2.5-inch or 7-inch cube—at the same distance, their gazing time neither increased nor decreased. However, when the infants repeatedly viewed either cube at 39 inches and then were shown the same cube 12 inches away, their gazing time doubled or tripled.

The infants' lack of interest in the cubes that were 39 inches distant had been foreshadowed by earlier observations that young infants are largely indifferent to anything in their visual field that is more than a foot away, a characteristic of which many caregivers are unaware. As infants grow older, they show interest in things at increasingly greater distances.

In the second experiment, one group of infants was shown the 7-inch cube at 12, 20, 28, and 39 inches. Another group of infants saw cubes of various sizes at the same four distances: larger and larger cubes were presented as the distance increased. In the first group, then, the image of the cube projected on the retinas of the infants' eyes grew smaller at increasing distances. In the second group, it remained the same. And yet in both groups of infants, attention time decreased with distance, indicating that their visual attention was dependent not on size, whether retinal or real, but on distance.

The studies of infants' visual perception so far described illustrate how much can be learned about infants by the exploration of their attention to objects and events. Infants are characteristically attentive to changes going on around them. They will respond to movements or objects appearing in their visual fields and orient to and track, for example, a moving hand or swinging object. They fixate with alert attention to a new noise or to being touched here and there, but drowse or go to sleep with rocking motions, continuous noises, or tight swaddling, that is, when the stimulus is constant or constantly repeated. They easily become habituated to repeated stimuli, paying less and less attention to them. So it is not surprising that continuous sensory stimulation, which also obliterates other stimuli that otherwise might attract attention, tends to quiet infants down.

Infants' rejection of the status quo and fondness for innovation and variability might seem a bit reckless. It seems that their security might better be served by concentration on the solid and unchanging, learning what can be counted on in the strange new world into which they have been thrust. However, by opting to attend to changes in their environment, infants best inform themselves about ongoing events that either promote or threaten their survival.[33, 34] And in human development, perception of the difference between the two kinds of events precedes the ability to seek the one and avoid the other. Long before children can flee from a stranger and run to mother, they have learned to distinguish between the two.

Infants are fascinated not only with something new but also with things that in themselves contain changing or varied elements. Infants prefer a light that flashes or moves to one that is steady or stationary. They prefer an array of dots to a blank square, and two dots to one dot. Their interest in change and variety is revealed as early as the first week of life, but as they mature, they like to look at more and more complex things. Even a slight advance in maturity reveals this tendency: In one study, premature infants looked longer at a white card with a single black square than at one with four black squares, while full-term infants, older by one month of gestation, preferred four squares to one.[35] Both, however, preferred the single black square to a blank white card. The attractiveness of complexity has its limits, however. When a pattern is too complex or crowded for infants of a particular age, it loses its hold on their attention.

A study of the examination by infants 1 to 4 days of age of a black triangle against a white background reveals an aspect of visual attention that is characteristic of newborns.[36] When viewing a blank, unchanging visual field, newborn infants simply scan the entire field, with their eyes moving here and there in a random manner. But in the course of many presentations of the triangle, the newborns, at least once, concentrated for a lengthy period on one vertex (point) of the triangle. Others, however, also scanned along one side of the triangle, or went over the whole figure with slight jerky ("saccadic") eye movements—which occur, for example, when adults read along a line of type.

The visual scanning of infants 1 and 2 months of age was later investigated in an extension of this study.[37] At 1 month of age, most of the infants would not look at a blank panel as newborns do, but instead fussed, cried, or fell asleep at this uninspiring visual scene. When presented with stimuli of black circles, triangles, squares, star shapes, or irregular figures, the 1-month-olds typically fixated on some point or part of the figure—even more so than the newborns. On the other hand, 2-month-olds tended to scan the figure broadly, not concentrating nearly so much on a single feature. This is in accord with the finding that 1-month-old infants, when presented with an image of the face of their mother or a stranger in a mirror, attend to the outside edges of the imaged face, again usually fixating on one spot, such as an ear, chin, or hairline. Two-month-old infants, however, concentrate on the inner features of the imaged face, such as the eyes, nose, or mouth. Mothers often report that by about 2 months of age their infants "look them in the eyes" or "recognize them," perhaps because of this change in attention.

Similar developmental changes in infant concentration on various facial features were reported in another investigation by Marshall Haith of the University of Denver and colleagues at Harvard.[38] The visual fixations on the mirrored faces of their mothers or strangers of infants 3 to 5 weeks old, 7 weeks old, and 9 to 11 weeks old were measured very accurately by the reflections of beams of invisible infrared light from the eyes of the infants. The youngest infants concentrated over half of their gazes on the edges of adult faces (the hairline, chin, cheeks, or ears), less than a third of their gaze on the eyes, and fewest on the nose and mouth. At 7 weeks, a dramatic shift occurred. Infants of this age gazed less than half as long at the periphery of faces as had the younger infants, and nearly twice as long at the eyes. Total fixation time on facial features quadrupled. This amount of concentration on the face was also seen in the oldest infants, although time spent looking at eyes dropped a few percentage points in this group.

As a possible explanation of their findings, the researchers suggested that by the age of 7 weeks infants found the eyes attractive "partly because they had acquired signal value in social interaction." However, whether the face was that of the mother or of a stranger made no significant difference in gazing at any age.

But does sudden interest in faces appearing at 2 months of age mean that eyes or other internal facial features are particularly attractive to infants of this age? In a study in which 2-month-old infants were presented with a small square or squares within a larger square, they tended to fixate on the small, internal squares in the figures, while 1-month-olds concentrated on a part of the external square.[37] The tendency of 2-month-olds to examine internal features is not limited to faces, then, but represents a general shift in infant visual scanning. The investigators speculated that by the age of 2 months a visual system in the cerebral cortex that controls attention to the internal elements of complex figures may have become functional. However, this does not foreclose the possibility that infants by this age are attracted to faces for other reasons.

In 1961, an investigator found that newborns would gaze longer at a schematic drawing of a face than at an abstract pattern, and this preference was promptly attributed to an early, even a "primitive," preference for faces.[39] It was suggested that the eyes and forehead of the face might serve as releasers of infant survival signals, in accord with ethological theory. Subsequent work during the 1960s showed that for very young infants, complexity of the stimulus, not facelike quality, constitutes the attraction. When the complexity of a meaningless drawing was equal to that of a schematic face, young infants seemed to show no preference. However, by 15 to 16 weeks of age, later studies indicated, infants look longer at faces than at designs, regardless of complexity.[33]

Then, in 1969, an investigation at Brown University of infants aged 4, 10, and 16 weeks cast serious doubt on the reality of infants' attraction to faces and again supported the role of complexity in determining fixation times at all these ages.[40] No evidence was found that infants aged 4 and 10 weeks prefer a facelike stimulus to a design of equal complexity. Although the 16-week-old infants seemed to prefer a photograph to a drawing of a human face, the evidence was borderline, and greater complexity was again implicated.

Much more recent and more sophisticated approaches have failed to resolve the issue entirely. In 1976, in a study done at the University of Toledo, 10-week-old and 15-week-old infants were shown two sets of three oval patterns, one pattern at a time.[41] One set consisted of scrambled facial features (mouth, nose, eyes, and so on, in the wrong places) increasing in complexity from the first through the third pattern. The other set consisted of three oval patterns with more and more facial features in the correct positions, also increasing in complexity.

In the 10-week-old group, fixation time increased with increasing complexity, but facial and scrambled patterns received almost the same amount of attention. There was some slight difference in favor of the most complex facial pattern over the scrambled pattern, but it was not statistically significant. The fixation time of the 15-week-old infants, however, although it also increased with stimulus complexity, was significantly higher for the most complex facial pattern than for the most complex scrambled pattern, implying that attraction to faces becomes a factor in attention in the period between 10 and 15 weeks.

Following on the heels of this investigation was another in which infants were shown four stimuli graded in their resemblance to a human face, ranging from (A) a blank oval, to (B) a face with scrambled parts, to (C) a facelike schematic drawing, to (D) a photograph of a real face.[42] The infants were shown these stimuli two at a time, and their preference would be indicated by longer viewing time. Genuine attraction to faces would be shown by a preference for the more facelike stimulus and increasing preference as "faceness" increased. The infants were divided into four age groups, 2, 3, 6, and 9 months, to see how preferences might develop with age.

The researchers found that for all age groups the most likely order of increasing preference was ABCD. The second most probable order was ABDC, interchanging the photograph and the schematic face. They concluded that from the ages of 2 through 9 months, infants demonstrate a preference for facelike forms. Since it is known that infants' responses to complexity change at 2 to 3 months of age and since no change in preference with age was evident in their data, they regarded it as unlikely that complexity of the stimuli could account for these findings.

The results of this study are not only in conflict with some earlier work but also with the discrepancy hypothesis, a theory relating to infant attention and supported by much experimental evidence, particularly that provided by Jerome Kagan and his colleagues at the Harvard Center for Cognitive Studies.[33] In terms of this hypothesis, by 3 to 4 months of age, infants have acquired a concept, or schema, of the human face and other familiar objects. Their attention will then be held longer by things that are moderately discrepant from a schema than by those that fit the schema or that are extremely discrepant from it. Thus, infants of this age should tend to fixate longer on drawings or photographs of human faces, which are moderately discrepant from the real thing, than on scrambled faces, with various features in odd positions, which would be extremely discrepant, or on actual, familiar faces, which would pose no discrepancy.

Although the findings of the 1976 study indicating that a preference for faces over nonfacial patterns emerges at 10 to 16 weeks is in accord with the postulate of the discrepancy hypothesis that a schema for faces has been formed by 3 to 4 months, those of the study just described are not, for they revealed a steady preference for faces from 2 through 9 months of age, with no sudden change at 4 months. However, some of the infants in this study preferred the schematic face to the photograph of a real face, perhaps finding the schematic face moderately discrepant, which may provide some support for the discrepancy hypothesis.

Further studies are obviously needed before the question whether infants have or have not a special interest in faces can finally be laid to rest. It could be, of course, that some infants are attracted to faces and some are not, depending on a multitude of factors among which might be the kinds of experience that have accompanied the appearance of a face within their field of view.

In the everyday world of infants, virtually everything is three-dimensional and in full living color, including faces. And real human faces are not static and bland but have constantly changing expressions. Thus, infants' reactions to two-dimensional black-and-white representations of faces might not accurately reflect their visual behavior in their natural environment, provided that infants are able to take in and sort out all the complexities of this environment. Aware of this possible bias, a group of researchers who wanted to find out how early an infant can discriminate faces from other stimuli provided an experimental setting more closely approximating real life.[43]

Eighteen female infants were studied weekly from 1 to 8 weeks of age. Each week the babies were brought to the laboratory by their mothers and placed in an infant seat that kept them partly upright. Their length of gaze was observed and recorded as the following stimuli were presented for a minute each at a porthole in the wall facing them: the actual face of their mother or a female stranger, either entirely still or nodding once every two seconds; the face of a store manikin; and a colander painted a flesh color with three different-colored knobs—two "ears" and a "nose"—on it. In addition to these stimuli, 12 of the 18 infants saw a female stranger (an experimenter) smiling and talking to them, and their mother, also smiling and talking.

Attention to all these stimuli increased over the eight weeks of the experiment. However, in all the sessions, covering the second through the eighth week of life, the infants' average attention time was lowest when viewing the mother, whether she was silent and expressionless, nodding, smiling, or talking. They looked significantly longer at the colander and manikin, devoting about equal time to each. The face of the friendly female stranger received roughly the same amount of attention as the nonhuman "faces." Furthermore, when the mother's face was the stimulus, the infants closed their eyes more and looked away more (even turning their heads) than when viewing either the manikin or the colander. They glanced to the side of the mother's head, keeping her face on the edge of their visual field. This furtive looking occurred less with the colander and least with the manikin.

Generally speaking, the infants' behavior passed through a sequence of approach and avoidance responses: direct fixation on the stimulus, looking away, closing the eyes, keeping the stimulus on the edge of vision, looking away again, and so on. This sequence occurred more often in the first month than in the second. At all ages, the duration and frequency of avoidance was greatest with the mother. The older infants often fussed when the mother's face appeared, as if in protest. This was followed by smiling and cooing, then by a sober-faced pause and more smiling and cooing, and finally by cries of distress. To the investigators, the older infants seemed to be "trying to alter the behavior of the stimulus. . . ." This might suggest, they said, that "the infant at this early age has learned that his actions affect his environment." Younger infants, on the other hand, seemed to be trying to control the "input from the stimulus" by approach-avoidance.

What mother would not be shocked to learn that her baby would rather look at a colander than at her? The significance of this preference will reassure her. It indicates, first, that infants as young as 2 weeks of age can distinguish the mother not only from inanimate objects that have facelike qualities but also from a strange human (and female) face. It could be said that the other stimuli were novel and therefore more attractive than the mother. But lack of interest in the mother's face would not account for the infants' strong avoidance reactions. The investigators proposed an alternative explanation.

Infants are not accustomed to seeing their mothers appear disembodied in a porthole. This is not the mother of their everyday experience, and yet she has the same face. Thus, the appearance of the familiar mother in "an unfamiliar guise" was probably too discrepant for the infants to accept. And so they peeked furtively at her, closed their eyes, and turned away, or when older, actively tried to correct this discrepancy.

This lack of attention to extreme discrepancies, which lends support to the discrepancy hypothesis, appears to hold for auditory as well as for visual stimuli. This was demonstrated in a study of the responses of 96 infants, 7½ months of age, to varied presentation of spoken syllables and musical notes.[44]

The infants sat in their mothers' laps in the laboratory after electrodes for recording their heart rates had been attached to stomach and chest. Decreases in heart rate (which indicate attention) and orientation to the sound source were used to measure the infants' attention. The infants were divided into eight groups, each of which heard one of eight different "episodes," repeated eight times to ensure habituation. Four of the episodes consisted of simple, six-note melodies played on either a French horn or a guitar; four others consisted of the enunciation of four syllables by a strange (to the infant) voice. In five 4-second episodes that followed habituation, the infants heard either the habituating episode repeated or a standard novel episode consisting of a six-note melody played on a French horn or four syllables enunciated by the same speaker as before.

The novel episode was assessed as slightly discrepant from the habituating episode when it differed only in pitch or in intonation (of the syllables); moderately discrepant when it differed in pitch and rhythm or contained two novel syllables; and extremely discrepant when it differed in pitch, rhythm, and timbre (the habituating melody had been played on a guitar) or consisted of four novel syllables that also differed in intonation from the familiar stimulus.

Slowing of the heart rate and orientation to the sound source were greatest when the novel episode was slightly or moderately different from the familiar episode. When the novel episode was the same or extremely discrepant, attention was minimal.

Infants, then, show a strong inclination to select from an array of stimuli those that provide novelty and variability and yet are not totally foreign to their experience. However, they are not averse to suggestions as to where they might direct their attention. This was revealed in an experiment with infants from 2 to 14 months of age.[45] The mothers brought their babies into the laboratory room, settled them in a high chair, and left the room. If the baby showed no sign of distress, a male or female experimenter then played with the baby. Seated in front of the infant, and at eye level, the experimenter first made eye-to-eye contact with the infant and then turned his or her head silently toward the left or right at right angles while video cameras followed the infant's head movements.

At 2 to 4 months of age, a third of the infants followed the direction of the experimenter's gaze, turning their heads to do so. Those who did not follow suit either kept their eyes on the experimenter or looked down at the tray of the high chair. By 8 to 10 months of age, two-thirds of the infants were following the experimenter's gaze, and by 11 to 14 months, all of them did so. Furthermore, the experimenter's pointing or saying "Oh, look" increased the tendency of the infants to follow his or her line of regard.

This inclination to look where others are looking remains very strong throughout life. We seem to be particularly compelled to do so when someone is looking at something we cannot see. Let someone stop and look upward on a busy street and dozens of people will also stop and gaze upward. In infants of a few months of age, the extent to which their following others' gaze is imitative or a more basic, almost a reflex response is open to question. In any event, such responses are not unique to human beings. Deer and antelope, for example, will respond to a danger signal from the lookout for their herd by raising their heads, gazing at the lookout, and turning in the direction in which the lookout is facing. Whatever its mechanism or function may be, the joint attention of infants early in development suggests that they are not as self-centered as we have assumed.

Infants' visual perceptual skills clearly exceed our expectations. However, as Bower has pointed out, infants' ability to perceive visual differences does not imply that they are aware of teeir significance.

Suppose a young infant is watching an object and the object moves to a new location. The infant's visual response to this event indicates that a change has been perceived. But what kind of change? Presumably, the infant has seen an object move from one place to another. At least this is the way an adult would view the situation.

The concept of the permanence of objects is deeply engrained in the adult mind—so much so that when Gertrude Stein wrote that "A rose is a rose is a rose," she was laughed at for stating the obvious: that an object is itself and not something else. But to young infants, this is not obvious at all. Their reactions in one of Bower's experiments with a moving toy train demonstrate this graphically.[31]

Three-month-old infants followed the movements of a toy train with flashing lights as it ran back and forth on a track. At first, the train remained stationary, directly in front of the infant. After 10 seconds, it moved off to the left, stopped for 10 seconds, and then returned to its original location. This sequence was then repeated 10 times.

Previous observations had shown that infants continue to track the path of a moving object after it has stopped moving, disregarding the now stationary object as they carry on their search. They cannot seem to identify a moving object that becomes stationary as one and the same object. With this in mind, Bower suspected that the infants might not see one train moving back and forth but a number of trains: a stationary train that vanished; another train that moved to the left and then also vanished; a third train that was stationary in a new location on the left and then disappeared; and a fourth train that moved to the right and vanished in front of them. His suspicion was confirmed. When, on the eleventh cycle, the train first moved off to the right instead of to the left and stopped on the right, all the infants, without exception, looked to the left, where the "second" train had always turned up before. No matter that the train, with lights flashing, stood in plain view on the right!

A mother must appear to an infant as somewhat like a moving train as she moves from place to place within the infant's field of view, disappears and returns, stops and looks down at the infant in the crib, and then vanishes again. Does the infant therefore see one mother as many mothers? Bower investigated this possibility in an experiment using an arrangement of mirrors that reflected multiple images.

Infants of various ages viewed two or three mirror images of their mothers on a screen.[29] Those up to 5 months of age found nothing bizarre about a mother in duplicate or triplicate, happily cooing, smiling, and waving their arms at each of the mothers in turn. With one image of the mother and two of a strange woman, all the infants ignored the strangers and concentrated on interacting with the mother's image. However, infants over 5 months of age were upset by the sight of a double or triple mother. Bower interprets their distress at this discrepancy as indicating that by 5 months of age the multiple mothers of the infant's earlier months have been fused into one.

CHAPTER 5
Learning

"All we have to start with in building a human being is a lively squirming bit of flesh, capable of making a few simple responses such as movements of the hands and arms and fingers and toes, crying and smiling, making certain sounds with its throat . . . parents take this raw material and begin to fashion it in ways to suit themselves."[1] Thus John B. Watson, dean of the school of behaviorism and a leading psychologist of the 1920s, expressed his belief that a human being is shaped by the environment as surely, he said, as a mass of hot metal is shaped by a blacksmith's hammer.

Watson spoke with a voice of considerable authority. In 1908, at the age of thirty, he had been appointed professor of experimental psychology at Johns Hopkins University. He brought to this post a background in animal experimentation and a conviction that the same objective and quantitative laboratory methods used to study animals should also be applied to the study of human psychology. At a time when most of his psychological confreres were preoccupied with the inner workings of the human mind, Watson boldly asserted that the outward behavior of human beings was the only proper subject for scientific inquiry, and he proceeded to apply this principle to the study of the human infant. His method was to chart every detail of the behavior of hundreds of infants from birth onward, to note the behavior patterns that seemed to be innate and therefore unlearned and the sequence in which they emerged, and to experiment with changing these patterns to demonstrate how learning takes place.[2]

Watson's experimental work with infants had been much influenced by the studies of the Russian physiologist Ivan Pavlov, who had discovered the conditioned reflex in the course of measuring saliva flow in his laboratory dogs. Pavlov had found that the salivary reflex, which is an unlearned, or unconditioned, response occurring when food is placed in the mouth, could be elicited by a neutral stimulus such as a bell, a ticking metronome, or a light after it had been paired with the presentation of food a sufficient number of times. From his extensive studies of the conditioned reflex, Pavlov had concluded that learning is simply "a long chain of conditioned reflexes," a proposition with which Watson entirely agreed and which guided much of his research.

Watson's most famous—or infamous—experiment was the conditioning of little Albert, age 11 months. Having determined that little Albert would happily reach out to touch a rabbit but was easily frightened by a loud noise, Watson "conditioned" him by striking a steel bar with a hammer whenever the baby made overtures to the rabbit. A strong fear of furry animals then developed in little Albert, and this conditioned fear became generalized to all furry objects, including fur neckpieces and Santa Claus whiskers. Watson had proved his point—but at considerable expense to little Albert's emotional health.

Watson's extreme environmentalist views sent shock waves throughout the psychological community. But his innovative use of quantitative methods and the techniques of the laboratory with infants and his insistence that psychologists confine their studies to observable behavior were to have profound and lasting effects not only on infant research but also on the methods and direction of research in general psychology.

We know now that infants' capabilities at birth extend far beyond a few simple reflexes, and the number of things infants were assumed to learn has consequently been reduced. The "material" is not quite so raw as Watson imagined. From the work of the behaviorist B. F. Skinner and of the cognitive psychologists such as Jean Piaget and Jerome Kagan, who study mental processes as well as behavior, new concepts of the learning process have emerged in which the conditioning of simple reflexes is of little or no importance. But none of this detracts from the contributions of John Watson, whose pioneering efforts paved the way to these discoveries and opened the door to scientific investigation of the infant.

In Watson's day the term "conditioning" meant the conditioning established by Pavlov's method, known as "classical" conditioning today. But if it were possible only to condition involuntary reflexes, conditioning would not play much of a role in the learning process. Its role was very greatly expanded when B. F. Skinner showed in the late 1930s that a pattern of behavior will recur frequently if it produces a reward. He demonstrated this fact by placing a rat in a box containing a bar that when pressed would release a pellet of food into a tray. After accidentally pushing down the bar a few times while running about exploring the box, the rat then began to press the bar over and over, stopping only to eat each pellet of food and returning again and again to the bar. This reinforcement of behavior by a reward is known in the lexicon of psychologists as instrumental conditioning. Using the same technique, parents who wish to increase the frequency of desirable behavior praise their child for being "good."

Classical conditioning of newborns has been tried by many investigators since Watson's time. Some have been successful and others have failed. Overall, these efforts have produced what has been called a "veritable mosaic of circumstances under which conditioning may or may not occur."[3] A leading Soviet developmental psychologist, N. I. Kasatkin, summarizing the extensive Russian experience with neonate conditioning, expressed general agreement with this view when he described the conditioned reflex in the first month of life as "with very few exceptions . . . notably unsteady."[4]

A major objective of infant conditioning studies has been to establish the earliest age at which conditioning—and, presumably, learning—is possible. In pursuit of this objective, David Spelt, an American psychologist, attempted to establish a conditioned response in fetuses of 8 to 9 months' gestation.[5]

His procedure was as follows: The mother lay on a bed with a vibrator (the conditioned stimulus) and a device to register fetal movements strapped to her abdomen. She was instructed to signal when she detected fetal movements during the experiment. Recording instruments were set up beside the bed, along with a wooden clapper that made a loud noise. Since loud noise had been shown to elicit fetal movement, the clapper served as the unconditioned stimulus. Two 7-month fetuses did not respond to the clapper, and therefore their mothers did not participate in the study.

Working with five fetal subjects and their mothers, Spelt found that after 15 to 20 paired stimulations of the clapper and the vibrator, three to four successive responses to the vibrator alone had been recorded; after further trials, as many as eleven successive responses were obtained. The mothers' signals that they had perceived fetal movements were in agreement with the record. Like other conditioned reflexes, the response gradually disappeared over time, although in one fetus it was retained over a period of 18 days.

Spelt's work was criticized on the grounds that he had not controlled all the factors besides the conditioning that could have produced the fetal movements.[6] And the failure of a subsequent attempt to condition fetuses adds to the uncertainty about their conditionability.

Considerable effort has been devoted, most of it in Russia, to the conditioning of infants born before term. In one such study, a Russian investigator had remarkable success in conditioning premature infants' response to changes in temperature.[4]

In newborn infants, particularly if premature, the reflex regulatory system that keeps body temperature constant despite changes in environmental temperature is not yet working efficiently. As a result, the infant's temperature fluctuates with environmental temperature changes, and so do breathing and heart rates. This physiological reaction was used as the unconditioned response in the Russian experiment, with an increase in incubator temperature serving as the unconditioned stimulus.

Two groups of infants, 89 full-term and 58 prematures, beginning with their first or second day of life, were removed from their regular cribs, swaddled, and placed in dark incubator cribs. This whole procedure constituted the conditioned stimulus. Their pulse and breathing rates and rectal and skin temperatures were recorded as the crib temperature was raised from 79° to 95° Fahrenheit over a two-hour period. The infants' responses to this temperature change was an increase in body temperature from 1° to 2° Fahrenheit, with concomitant changes in respiration and heart rates. This sequence was repeated four to five times. Following these conditioning trials, the infants were again swaddled and placed in the darkened incubators, but this time incubator temperature was kept constant. Nonetheless, the infants' temperatures—and their respiration and heart rates—rose as before. This occurred both in the full-term infants and in the prematures, regardless of their degree of maturity. After six to seven trials in which the conditioned stimulus alone was given the infants, the conditioned response gradually diminished and finally disappeared. Called "extinction," this typically happens to a conditioned response that is not occasionally reinforced by presentation of the unconditioned stimulus.

It is difficult to consider the conditioning of a physiological response as learning in the usual sense of the word. However, the range of behavioral responses available for conditioning in newborns is narrow because of their limited ability to act. But this limitation does not apply to a hungry infant, whose reactions to food are forthright and unmistakable—and ideal for attempts at conditioning.

In an experiment closely following the Pavlovian design, an American investigator, Dorothy Marquis, studied the responses of bottle-fed infants during their first 10 days of life when a buzzer was sounded for five seconds before they were given the bottle and continued for five seconds as they sucked.[7] The buzzer was sounded again each time the nipple was reinserted in the infant's mouth during feeding. By 10 days of age, 7 of the 10 infants responded to the buzzer with mouth opening and sucking—and a decrease in crying and body movements.

In a later Marquis experiment, newborns on a three-hour feeding schedule were shifted to a four-hour schedule on the ninth day after birth.[8] During the extra hour, there were marked increases in the infants' bodily movements, which were attributed to the frustration of their expectation that they would be fed. Had the infants been conditioned by the schedule? Or were they just reacting to hunger pangs? The increase in movement was so striking that Marquis was inclined to call it a conditioned response.

It is common knowledge that about 10 days after birth infants tend to settle into a fairly regular feeding schedule, whether they are fed on demand or every three or four hours. In the light of Marquis's observations, this adaptation to a schedule suggests that infants may, in fact, become conditioned to the passage of time, which then arouses the conditioned responses of increased bodily activity and of sucking at about the usual time they are fed.

The Russian investigator, Bystroletova, observed the responses of bottle-fed infants during their first 10 days of life, separating them into groups placed on three different feeding schedules: 3, 3.5, and 4 hours.[4] The sucking and head movements of the infants were recorded for three to four minutes every quarter of an hour. By the third to fifth day, an increase was detected in their sucking and head motions before feeding, no matter what the schedule, and they were beginning to wake up a few minutes before feeding time. By the seventh to eighth days these responses had become more distinct, and the investigator was convinced that the infants had been conditioned to the feeding schedule. Again, hunger pangs rather than the passage of time could account for the increase in activity. As Kasatkin remarked in discussing the experiment, changes in a neonate's sucking responses can have many causes. These are impossible to rule out by any kind of experimental control.

Beginning with the sixth day of life, most neonates show a rise in white blood cell count one hour after feeding. After the eighth day, a rise is observed 15 minutes before feeding as well. When infants on a three-hour schedule were changed to a four-hour schedule, the cell count at first continued to rise according to the old schedule.[4] After two to three days, this response was extinguished, and the cell count now rose 15 minutes before the new feeding time. This demonstration of a conditioned physiological response to a change in feeding schedules adds credibility to Marquis's and Bystroletova's interpretations.

To establish conditioned responses in infants, it is not always necessary to sound buzzers, tinker with feeding schedules, or move infants from crib to crib. Several Soviet researchers have explored conditioning under what are, for Russian babies, perfectly natural circumstances.[4] Newborns were swaddled according to Russian custom and then placed in the typical nursing position, held to the breast of the experimenter and cuddled against her body. By the tenth day of life, a fourth of the infants began searching and sucking movements when swaddled and held in this position, and two-thirds were doing so by the eleventh day. Four to six days later, the conditioned response occurred just on placement in the nursing position, without prior swaddling.

The manner of taking food also has conditioning potential—at least in older infants. This was revealed in a study of 4- to 7-month-old Russian infants who had become accustomed to being fed yogurt from a bottle and cereal from a spoon.[4] In these infants, the yogurt, but not the cereal, normally produced an increase in the frequency of urination but a decrease in its amount. Then the method of feeding the infants was switched, with the cereal given in the bottle and the yogurt fed with a spoon. When the infants sucked cereal from the bottle in amounts equal to the amounts of yogurt they usually took, the frequency of urination increased as before.

As noted, attempts at classical conditioning of newborns sometimes fail. Ruefully entitling their report "Evidence for the Unconditionability of the Babkin Reflex in Newborns," three American psychologists described one of the unsuccessful attempts.[9] The Babkin reflex, as described earlier, is present in the fetus and from birth to about 4 months of age. It is a response to simultaneous pressure on both the infant's palms and consists of opening the mouth or gaping, raising or bending the head, turning it to the midline of the body, and, often, closing the eyes and bending the forearm. In two prior studies some rather dubious conditioning of this reflex had been achieved by combining palm pressure with raising of the infant's arm. Nonetheless, the investigators decided to use arm raising again as the conditioned stimulus, but with controls that had been conspicuously absent in the previous experiments. Their subjects were normal infants 1 to 3 days of age.

The title of the report gives the results of this experiment in capsule form. It was plagued first of all by infants crying and fussing or getting drowsy or falling asleep. More serious was the frequent occurrence of mouth opening and gaping to arm raising alone. Had this been predictable, arm raising would never have been used as a conditioned stimulus. Concluding that the experiment had been an exercise in futility, the researchers strongly advised that attempts at classical conditioning of newborns be abandoned until more is known about their unconditioned behavior.

From the age of 1 to 3 months, infants are much more susceptible to conditioning. In fact, in a 1967 experiment, 32 infants from 1 to 3 months of age proved to be more conditionable than adults.[10] This was a special case, however, since the experiment involved the conditioning of the pupillary reflex—the automatic contraction (or expansion) of the pupil to increase (or decrease) in light intensity. This reflex is exceedingly hard to condition in adults. Even in successful experiments, it is unconditionable in a large and stubborn minority of the adult subjects.

In the infant experiment, the turning on or turning off of a 100-watt blue light bulb placed 15 inches from the infants' eyes was used as the unconditioned stimulus. Conditioning was tried with six different pairs of stimuli, one pair in each of six groups of infants: a loud sound from a loudspeaker followed by the light (on or off); a 20-second interval between presentations of the light (on or off); a 20-second interval followed by the loud sound and then by the light (on or off). Pupillary diameters were measured by a computer from an enlarged film of the infants' responses.

The researchers' choice of a time interval for a conditioned stimulus was related to a second goal of the experiment. They had been impressed, but not convinced, by the reports that infants could be conditioned to a feeding schedule. Therefore, they designed their experiment to test the conditioning potential of time under stricter controls than had been possible in the feeding-schedule studies.

As indicated by pupil contraction or dilation after 20 seconds and in the absence of the light stimulus, a conditioned pupillary reflex to time was firmly established in these infants. This occurred both with the time interval alone and in combination with the sound stimulus. Sound alone was totally ineffective.

How can an infant "perceive" the length of an interval of time—and with such accuracy? Infants are not unique in this ability. Pavlov conditioned his dogs to respond to time intervals, and time perception can be inferred from the behavior of many animal species. All this has led to the concept of a "biological clock" that ticks away somewhere in the nervous system, registering the passage of time. Various suggestions have been made as to its location, but even the existence of such a mechanism has yet to be proved. After extensive study of time perception using conditioning techniques, Pavlov concluded that it must be a capacity common to all the senses, but he declined to speculate about its nature or modus operandi.

Skinner's discovery that behavior could be conditioned by reinforcement had little immediate impact on infant research. By the 1960s, however, reports of instrumental conditioning in infants began to appear in significant numbers. It was evident in all these reports that infants are extremely sensitive to the environmental consequences of what they do; they learn very quickly that the "right" behavior will produce a reward. This sensitivity was well documented, for example, in a series of experiments done at Brown University by Einar Siqueland and Lewis Lipsitt, in which a reward was contingent on a specific head-turning response.[11]

Infants sometimes, but not always, respond to stimulation on the cheek, especially near the mouth, with the rooting reflex, that is, they turn their heads in the ipsilateral direction—to the left when stimulated on the left and to the right when stimulated on the right. In the first experiment of this series, infants averaging 3 days of age were stroked three times on the left cheek while a buzzer was sounded (to make sure the infants were awake). In each of 30 trials, of the infants who turned to the left, half were given an immediate reward of a two-second suck on the nipple of a bottle containing 5 percent sugar solution, and half were given the sugar suck 8 to 10 seconds after the head turn. Head turns were recorded by a device attached lightly to the infants' heads.

As the trials proceeded, infants who were not immediately rewarded showed a relatively stable but somewhat decreasing incidence of left (correct) head turning. However, in the infants whose left head turns were immediately reinforced, the incidence of left head turning increased from 30 percent in the first trial to 84 percent in the thirtieth trial.

In the second experiment, infants 2 to 5 days of age were stimulated alternately on the right or left cheek. This time, an immediate reward for the correct head turn (right or left) was given on an individual basis. After six trials had shown that a particular infant was more likely to respond correctly when stroked on the right cheek than when stroked on the left, that infant was thereafter given a sugar solution to suck after a correct turn to the left but not after a correct turn to the right; infants who preferentially turned to the left were rewarded only when they correctly turned to the right. In other words, the infants had to turn in a direction contrary to their preferences if they were to receive the reward.

Reinforcement proved to be highly effective in altering the infants' natural responses. The incidence of correct head turns increased from a low of 18 percent in the first trial to a high of 73 percent in the last, while the incidence in two groups of unrewarded infants decreased.

In a third experiment, infants 2 to 5 days of age were divided into two groups. In one group, right-sided head turns to stimulation on the right cheek were rewarded when a tone was sounding but not rewarded when a buzzer was sounding. The other group had to respond to the opposite contingency to obtain the reward: buzzer—right turn—reward; tone—right turn—no reward. In both groups the incidence of right head turning continued to increase throughout the experiment.

Then, the contingencies to which the infants had previously had to respond were reversed. Infants who had learned tone—right turn—reward now had to learn buzzer—right turn—reward. Similarly, the infants who had been rewarded for a right turn with a buzzer sounding were now rewarded only when the tone was sounding. The infants' responses in both instances clearly reflected the reversal. The incidence of right head turning decreased with the sound stimulus formerly associated with a reward and increased with the sound stimulus that had previously produced no reward.

In commenting on this experiment, T. G. R. Bower, who takes the cognitive point of view, noted that its implications are staggering in terms of the number of data the infants had to "process."[12] First, they had to discriminate between two sounds. Further, they had to distinguish the feeling of a right from the feeling of a left turn. They also had to group the particular combination of events (buzzer—right turn, or tone—right turn) that would produce a reward. And finally, they had to select the only relevant stimuli—buzzer or tone, feeling of right head turn—from all the stimuli present in the experimental situation. Bower saw these infants as "[testing] all possible responses" to find the one that would work. He regarded infants' typically high activity at the beginning of conditioning sessions as evidence that such testing does, in fact, take place, and he was not averse to calling it problem solving.

The fine powers of discrimination displayed by these infants might be most useful in the normal feeding situation. As the investigators pointed out, breast-fed infants are likely to receive tactile stimulation on the left side of the face when held in the nursing position at the right breast—and on the right side of the face when held at the left breast. With ipsilateral head turning in either case, the infant would find the nipple. Thus, head turning in the correct direction would be reinforced, increasing the probability of continued success in obtaining nourishment.

The fact remains, however, that in the protective environment of infants there is very little real need to use these particular capacities, and except for head turning and a few other motor responses, the ability of infants to "operate" on their environment and produce the effects they desire is very limited. Thus, as one investigator remarked, the first three months of infancy is a "period of 'natural deprivation' of learning experiences."[13] Whatever their abilities, infants have little opportunity to exercise them during this period, and this lack of exercise may affect their long-term intellectual development.

An immediate result of this deprivation is seen in the decline in infants' performances in conditioning experiments after 3 months of age. However, if infants are given learning experiences in the first three months, the picture changes radically. This was evident in a study comparing the conditionability of two groups of infants 3.5 months of age. One group had not experienced a conditioning procedure until they were 3 months old. The other group had participated in conditioning experiments from birth. It required almost twice as many trials to establish conditioning in the novice group as in the "veterans" of the same age. This beneficial effect of early training has been confirmed in other conditioning experiments.[13]

When infants turn their heads spontaneously to attend to a stimulus (as opposed to reflex turning), they are said to be demonstrating the "orienting response." Movements of the head, whether lateral or up and down, are basic to orientation. This is reflected in such common expressions as "heading in that direction" or "heading for town." Since orienting responses are essential in securing and holding an infant's attention, it would be helpful to find out what kinds of reinforcement are effective in maintaining such responses. Using considerable imagination, a Czechoslovakian investigator who was interested in this problem devised a variety of scenes and tested their effectiveness as reinforcers of spontaneous head turning in 2-month-old infants.[14]

The infants were placed in an enclosed crib with two windows on either side of their heads and a sound source near their feet. One window was used for observation by the experimenter. Eight seconds after a sound signal was given, one of five different reinforcers appeared at the other window: the mother, speaking to the infant; an adult stranger, also speaking to the infant; various noise-making toys, changed with each trial; a stranger showing a different toy with each trial; and a stranger who picked up the infants and rocked, cuddled, dandled, and talked to them. These stimulating reinforcers were repeated for 10 times in a session, following the sound. If the infant did not turn his head spontaneously to the reinforcing stimulus within eight seconds after hearing the sound, the experimenter turned it for him so that he would receive the reinforcement.

It was extremely difficult to establish conditioned head turning (that is, turning to the sound alone) when the reinforcing stimulus was the mother's face and voice. Here, the maximum incidence of head turning was only 10 percent. Some of the infants eventually became openly negativistic and actually turned their heads away from the mother. Some even resisted the experimenter's attempts to turn their heads toward the mother after the eight-second interval and subsequently became very cranky.

The stranger in her various appearances was a much more effective reinforcer. The maximum incidence of conditioned head turning to the stranger's face and voice was 28 percent—and 37 and 39 percent respectively to the stranger with different toys and the stranger who picked up the infant. The most successful reinforcement, resulting in a 45 percent incidence of head turning, was provided by the noise-making toys that changed on each trial. And conditioned responses were established earlier with these reinforcers than with any of the others.

In summarizing the results of his experiment, the investigator explained the relative ineffectiveness of the mother as a reinforcer as follows: Infants are accustomed to seeing their mothers under circumstances that are connected with the satisfaction of needs—being picked up, talked to, fed, and petted. But in the experimental situation the mother's familiar and unchanging face and voice, unaccompanied by any pleasant feelings, provided very weak reinforcement and in time produced aversive reactions. This is reminiscent of the infants' reactions in the mother-versus-colander experiment. The stranger's face and voice were novel and therefore excited more interest, although this, too, was an unchanging stimulus that eventually palled. The different toys, the stranger with a new toy each time, and being played with by a stranger all offered something new—and changing. Thus, novelty seemed to be the most important element in the conditioning of these infants.

There is nothing novel about a mother standing by the crib and smiling at her baby. Yet this situation provides strong reinforcement of the baby's own smiling. This is not an "experimental" mother appearing and disappearing at a window but the mother of the infant's everyday experience. A study of infants in their third month showed that this seems to make a difference.[15]

The infants' mothers or female strangers stood for five minutes beside the infants in their cribs and reinforced any smiling on the infants' part by saying "Hi, [infant's first name]," smiling, and lightly touching the infants' chests. The number of smiling responses was then compared with the number that had been observed during a prior five-minute period when the mother or stranger simply stood motionless in view of the infant. Smiling is a rather constant and consistent kind of infant behavior that occurs, as it did in the baseline period, with another person simply in view and doing nothing to evoke a smile. But even in this situation, the infants in this experiment smiled much more often at their mothers than at the strange women.

Further, during reinforcement, the infants' smiling at the mothers increased more than 50 percent over the baseline rate, while smiling to the strangers exceeded the base rate by only 22 percent. But although the mothers were by far the more effective reinforcers of smiling behavior in these infants, it is noteworthy that smiling at the mothers, as well as at the strangers, markedly diminished after four minutes of exposure to the same situation, probably as a result of habituation.

The obvious preference for their caregiver shown by these infants suggests that by 3 months of age, infants have begun to develop a social attachment to specific adults. It had previously been assumed, on the basis of other criteria, that infants do not form such attachments until they are 6 to 8 months of age.

A pioneer study carried out by developmental psychologist Yvonne Brackbill had laid the groundwork for the use of instrumental conditioning to explore the effect of adult social behavior on infant social responses.[16] Brackbill studied smiling behavior in 3.5- to 4.5-month-old babies in their homes. Her goal was to determine whether continual or intermittent reinforcement of the infants' smiling would be more effective, that is, responding to every smile or only to some smiles. Throughout the experimental period, the infants were placed on a schedule of emotional deprivation, with a minimum of bodily and social contact with other persons except for that necessary to maintain the infants' well-being. This was to assure that the smiling and protest behavior of the infants in the experimental situation could be attributed to the effects of previous stimulation.

In each experimental session, the experimenter first stood motionless and expressionless near the infant's crib after the infant had awakened and been fed and diapered. She observed and recorded the infant's spontaneous smiling behavior for five minutes. The average baseline rate for all the infants' smiling was two to three smiles per five-minute period. After the incidence of spontaneous smiling had been determined, the infants had a three-minute rest in the crib. This was followed by a five-minute period in which spontaneous smiling was reinforced. When the infants smiled, the experimenter immediately smiled in return, picked them up, and for 30 seconds held, jounced, and talked to them. Some infants were given reinforcement after each smile throughout the experiment. Others were given continuous reinforcement only until they smiled at least four times in 10 of the five-minute periods. At this point they were switched to an intermittent reinforcement schedule: one reinforcement for two smiles, one for three smiles, and, finally, one for four smiles, with less and less reinforcement as the experiment continued. Then, all infants were observed for 13 five-minute intervals during which no reinforcement was given and their conditioned smiling responses were gradually extinguished.

The smiling rate of the regularly reinforced infants was twice as high as their baseline rate, averaging five smiles per five-minute period, but infants on an intermittent reward schedule smiled much more. Those rewarded for every second smile averaged over six smiles per five-minute period. The group rewarded for every third smile smiled eight times on the average, and those rewarded every fourth smile averaged 13 smiles per five-minute period.

The greater effectiveness of intermittent reinforcement, which has been demonstrated in many learning experiments, was also evident during the extinction trials, when the infants were again confronted with the motionless unsmiling experimenter. Conditioned smiling disappeared rapidly in the regularly reinforced group, reaching a zero rate before the end of the experiment. This represented a drop from their smiling rate before conditioning. The infants who had received intermittent reinforcement, on the other hand, although their smiling rate was markedly reduced, never stopped smiling altogether.

When the continuously reinforced group had ceased to smile, their behavior toward the experimenter changed in other respects. They stopped looking at her, turned heads to the side, and kept them there. When their heads were propped by pillows so that they could not turn away, they raised their eyes up toward the ceiling, refusing to look at her. This she interpreted as frustration at no longer receiving her reinforcing attention.

Brackbill had decided in advance that infants who cried or fussed too much would be disqualified as subjects because they would interfere with the work in progress. For this reason it was necessary to record crying and fussing, which she called "protest," during the baseline period and for a few conditioning trials. But once embarked on this project, she continued to record protests throughout the experiment, although she had no particular purpose in mind. In reviewing the data, she discovered a significant negative relationship between the protesting and smiling: that is, while smiling was increasing during reinforcement, protests were decreasing, and, during the extinction trials, protesting mounted again. Conditioning of smiling, then, resulted in the counterconditioning and extinction of protesting responses. Answering potential objections that infants cannot, of course, cry and smile at the same time, she noted the following: All the infants had periods when they neither protested nor smiled. If the protesting response had not been counterconditioned, the infants could have protested during these periods. Smiling, then, did not preclude protesting.

Brackbill inferred from this extinction of crying with the reinforcement of smiling that the strength of the habits of crying and smiling had been affected by the conditioning. Before conditioning, the habit of crying may have been stronger, even dominant, in some of the infants, but it weakened as smiling was reinforced. When the new habit of smiling was blocked by lack of reinforcement, the habit of fussing and crying came back into its own. When habits of this sort compete, they can affect each other in this way—a characteristic of habitual responses that can be used to advantage in correcting undesirable behavior by counterconditioning. The case history of Anthony, a 6-week-old *enfant terrible,* will illustrate concretely just how counterconditioning works.[17]

Anthony had been in the well-baby boarders unit of a children's hospital from the age of 2 weeks. He was considered a healthy infant except for some rapid breathing earlier in life. However, he fussed and cried a great deal, when he would often be picked up by an aide or volunteer, rocked, and soothed. Observations of Anthony's behavior in the nursery in comparison with that of three other infants revealed that he cried as often as the other three combined, and he was held in someone's arms twice as much. To put it bluntly, Anthony's crying was being strongly reinforced by all this loving attention. Because of his unprecedentedly high crying records, the experimenters classified Anthony as a member of the species *Infans tyrannotearus* and scheduled him for treatment.

So Anthony was placed in a carriage, wheeled down a corridor, and taken via elevator up to the experimental room on the next floor to begin a 15-minute-daily course of counterconditioning. In the experimental room, he was placed in the center of a U-shaped screen at the end of which he could see the head and shoulders of an experimenter when the window shade over an opening was raised. Whenever Anthony cried, he only saw a neutral, expressionless face. Reinforcement was given when he stopped crying, made eye contact with the experimenter, and smiled. With such direct attention, Anthony's smiles were more easily evoked. For rewards he was shown a glinting, gold-colored child's tea saucer, or various bells were rung, hand puppets worked, or toy whistles and crickets sounded. After his "partial" smiles came more frequently and became more wholehearted, the experimenter rewarded Anthony with a broad smile and a "Good boy, Anthony," nodding his head up and down. By the end of his nine-day reinforcement extension course, Anthony had become an accomplished smiler, keeping his eyes on the experimenter most of the time and breaking into frequent grins. His crying and fussing in the experimental room greatly diminished, for they were counter to his regimen of smiling. He did not cry at all in the last three days of conditioning. Throughout this procedure, his crying in the nursery continued and was still being reinforced. Clearly, he was able to distinguish between conditions in the nursery and in the experimental setting.

Anthony's smiling continued to increase the first three days of no reinforcement and then dropped gradually, though not to its low level before conditioning. Meanwhile, crying had returned, which was attributed to the reinforcement of crying in the nursery as conditioned smiling gradually diminished.

Then, after nine days of no reinforcement in the experimental room, the head nurse announced that Anthony had become "spoiled" and laid down the nursery rule that no one was to pick him up when he cried. (Certainly, such treatment cannot be recommended generally. Normal crying benefits from prompt attention to it, as noted earlier.) With this dictum in effect, Anthony had only one short episode of crying in the experimental room for the next seven days. At this point, a quarantine was imposed on the nursery because of a case of chickenpox, and the experiment had to be stopped. But it had shown that in infants in the second month, reinforcement of a desirable response can be followed by gradual extinction of an undesirable one. And that even at this early age, infants readily learn the conditions under which reinforcement is or is not given.

Since infants respond so sensitively to instrumental conditioning, then they should demonstrate some of its peculiar effects as well. One of the infants in the Brackbill smiling experiment did just this, displaying a clear case of what B. F. Skinner called "superstitious behavior" when he observed it in some pigeons that were being instrumentally conditioned—but in a rather unusual way.[18] At regular intervals during his experiment, a food hopper attached to the pigeon's cage was swung into a position that enabled the pigeon to eat from it. Thus, no matter what the pigeon happened to be doing at the time, his behavior was reinforced. This resulted in the repetition of some extremely bizarre goings-on, such as pigeons hopping from side to side or spinning around in a circle several times, although none of these responses had "caused" the food hopper to appear. Superstitious behavior such as wearing a "lucky charm" probably has a similar origin. The object was once present by chance when the wearer was lucky, and so he sees the object as responsible for his good fortune.

The "superstitious" infant in the Brackbill study regularly kept his left fist in his mouth during the reinforcement of smiling. Then, when returned to his crib, he would take his fist out of his mouth and keep it suspended in the air while he was smiling. The moment reinforcement of this smiling began, he would again pop his fist into his mouth, turn his head to the left, and stiffen. This stereotyped behavior began when a conditioned smiling was first established. It continued to recur except during a brief period of illness. But it gradually diminished and had disappeared by the end of the experiment. In some fashion, the baby had associated this behavior with the experimenter's reinforcing attention. The results of more recent studies (with pigeons) suggest that such apparently "superstitious" behavior is hypothesis testing or "playing long shots," occurring because the animal is not sure whether or not there is any relationship between its behavior and the reward.[19] Under such circumstances, "superstitious" behavior is adaptive, not irrational.

So far, the terms "reinforcement" and "reinforcer" have been used in a general sense. But in learning by instrumental conditioning, a distinction is normally made between primary and secondary reinforcement and reinforcers, a primary reinforcer being one that is naturally reinforcing—as food is for a hungry child, for instance. A secondary reinforcer, on the other hand, is neutral, with no inherent reinforcing power in and of itself; it becomes reinforcing by being associated or paired with a primary reinforcer. Money is a particularly good example. If the small rectangles of paper called dollar bills were not associated with the satisfaction of many needs, who could be induced to work for them?

The words of praise and looks of approval that infants receive from their caregivers are believed to be secondary reinforcers because of their association with various good things. It has often been asserted that it is by this kind of reinforcement that infants are trained in the ways of their culture. Yet this claim was made in the absence of any credible experimental evidence that infants can learn by secondary reinforcement. In 1972, an investigator reported that he had obtained such evidence in an experiment with 10-month-old infants.[20]

The infants were brought into the experimental laboratory by their mothers and placed in a seat in the center of an infant feeding table. A slide projector housed above the infant's head could project three "targets" onto the table: a patterned yellow and black cross centered on the tabletop and two identical red circles, one on either side. Photoelectric cells were embedded in the table underneath the targets, so that touching a target would activate either a continuous or a pulsating tone and then trigger the delivery of a tidbit. Each infant had a conditioning session with up to 20 reinforcements and lasting 20 to 30 minutes. This was followed by five minutes of testing to determine whether or not conditioning had taken place.

In the conditioning phase of the experiment, only the center target, the patterned cross, was switched on. When the infant touched it, a continuous or pulsating tone was automatically sounded for three seconds. After one and one-half seconds of the tone, a piece of Froot Loop cereal was delivered through a concealed tube to the tabletop near the target, where the baby could pick it up. One or the other tone was used consistently for each infant. Then, at a random time in a 20-second interval following the appearance of the tidbit, the other tone (either pulsating or continuous) sounded for three seconds.

In the testing that followed, the center target was switched off and one of the two red circles was switched on. When the infant pressed one of the circles, this produced the three-second sound that had preceded and accompanied the arrival of the Froot Loop during training. The pressing of the other red circle activated the three-second tone that had been associated with the 20-second period of no reinforcement.

Testing, without reinforcement, revealed a significant difference between responses to the two targets, even though neither target had produced a reward in the training sessions. The infants pressed the red circle yielding the Froot Loop–associated tone twice as often as the red circle that activated the "neutral" tone, indicating that a particular tone had come to "stand for" a reward. Their ability to respond selectively in a novel situation by applying their experience in the training session was a convincing demonstration that secondary reinforcement can be highly effective in infant learning.

A need-satisfying or stimulating event is usually sufficient to establish a conditioned response in infants. But this is not always the case. Reinforcement, however carefully planned, sometimes fails. The concept of the "setting event" was proposed to explain this variability. It was defined as a factor in an experimental or real-life situation that contributes to or interferes with the effectiveness of reinforcement. For example, praise from a younger sister probably would not reinforce the behavior of a female child, but praise from her mother would be effective. Or infants in a conditioning experiment might respond to reinforcement only when an adult was present. Possibilities of this kind were much discussed, but there was no experimental verification of the setting event concept until recently. This came out of an experiment in which the relationship between eye contact and the effectiveness of reinforcement was investigated.[21]

Many studies have been made of eye-to-eye contact between infants and adults and have shown that it plays a significant role in infant behavior. Researchers have found, for example, that autistic infants do not make eye-to-eye contacts, that after eye contact an infant will often follow the shifting gaze of a caregiver, that eye contact with an adult will elicit smiling in an infant, and that eye contact is involved in the development of attachment to the mother. Such findings suggested to the infant investigator Kathleen Bloom that eye contact might be used experimentally to test the concept of the setting event. She selected infant vocalization as the behavior to be reinforced and provided or prevented eye contact by wearing eyeglasses with specially designed lenses throughout the experiment.

Vocalizations (defined as voiced sounds) in 11 infants ranging in age from 10 to 14 weeks were recorded in the infants' homes. To obtain the baseline vocalization rate, the investigator simply leaned over the crib and kept a face-to-face position vis-à-vis the infant but did not respond to any of the infants' vocalizations. In the reinforcement sessions, the experimenter responded to each vocalization by touching the infant's face, smiling, and saying "Tsk, tsk, tsk."

The infants were divided into four groups, each of which saw the experimenter wearing eyeglasses with two of four different pairs of lenses, one pair for each half of a session: clear plastic lenses; lenses covered with life-sized photographs of the experimenter's eyes with either direct or averted gaze; and lenses covered with skin-colored opaque shields. Pinholes were made in all but the clear plastic lenses, so that the experimenter could keep her gaze directed into the infant's eyes.

The clear and opaque lenses were used for three infants. Three other infants saw the clear lenses and direct-gaze photos. The opaque lenses and direct-gaze photos were used in the third group of three infants. And two infants saw the direct-gaze and averted-gaze photos.

During the baseline period, the change in lenses during sessions had no effect on vocalization rate in any of the infants. But when the experimenter socialized with the infants after each vocalization, the rate continued to increase whether she wore clear lenses or lenses with direct-gaze or averted-gaze photographs of her eyes. When she wore blank, opaque lenses, however, reinforcement had no effect on vocalization rate.

Judging from this experiment, at least, eye contact, whether with real eyes or two-dimensional representations of eyes, appears to be an essential element in infant learning. As the investigator put it, eye contact acts as a sort of catalyst—a setting event—for social reinforcement. Thus, even though reinforcement is given consistently, an extraneous factor, the absence of eye contact, can destroy its effectiveness. Reinforcement, then, is not always a sufficient condition for learning.

Does learning involve more than conditioning theory allows for? To developmental psychologists of the cognitive school the simple conditioning formula of the behaviorists is totally inadequate to account for such complex processes as reasoning, understanding, and using knowledge to solve problems. In the cognitive view, active processing of information from the environment is interposed between stimuli and responses: stimuli are compared, differences are seen, and decisions are then made as to how to respond. In short, cognitive psychologists regard mental activity as an integral part of the learning process. Their approach is exemplified by Bower's interpretation of the results of the reversed contingency head-turning experiment as a demonstration of infant problem solving. He did not see the infants as being conditioned by reinforcement but as testing out various responses to find out which one would yield the reward.

Lucienne, Jacqueline, and Laurent Piaget are probably the most famous of all the infants whose learning processes have been subjected to the scrutiny of infant investigators. Their father Jean Piaget, the most prominent figure in the cognitive school, derived from his daily observations of their behavior from birth onward—as well as from observations of many other children—a theory and a timetable of cognitive development that have had a major influence on developmental psychology and infant research.[22] A significant proportion of infant studies today involve experimental testing of Piaget's observations.

Piaget does not use the term "learning." Rather, he conceives of all behavior as adaptation to changes in the environment that is achieved by means of two complementary processes, assimilation and accommodation. In assimilation, the infant, encountering a new situation resembling those with which he is familiar, responds with a pattern of behavior that has already been established—or a behavioral *schema*, as Piaget calls it. The infant who has a schema for grasping a rattle will also grasp a spoon that is handed to him, and the spoon is then incorporated into the existing schema. In accommodation, on the other hand, the infant encounters a new situation that cannot be dealt with by an established schema, and so he will have to modify his behavior to adapt to the new situation. Thus, when handed a large toy that he cannot grasp with one hand, the infant will eventually find that two hands must be used to grasp large objects, and this new pattern of behavior will itself become a schema.

Through this interplay between assimilation and accommodation, more and more complex schemata will be formed, combined with each other, and organized into patterns, making infants increasingly capable of dealing with the complexities of their environment, or as Piaget views it, increasingly capable of intelligent behavior.

Piaget believes that the development of intelligence proceeds sequentially and without exception through four periods, in each of which the child's behavior and mental processes are qualitatively different. The first of these—and the one that concerns us here—is the sensorimotor period, which lasts from birth to about 2 years of age.[23] In this period, the infant acquires information about the environment solely by motor activity and sensory impressions, and this information is coordinated in increasingly complex behavioral schemata. Since infants cannot use language symbolically to stand for objects or events, Piaget does not regard them as capable of thinking in this period of development, and therefore their schemata are not cognitive but sensorimotor only in his view.

During the first stage of the sensorimotor period, corresponding approximately to the first month of life, reflexes and fixed-action patterns are exercised and expanded. During the newborn's first feedings, for example, he simply reacts mechanically and passively by sucking when anything touches his mouth. This occurred in Piaget's three children almost immediately after birth. Very soon, however, the infant will begin to grope around with his mouth in response to visual, tactual, or olfactory cues, actively seeking the nipple, and a new schema will be established, incorporating these stimuli. For example, when Laurent was 3 days old, he began to grope for the nipple the moment his lips touched the skin of the breast.

Piaget suggests that the newborn is geared to shift from passive reaction to active groping because the exercise of a function, such as sucking, is intrinsically satisfying in its own right—and the more so the more fully the function is performed. The newborn performing his natural functions earns his own reward, in other words, and is kept moving on to higher levels of adaptation through assimilation and accommodation.

In the second stage of the sensorimotor period, lasting from 1 to 4.5 months of age approximately, sensorimotor schemata begin to become coordinated with each other. Thus, sucking is accompanied by grasping as the newborn's hands go to the breast or bottle while he is sucking. Bringing the hand to the mouth will be combined with sucking in a new thumb-sucking schema. And sight of the bottle or breast alone will now initiate sucking and grasping by the newborn. Thus, stimuli from all the senses can be related to one another and the schemata modified to include them in broader patterns of behavior. Now, when an infant is picked up from the crib, wrapped in a blanket, and held against the mother, he is likely to begin to suck. Piaget would say that the infant has accommodated his schemata to include these stimuli and now assimilates them under a much fuller schema. The behaviorists would say that being picked up, wrapped, and held have been paired with the stimulus of milk and that this sucking is a conditioned response.

During the third sensorimotor stage, from 4.5 to about 8 or 9 months of age, the infant may be said to reverse his earlier coordinations, say between sucking and grasping. Now he grasps toward the bottle in order to suck, with apparent anticipation of the results of his actions. Rather than simply looking at swinging objects nearby, smiling in response to the sight, the infant may now kick up his feet to make them swing, smiling in satisfaction with recognition of his accomplishment. He now dimly begins to see a connection between his actions and changes in the environment, but with no real understanding of cause and effect. This was shown very clearly by Laurent's reaction when Piaget snapped his fingers as Laurent was striking a cushion—"one of his favorite schemata." Laurent smiled and then began striking the cushion harder and harder, meanwhile staring at his father's hand. When Piaget finally snapped his fingers again, Laurent stopped hitting the cushion, "as though he had achieved his object."

The infant at this stage begins to get a sense of the permanence of objects and will actively search visually for an object that he or someone else has dropped. However, if an object is hidden in his sight, he will promptly forget it.

Recognition of familiar objects is expressed by foreshortening of behavioral schemata at this stage. At 6 months of age, when Lucienne saw a doll that she had swung many times, she made a brief swinging movement with her hands. A month later when she saw the doll, she merely opened and closed her hands. It was, Piaget said, "only a sort of acknowledgment." This behavior may represent the dividing line between motor activity and the beginning of cognitive processes.

In the third sensorimotor stage the infant also develops a capacity for what Piaget calls pseudoimitation, "pseudo" because the behavior that is imitated is initiated by the infant. Piaget reported that at 5 months of age, after Lucienne had put out her tongue and he had imitated her, she showed great interest and put out her tongue again. This interaction was repeated several times.

From the age of 8 to 9 months to 11 or 12 months, the infant passes through a fourth stage in which he coordinates two or more familiar schemata in order to deal with new situations, with his behavior consequently becoming even more complex. Thus, an infant may turn on one side and pull on a string, to bring an object near enough to grasp it, or he may push aside several objects in order to reach an object behind it. Piaget believes this coordination of schemata to achieve an end signals the beginning of genuinely intelligent behavior. At this stage, the infant clearly recognizes and anticipates the effects of others' actions as well as his own. An infant will cry, for example, on seeing his mother put on her coat, since this signifies to him that she is about to depart.

The infant's notion of the permanence of objects improves during this stage, as he begins to group things that are alike, as well as separating himself and his actions (me) from other things and actions (not me). But at this stage, after an infant has seen an object hidden, say under a pillow, twice in one place and found it there, then watched the object hidden in another place, he will continue to search for the object under the pillow. According to Piaget, the infant still does not conceive of an object as something than can move from place to place and yet remain the same object. Bower places the achievement of object permanence considerably earlier.

At this fourth stage, the infant begins to play more obviously, repeating many assimilated activities with evident relish. He gradually advances from flitting from one random activity to another to meaningful sequences, such as pretending to go to sleep—playfully lying down, sucking his thumb, and pulling up his blanket. And he is now capable of genuine imitation of the actions of others and of learning by imitation, Piaget states. Thus, at about 8 months of age, when Piaget said "ga-ga" Jacqueline made a sustained effort to imitate him, first saying "ma-ma," then "ba-ba," "va-va," and finally "pa-pa."

Piaget's observations with respect to the age when learning by imitation begins have been generally confirmed by a recent experiment with infants at 6, 9, 12, and 15 months of age.[24] The infants sat in their mothers' laps at a table across from the experimenter and their reactions to the experimental procedures were videotaped for later detailed analysis. The experimenter modeled 22 different "actions" for each baby. For example, she placed four red cubes on the table and stacked one atop another, leaving two cubes near the baby to see what he would do with them. In another action, she placed two red crayons and a sheet of paper on the table and scribbled with one crayon on the sheet, leaving the other crayon near the baby. In others, a white and yellow plastic duck was squeezed with or without a quacking sound, or a bell was shaken with or without sounds, to see if sounds stimulated more imitation. Thirteen of the actions involved objects, so that if they were imitated, the infants could observe their own imitative behavior. Six of the actions, however, were facial and head movements, which the infants could not see themselves imitating, such as smacking lips, protruding the tongue, shaking the head, and looking at the ceiling. And three of the actions involved pat-a-cake, performed silently in one action and with sound in two others.

A group of control infants was also used at each age level. These infants were simply presented with the objects as they sat in their mothers' laps at the table, to assess to what extent infants would spontaneously perform an action, such as stacking blocks, without any model to imitate and thus guarantee that the experimental groups' actions were actually imitative.

Infants at each age level imitated many of the modeled actions, although at 6 and 9 months the imitations were more often incomplete than complete. The frequency and completeness of imitation increased with age, with substantial increases between the ages of 9 and 12 months and 12 and 15 months. Actions that made sounds did not significantly stimulate infant imitation in this experiment, but actions with objects were imitated more than actions without them. No signs of significant sex differences in imitative ability were found.

Attempts have been made to explain infants' imitative behavior in terms of the principles of classical and instrumental conditioning, but these explanations seem inadequate to account for the complex nature of imitation. In pseudoimitation, for example, an infant must recognize the similarity of his own and another person's behavior, sometimes when his own actions are not visible to him.[25] Lucienne's early tonguing involved such recognition. But more is involved in imitation than merely recognizing similarities. When Jacqueline searched for a way to match Piaget's "ga-ga," she was experimenting with sound she had neither heard nor made herself. Somehow she recognized that this sound was produced by movements of the mouth and vocal cords and "knew" that she, too, was capable of making these movements. And to imitate an action such as stacking cubes, the infant must reverse some of the movements he has seen modeled if he is to make a match. For example, the model's hand moves *toward* the infant to grasp the cube, but the infant must move his hand *away* from his body to do so. It is difficult to see how conditioning principles can satisfactorily account for the recognizing, translating, and matching that imitation requires.

Several preliminary reports have suggested that infants may be capable of simple imitation in the first months of life.[54] One thoroughly controlled series of experiments with infant imitation was recently carried out by Andrew Meltzoff and Keith Moore of the University of Washington, Seattle.[26] The experiments were conducted in a laboratory room that was free of noise and other distracting stimuli. Alert infants, 12 to 21 days of age, were seated in reclining chairs and watched while the experimenter, standing directly in front of them, stuck out his tongue, opened his mouth, protruded his lips, or opened and closed his hand by moving successive fingers. The babies imitated these actions in a highly significant proportion of instances.

Meltzoff cautions that

> ... We should be careful not to mislead parents into thinking that all they need do is poke their tongue out at their baby and they will see him imitate in return. ... The normal home environment is usually (not always) too noisy and too full of distractions for the infants to display their true imitative competence. In order to document this

remarkable ability, we were forced out of the home and into a rigorously controlled experimental environment. . . . My experience has shown that parents often try to test out new ideas with their babies, and may then become worried or even upset if their baby does not respond "properly." I would hate to think that this might happen because of this research on infant imitation.[27]

Parents should also keep in mind that the same kind of reservations hold for other infant capacities that may be easily affected by distracting conditions.

Meltzoff and Moore discarded the possibility that the infant subjects had learned how to imitate adult facial expressions and gestures either at home or during the experiments. None of the parents recalled seeing their babies imitate, and most expressed surprise when they heard of this capacity. Furthermore, six younger infants, one only 60 minutes old, were also observed imitating adult facial expressions. Nor could the researchers accept the explanation that the imitative responses were fixed-action patterns, released by the corresponding adult action (sign stimulus), since they were not stereotyped enough to qualify as fixed action. Instead, Meltzoff and Moore proposed that intermodal matching of infants' visual sensations and their own muscular movements must be involved, probably made possible by some kind of "abstract representations" of the adult movements that are no longer going on at the time of imitation. If this ability is innate, the investigators said, "we must revise our current conceptions of infancy, which hold that such a capacity is the product of many months of postnatal development."[26]

T. G. R. Bower has discussed the implications of this infant talent. It implies, he said, that the infant has a sufficiently elaborate image of his own body to permit him to identify its parts with parts of other people's bodies. "This is intersensory coordination with a vengeance! Remember that we are talking about newborn babies, who have never examined themselves in mirrors or done any of the self-discovery things that adults can do."[28]

Near or at the end of the first year, the infant begins to manifest the developments of the fifth sensorimotor stage, which lasts through 18 months to 2 years of age, as charted by Piaget. In this stage, the infant can search for and find objects hidden in a second place after first seeing them hidden elsewhere, apparently conceiving of the objects as having a permanent existence. At the same time, the infant becomes interested in manipulating things in a variety of ways, curious now to see what can be done with them. This soon leads the infant to the use of the simple process of trial and error to discover new ways to effect his goals. An infant observes, for instance, that objects fall when he lets go of them and is fascinated by their motion or the glorious noise when they strike the floor. The baby will then try out various ways of letting things go and may soon discover that swinging his arm as he lets go results in even greater motion and more delightful crashing sounds. More trials of diverse methods of arm swinging and perhaps some imitation of others, and he soon becomes an expert thrower.

Thinking can be described as an internal trial-and-error method of problem solving in which solutions are formulated as hypotheses and then tested to determine which one works best. According to Piaget, children are not capable of genuine thinking until they are well into the sixth sensorimotor stage (beginning at 18 to 24 months), when language development permits the internal symbolization of schemata. However, Jerome Kagan, of the Harvard Center for Cognitive Studies, on the basis of several lines of evidence, holds that cognitive activity is apparent in infants around the end of the first year.[29]

Kagan notes, for example, that the duration of infants' fixation on masks of the human face diminishes from 2 to 9 months of age, as if they could be more and more easily assimilated in the infants' maturing schemata for faces and so require less and less attention. However, from 9 to 36 months of age the concentration of infants and children on masks increases. This change has been found not only in children in the United States but also in Guatemalan and African !Kung (Bushman) infants. Kagan proposes that this shift manifests the emergence of a cognitive process in which infants formulate hypotheses to explain unfamiliar events. It is as though the infant now says, "Here is a face [the mask's] that is not like the faces I know"— and is attempting to understand the discrepancy.

Although cognitive activities can only be inferred by this change in attention to masks after 9 months of age, Kagan points out that more direct evidence is available. Studies have shown that the heart rates of children, as well as those of adults, tend to decrease when they are attending to interesting events, but to increase when they actively think about things, as in memorizing words or making calculations.

These findings have been replicated in a number of infant studies. For example, in two separate but similar investigations, infants 5½ to 11½ months of age heard 8 to 12 repetitions of a speech phrase followed by a discrepant phrase. In one study the phrases were meaningful, and in the other the infants heard nonsense phrases. In both studies, heart rate increases occurred in response to the discrepant phrase. However, they occurred in only 20 percent of the 5½-month-old infants, but in over 60 percent of the 11½-month-old infants. If heart rate increases in infants signify an increase in cognitive activity, as they do in children and adults, the age of reason has taken a quantum leap backward to age one.

CHAPTER 6
Delight and Distress

Overshadowed by his monumental *Origin of Species*, Charles Darwin's *Expression of the Emotions in Man and Animals*, published only thirteen years later (1872), was a work of equally great imagination. In her preface to a modern edition, published in 1955, Margaret Mead said of Darwin's innovative approach to the expression of emotion that "his list of ways in which the subject might be studied has not been improved upon." And with some minor exceptions, his precise delineation of the behavior associated with emotional expression still stands today.

For more than forty years, Darwin gathered material on expressive movements and facial expressions in emotion in people around the world, in the insane, in great paintings and sculpture, in primates and domestic animals, and in infants. His book contained minutely detailed descriptions of the physiological and muscular changes involved in the expression of emotion. These were documented by photographs and drawings of animals and human beings in the grip of a variety of emotions, giving the book a peculiarly modern flavor. Such captions as "Cat in an affectionate frame of mind" and "Chimpanzee disappointed and sulky" foreshadowed his conclusion, based on overwhelming evidence, that the expression of emotion in animals and human beings of all cultures is remarkably similar. Noting that this confirmed his hypothesis that "man is derived from some lower animal form," he added a typical Darwinian touch: ". . . as far as my judgment serves, such confirmation was hardly needed."

In his "Biographical Sketch of an Infant,"[2] published some five years later, Darwin concentrated exclusively on the expression of emotion in infants as seen in one of his own children. The infant of the biography was Darwin's firstborn son, whose emotional development in infancy and early childhood he had followed and recorded with great care, as he was to do with all his children.

Infants express pleasure, Darwin said, by their "swimming eyes" while sucking, as well as by their "real" smiles, in which their eyes brighten and their eyelids close slightly. These real smiles appeared in his own children at about a month and a half of age. Mothers usually cause such smiles, he said, but infants sometimes smile for no reason at all—just from "some inward pleasurable feeling." He saw expressions of humor in his infant son at the age of 110 days and observed that it followed surprise as it almost always does in adults.

Darwin was uncertain when his son showed anger for the first time. The baby first frowned before a crying fit (which became a typical pattern) at the age of 8 days, which Darwin was inclined to attribute to pain or distress. At 10 weeks of age, his son frowned continuously while sucking on a bottle of cold milk, "much like a grown-up . . . made cross from being compelled to do something . . . he did not like." By 4 months of age, he showed unmistakable signs of anger, with reddening of the face and scalp, thrashing of the arms and legs, and screaming. At this age, Darwin said, "he easily got into a violent passion. A small cause sufficed."

Fear is probably one of the earliest feelings that infants experience, Darwin said. This is shown by "their starting at any sudden sound when only a few weeks old, followed by crying." At 2 months of age, his son became frightened when Darwin suddenly sneezed, and for an hour afterward jumped at the slightest noise like an adult in a nervous state.

Darwin observed expressions of "affection" in his son before 2 months of age, manifested by smiling at "those who took care of him." By 6 months of age, "with respect to the allied feeling of sympathy" the baby assumed a melancholy expression, with the corners of his mouth turned down, when his nurse pretended to cry. And in keeping with the concerns of the Victorian era, Darwin looked for and found the first sign of a moral sense in his infant son at 13 months of age. Even though he "had never in any way been punished," he showed signs of discomfort at being called "naughty" for refusing to give his father a kiss.

Darwin's evident enjoyment of his infant son's company was

unique at a time when a proper father kept a safe distance between himself and the nursery. Nor would it have occurred to most scientists of his day that infant watching could be scientifically productive. It was the essence of Darwin's genius that he was able to delight in something so ordinary as the expression on an infant's face while carefully noting its connection with the behavior of the species to which the infant belonged.

Infant facial expressions have received very little attention since Darwin's time, although those involved in such common human emotions as happiness or joy, surprise, fear, sadness or suffering, anger, and disgust or contempt have been extensively studied and analyzed in adults. A brief and admittedly preliminary infant study was reported in 1976 by Jeanette Haviland of the Educational Testing Service in Princeton, New Jersey.[3] She made videotapes of her fraternal twins Alex and Lizbeth from the time they were 2 weeks old until they reached the age of 2 years and then analyzed and compared their facial expressions over their first six months. She noted that still photographs reveal very little about mobile facial expressions, but when registered and viewed on films or videotapes, they become much more meaningful. The twins' facial expressions differed from the beginning, and these differences remained remarkably stable throughout the two years of the study.

Haviland's analysis of her children's facial expressions over the study period showed that their eyebrow positions were similar, most often relaxed, but also contracted to a frown on occasion and sometimes were raised in a curious, quizzical look combined with opened eyes that seemed to indicate interest or surprise. The twins differed, however, in their eye openness, with Lizbeth's eyes widened more often than Alex's and Alex's more often narrowed. Lizbeth also glanced much more often to the side or up than did Alex, who seemed to prefer to look down or down and to the side. Because of his narrowed eyes and the direction of his glances, Alex seemed to avoid eye contact, but Lizbeth, looking up with widened eyes, appeared to seek it. The frequent and varied movements of Lizbeth's mouth and lips made her seem the more active infant, while Alex's mouth and lips, usually still and relaxed, made him appear more passive. But as a result, uncommon movements of his mouth against the background of its usual calm made him more expressive than his twin.

Friends, visitors, and even passersby tended to "read" emotions, temperament, and even character into the twins' facial expressions, Haviland noted. Alex was called the "judge" and "cool customer," while Lizbeth was dubbed "sweetie," "woozel," and "little pumpkin." Alex was regarded as interested in things rather more than in people because of his calm, relaxed face, his gaze aversion, and his relative lack of emotional response. Lizbeth was considered affectionate and creative because of her eye openness, upward gaze, mobile mouth, and emotional responsiveness. With commendable scientific detachment, Haviland herself did very little interpreting of her children's facial expressions, but merely noted their appearance and their similarities and differences.

A very detailed ethological analysis of the videotaped facial and vocal expressions of some 75 infants in the last quarter of their first year was published in 1977 by Gerald Young and Thérèse Gouin Décarie of the University of Montreal.[4] The laboratory procedure was arranged to produce a variety of infant emotional reactions: exploring a new room in the presence of the mother; playing directed by the mother; the mother taking a toy from and physically restraining her infant; approach of a stranger with the mother present; the mother departing and then returning to her infant. All the social, emotional, or communicative actions of the babies in these situations were then studied on the tapes, distinguished, and made up into a tentative catalogue of some 42 distinctive facial expressions and 10 different vocalizations.

Young and Décarie found that, like adults', infant expressions usually affect many parts of the face. An expression may include changes in the brow, eyes, mouth, cheeks, nose, jaw, chin, and throat, as well as varied vocalizations. For example, a baby's expression called "play face" usually involves an uncreased brow, sparkling eyes (with tear secretion) with wrinkling of eye corners and narrowing of lids, oval opening of the mouth at a fast rate, bulging of the cheeks, dropping of the jaw, and sometimes throwing back of the head, often accompanied by laughter. The features involved in such expressions are revealed much better by videotapes than by photographs.

The researchers put the infant facial expressions and vocalizations they observed into three main groups: positive, or expressing pleasure; neutral, or undifferentiated; and negative, or expressing displeasure. In these terms, they placed a brightened face, play face, and various kinds of smiling, including coy and shy smiles, under positive facial expressions and classified babbles, coos, laughs, and squeals as positive vocalizations. Neutral facial expressions included the attentive, the detached, and the frozen faces, the sober stare and frown, the perplexed and the surprised faces, and the sigh and yawn, with ambivalent or undifferentiated vocalizations as well. Negative facial expressions included disgust, fear, and sad faces, the pout and the frown, the "clenched teeth" and the "square-mouth" and "kidney-mouth" faces, and the "tremble-face" among others. These expressions may be accompanied by wails, ranging from soft to harsh.

As any caregiver will testify, various infant facial expressions and vocalizations are often combined, or follow each other successively, to create identifiable feelings or emotions. For example, when a mother takes a toy away from her baby and holds him in her lap so he can no longer play, an attentive face may be followed swiftly by surprise or perplexity, and then perhaps by a square-mouth face and a harsh wail as well as brandishing of arms and legs. Such behavioral sequences often appear in the expression of infant emotions. This kind of analysis of the specific facial and vocal events making up such patterns may be useful in the study and eventual understanding of infant emotions, the investigators concluded.

For over fifty years after the publication of "Biographical Sketch of an Infant," scientists showed little or no interest in the emotional life of infants. A few scientist parents observed their own infants and sometimes recorded and reported their development in biographies, but with only passing reference to the emotions. Other occasional reports on infant emotions simply presented anecdotal evidence or generalizations based on a few cases. It was not until the 1920s, when infant psychology became a fledgling scientific discipline, that data on emotional development in large numbers of infants began to accumulate. The work of two investigators in particular—the behaviorist John Watson and the Canadian psychologist Katherine Bridges—marks this transition.

Watson's observations and experiments with hundreds of infants at Johns Hopkins University and nearby institutions had convinced him that infants at birth are capable of only three kinds of emotional response: fear, anger, and love.[5] All other emotions, although based on these three, are the result of environmental conditioning. Behaviorist to the core, Watson hastened to add that these words must be stripped of their "old connotations." They are simple responses, as neutral as the heartbeat and breathing, he declared. Watson's own statement with respect to fear epitomizes his no-nonsense approach:

> Our laboratory work shows the fear life of the newborn infant is simplicity itself. From birth the child will show fear whenever a sudden loud sound is made close to its head and whenever it is thrown off its balance, as for example, when its blanket is quickly jerked. . . . No other fears are natural, all other fears are built in.[6]

Unconstrained by the stringent ethical standards that guide infant research today, Watson experimented with fear in infants by striking a steel bar with a hammer behind their heads. Because he was not averse to trying to condition fears in infants and did so successfully, he strongly recommended that parents protect their babies from exposure to loud noises. Any such stimuli as the banging of pans, a window shade zipping up, or a door slamming could elicit infant fears and would then be associated with whatever was going on at the time. A new fear would thereby be "built in." A number of investigators have failed to confirm Watson's contention that all fears except fear of loss of support and loud noises are conditioned.

From birth on, Watson said, gently but firmly restraining an infant's head, arms, legs, or trunk so that he cannot move will "almost invariably" call out anger or rage. "Temper and rage displayed in any other situation is home made," he asserted. To such restraint, the infant first responds by struggling and then crying. This is followed by breath holding, stiffening of the body, opening of the mouth to its greatest extent, and flushing of the face to deep purple. No amount of training can ever extinguish this innate response to restraint, Watson said, but it, too, is very easy to condition, and he described how it was done.

> Here is a youngster in front of me whose movements I have interfered with from the day of his birth. In order to carry out a certain test upon him, I hold his hands until they begin to stiffen. I shake him a little, sometimes hold his nose. This brings out the grasping reflex in the hands. I then slip a tiny stick into his hands. He grasps it tightly. I lift him and let him support himself over a . . . pillow. Just the instant he begins to release his hold my assistant catches him. Nearly always he goes into a rage the moment this test starts. After three or four such

tests the mere sight of my face drove the youngster into a rage. *I no longer have to hamper his movements.*[6]

Some two months later the infant would still fly into a tantrum whenever Watson came within 8 feet of his crib.

Following Watson's prescription, a German investigator pressed the arms of 100 newborns to their sides in the hope of eliciting anger; 12 cried, 2 grimaced, and the rest had a variety of reactions.[7] Holding the infants' arms firmly over their heads was more successful, since 61 cried or grimaced angrily at this assault on their freedom. But a 61 percent response is far from Watson's "almost invariably."

Only one stimulus can elicit the infant's "love response," Watson said: touching and stroking "its skin, lips, sex organs and the like," which elicits smiling and cooing and quiets the infant. The love response, he added, is "the clay out of which all love . . . is made."[6] Watson conceded that affectionate responses are a social necessity, but he advised parents to keep their own and their infants' under firm control. Too much "coddling" in infancy, he said, gives rise to overdependence and will only stunt the child's development.

> Mothers just don't know, when they kiss their children and pick them up and rock them, caress them and jiggle them upon their knee, that they are slowly building up a human being totally unable to cope with the world in which it must later live. . . . All too soon, the child gets shot through with too many of these love reactions.[6]

Watson was not among the parents, if any, who put these spartan regulations into practice. In rearing his own children Watson was described by a friend as a most affectionate and very indulgent father.[8]

Katherine Bridges's gentler approach to infants yielded quite different results. In her observations of some 60 infants from 2 weeks to 24 months of age in the Montreal Foundling and Baby Hospital in the early 1930s, she found no evidence that infants start life with "[three] fully matured pattern reactions, such as have been mentioned by behaviorists."[9] In their first month, the infants she observed reacted to loud noises, restriction of the arms, sudden picking up, and other strong stimuli with generalized agitation or excitement that involved tensing of the arm and hand muscles, jerky kicking movements, increased respiration, crying, and opening of the eyes. This undifferentiated response, Bridges said, "must surely be one of the original emotions, if not the only one." Noticing a similar pattern of behavior when infants awakened from sleep, she suggested that waking must also call for an emotional adjustment on the part of the infant.

The "love responses" that caused Watson such concern were not apparent in Bridges's infants.

> The baby under a month old is either excited or quiescent. Gentle stroking, swaying and patting soothe him and make him sleepy. When satisfied after a meal he ... is ... either tranquil or busy mouthing and staring at distant objects. When he is *over two weeks old* he will sometimes give a faint reflex smile upon light tapping at the corners of his mouth. This is hardly an emotional response.[9]

She reported a similarly undramatic response to rocking, which she said merely soothed some agitated infants and caused a quiet infant to "open his eyes attentively." But, in fairness to Watson, it should be stated that Bridges's sample of infants included only three under the age of 1 month.

The next step in the "evolution of the emotions," Bridges said, was the emergence of the emotions of distress and delight from the undifferentiated pattern of excitement. The characteristics of distress, which could be distinguished from excitement in infants by 1 month of age, were extreme muscular tension, disruption of movement and breathing, closing of the eyes, and a high-pitched, loud cry.

Delight, Bridges said, cannot be differentiated from excitement before the age of 3 months, although she observed "fleeting smiles" in 2-month-old infants in response to being fed, tickled, or gently rocked. She described the first manifestations of delight as free and rhythmic motions of the arms and legs, open eyes, approach movements, cessation of crying in response to an adult voice, smiling at an adult, soft vocalizations while being fed or rocked, and "prolonged attention to the object of interest."

From her observations of infants from 3 through 24 months of age, Bridges concluded that the negative emotions of fear, anger, and disgust and the positive emotions of joy, elation, affection, and love are gradually derived from the emotional "syndromes" of distress and delight.

Bridges's work would not pass muster today. She said nothing about her methods of observation or recording and provided no quantitative data to support her conclusions. Furthermore, some of her observations have not been confirmed by other investigators. And with respect to her evolutionary theory, the emotions she described, although they were observed in many infants, "evolved" from only three. However, she was the first to explore the emotional development of many infants in their everyday environment, and thus her work, as well as Watson's, has an important place in the history of developmental psychology.

Heavily influenced by psychoanalytic and ethological theories of infant development, developmental psychologists today approach the study of infant emotions in an altogether different way. Both of these theories stress attachment to the mother as the emotional center of the infant's life. As a result, research efforts in the area that used to be called "the emotions" have become concentrated on exploring the development of the mother-infant tie. What infants do to promote this tie, and therefore ensure their survival, is of particular interest to the ethologically oriented researcher, who focuses on the biological foundations of behavior.

Since the smile is considered one of the infant's most valuable tools in promoting attachment to the mother, the development of the smile has received a great deal of attention from infant investigators.

The faint reflex smile or grimace that Bridges observed when she tapped a 2-week-old infant at the "corners" of his mouth can be seen in infants shortly after birth. As she noted, this is not an "emotional" type of smile. It consists only of contraction of the muscles around the mouth, so that it is pulled sideways and upward. The rest of the face is relaxed, and there are no crinkles at the corners of the eyes as in a "real" smile. This reflex smile can be elicited by tapping or stroking. It also occurs spontaneously, most often during REM (active) sleep, a period during which other facial expressions are commonly seen on the faces of infants.

In one series of observations of infants in active sleep, reported by Evelyn Thoman of the University of Connecticut, facial expressions were seen about once a minute on the average.[10] Two-thirds were classified as grimaces—fleeting facial movements that had no particular pattern or resembled adult facial expressions in various emotional states. The rest were definite smiles or frowns. Although the frowns outnumbered the smiles two to one, the infants smiled on the average about every six minutes. Since these spontaneous smiles—and the frowns, startles, jerks, and so on, typical of REM sleep—occur at fairly regular intervals and have no apparent cause, it has been suggested that they represent some sort of rhythmic discharge from the nervous system. If they are simply physiological events, as it appears, these smiles are unlikely to have any emotional significance.

An indefatigable infant researcher, Peter H. Wolff, working in Boston, watched the smiles of eight infants evolve over the first four weeks of life from rhythmic discharge patterns to broad grins.[11] By prearrangement with the family, Wolff was present at each infant's birth and made daily observations of his eight subjects while they were in the hospital nursery. When the babies left the hospital, he visited their homes six days a week, observing the infants' reactions to various smile elicitors for a total of 30 hours per week for four weeks. After the first few visits, the family took his presence as a matter of course, and he was treated much like a member of the household. Thus, his presence did not appear to disturb the infant's natural environment. However, the evolutionary process may have been speeded up in these infants, Wolff felt, because some mothers openly competed with him by trying to outdo his smile production rate.

To elicit smiles in these infants in the first two weeks, Wolff used a variety of sound stimuli, including a brass bell, an Audubon bird whistle, his own voice in falsetto, and tape-recorded voices of mothers talking to their babies. In a single experiment, one of these sounds was presented five times at regular intervals during active sleep. In the first week, only one or two of five stimulations produced any smiling, and infants who smiled smiled within seven seconds. This seven-second interval between stimulus and response in active sleep was constant through the fourth week. Some infants smiled more to the voices than to the bell. Others smiled more to the bell than to any of the other stimuli, but for all the infants, no one stimulus was consistently more effective than the other. All the smiles were of the reflex type—Wolff called them "grimace-smiles." Except in two "precocious" smilers, there was no spontaneous smiling in the awake state in the first week, nor could smiling be elicited when the infants were awake.

During the second week the infants began to smile with greatest frequency to a high-pitched voice, whether it was the mother's or a strange woman's or the experimenter's falsetto and whether they were in active sleep or in a glassy-eyed awake state after a meal. By this time the smile had undergone a metamorphosis: The mouth was stretched farther and sometimes opened; the muscles of the cheeks contracted and there was some crinkling around the eyes. Coupled with the infants' glassy eyes, drooping eyelids, and generally "tipsy" appearance, these smiles were a source of great amusement to the parents.

During the third week, the infants were tested with the brass bell and the whistle, a rattle, the experimenter's voice, both normal and falsetto, the mother talking baby talk, and tape recordings of other mothers talking to their children. All responded consistently to a high-pitched, unrecorded human voice—either the mother's or the experimenter's—by smiling broadly while they were fully awake, bright-eyed, and with their eyes apparently focused. Toward the end of the week, the first voice stimulation often stopped any crying, and the second would sometimes produce a smile. And in two of the infants, a nodding head—the mother's or the experimenter's—accompanying the voice produced even more smiles, indicating that visual stimulation was beginning to have a role in smiling. The nodding head alone was ineffective, however.

Although the voice continued to be the best smile elicitor during the fourth week, it was during this period that Wolff saw the first indications of smiling to the face alone—and the first occurrence of eye-to-eye contact. In the first three infants who made eye-to-eye contact and smiled, he observed the same sequence of events: The infant would scan the experimenter's face with great thoroughness, and then, on making eye-to-eye contact with him, would break into a broad grin. Within two to three days after this first occurred, the infants' mothers suddenly began to spend a great deal of time playing with them, commenting that the baby was now "fun to play with" or could now see her, although they were not aware of what exactly had changed. As other investigators have also found, it is not until the appearance of this social smile on eye-to-eye contact, when the mother first feels that her attention is finally reciprocated, that she begins to interact socially with her baby.[12] And developmental psychologists believe that social interaction with the mother plays a key role in the infant's emotional development.

In a series of studies carried out by T. Berry Brazelton, Edward

Tronick, and their colleagues, films were made of the face-to-face interactions of 12 infant-mother pairs beginning when the infants were about 2 to 4 weeks of age and continuing until they were 5 months old.[18] After a get-acquainted home visit, the mothers were asked to bring their babies into the laboratory for weekly videotaping sessions. The mothers were given the details of the procedure and reassured that the purpose of the filming was not to judge their behavior but to study the normal development of infant social abilities.

In each session, after chatting with the experimenter and changing and feeding her baby if necessary, the mother settled him in a reclining chair placed on a table within a curtained alcove. Then she left the alcove for a moment, reentered past a curtain, and sat down on a stool in front of her baby with her face on a level with his and about 18 inches from it. Two unobtrusive mirrors reflected the infant's and mother's faces side by side into the lens of a TV camera. The videotaping was started as the mother entered and sat down. She interacted and played with the infant for three minutes, left for half a minute, and returned for another three-minute session. If the infant became fussy or seemed bored, the filming was stopped while the mother handled or rocked him.

The videotapes were then played back at one-seventh normal speed to analyze and categorize the interactions. Somewhat as a microscope brings into view things not visible to the naked eye, the videotapes reveal minute details of the infant-mother exchange too fleeting to be detectable under ordinary circumstances.

The investigators identified five major phases through which these interactions pass. In the first phase, the phase of initiation, the mother's face brightens or she talks baby talk to an unsmiling infant, or the infant vocalizes to or smiles at the silent mother. Then mutual orientation occurs, followed by the next phase, greeting, in which infant and mother smile at each other, the mother may utter brief phrases such as "Hi, hi," or "Here we are!" and there may be much or little body movement. A play-dialogue phase then develops, with smiling and vocal exchanges between mother and infant, much baby talk, touching, and stroking by the mother and cooing and waving of arms and legs by the infant. In the last phase, disengagement, either mother or infant may stop the mutual interaction, the baby by sobering or looking away, the mother by turning away or talking in an adult manner.

In interacting with their mothers, the infants may pass through up to four or five cycles a minute of looking at the mothers for a time, looking away, then looking back, and so on. When the interaction begins, the infant's eyes may be dull, his face relaxed, and his body and limbs moving slowly. But as he turns toward he mother, with orientation and greeting, his eyes brighten, and his fingers and toes point toward her. As the mother responds in the play-dialogue phase, the infant attends fully to her. In this state of attention, fleeting smiles, vocalization, and reaching of the extremities toward her alternate with settling back and relaxation of tension. It is as though the infant, having signaled, is waiting for the mother's response, as in the back and forth of a conversation. As the interaction builds toward a peak, intense bodily activity precedes each vocalization. The infant watches the mother's face intently, responding to her smiles by smiling for longer periods than before. This is accompanied by rhythmic pumping of his arms and legs, tonguing, and spitting up. The mother's actions become almost continuous, consisting of rhythmic patting of the baby, constantly varying speech, and rhythmic movements of her body. Such actions, known as "continuates," also occur in adult communication, with head nodding and gesturing, for example, but they are less frequent and dramatic than the actions of a mother with her infant.

As the peak of attention is reached, the infant's intense activity alternates with what appear to be attempts to control his excitement—yawning, sucking his tongue, or holding onto his hand. This is followed by a gradual deceleration of bodily activity, with fading of smiles, decreased vocalization, yawning, fingering his head or ears, or sucking his thumb, and then either by a renewal of attention or by withdrawal from the mother in disengagement. Withdrawal may take the form of simply looking away from the mother, vocalizing into the room, smiling into the distance, and absentmindedly fingering the mother's hand. Or the infant may orient toward some object in the room and briefly fix his attention on it. However, when interaction with the mother has been unsatisfactory, the infant may shrink away from her, or push with his hands and feet as though pushing her away, or he may fuss or cry or go to sleep. Then after a period of this withdrawal and quieting or attention to something else, the infant may respond to the mother again, and a new cycle starts.

As their babies begin to withdraw their attention, some mothers may redouble their efforts to maintain it, but this is usually to no avail. Others may look away, relax, or lean back when the infants do, lowering their voices or simply waiting quietly for the infant's gaze to return as the next cycle begins, again with greeting and further play-dialogue. Mothers who thus made adjustments to the infant's cycling needs gained more of their babies' attention and responses for longer times, and with harmonious cycling, mother-infant interactions appeared to the observers as positive and full. When mothers kept interacting while the infants looked away, the interactions became desynchronized, as it were. Instead of helping the infant to learn how to communicate and express his feelings, the mother's behavior disrupted the infant's cycle of attention. When not responding to the infant's own rhythm of attention and withdrawal, or when attempting to regulate the infant's rhythm to her own, the mother got out of phase with her baby, and their interactions became less frequent, briefer, and seemed less positive and satisfying.

In some of the sessions, the infants were shown an object, such as a toy monkey, and their reactions to it were filmed. Even in infants as young as 2 to 3 weeks of age, the investigators felt they could distinguish clearly between the infant's attending to the object and his attending to his mother. The infants often became "hooked" on the object, with tension building up and bodily activity increasing, the infant flailing toward it. Then tension would quickly become too great and they would turn away, sometimes with fretting and crying. This sequence occurred much more rapidly—and the infant's behavior was much less organized—than when "conversing" with the mother, from whom a response was quite obviously expected.

The adaptability of infants to changes in the interactions was explored by having the mothers alter their approach to the baby. When the mothers slowed down their speech rate markedly, their other actions also slowed down, changing their normal interactive rhythms. At first, the infants sometimes seemed perplexed, but they were not disturbed, and their smiles and vocalizations became more frequent and their intensity more sustained. The slower rhythm often yielded very successful communication. When the mother sat with her head turned in profile, the baby would fasten his gaze on the mother and watch her intently. He would often lean forward, coo, and make calling vocalizations, but would rarely smile. Long periods of intense watching were interspersed with the vocalizations. Fussing sometimes occurred when the mothers sat in profile, and they were reminded of similar behavior when they were driving the car and could not face the baby.

Stronger infant responses developed when the mother simply sat still faced, in front of the infant, saying and doing nothing. When the infant greeted the mother with a smile and had no response, his face would sober and he would look away. Then he would shoot glances at the mother, sometimes with a fleeting smile. After some minutes, finding there was nothing to be done about the situation, the infant would withdraw into self-comforting behavior, sucking a finger or rocking his head and eventually becoming downcast and listless in a way reminiscent of the behavior of institutionalized infants separated from their mothers.

All these changes in the mother's interactive behavior were apparently noted by the infants, and they adjusted their responses to cope with the changes. Far from being passive spectators, they did their best to keep their communicative interchanges with the mother in working order.

In a laboratory study of face-to-face interactions at the University of Massachusetts, mothers interacting with their 3½-month-old infants were asked to (1) imagine that they were at home at the kitchen table playing spontaneously with their infants, (2) imagine that their husbands were taking a home movie and that they (the mothers) were trying to keep the infants looking at them face to face, and (3) imitate all the actions of the babies just as they occurred.[14] The babies interacted least during the attention-getting, home-movie approach, with more looking away. There was more face-to-face interaction with spontaneous play, but imitation proved to be the most potent facilitator of face-to-face interactions in this study. Furthermore, the imitation sessions yielded more smiling and laughing by the infants, who made a gleeful game of it. In trying to imitate her baby, the mother is watching him more closely and is more aware of his looking and not looking signals, the investigator noted, and the mother's imitative actions tend to be slower and more exaggerated than those of spontaneous play or intentional attention-getting, factors that tend to improve communication.

Brazelton and his colleagues have suggested that the cycles or modulations in looking and not looking observed in infants interacting with their mothers may be controlled by a homeostatic mechanism such as those that regulate breathing, temperature, heart rate, and perhaps sleeping and wakefulness. After the excitement involved in the infant's attention to the mother becomes strong and peaks, the infant gradually withdraws and relaxes, fastening his attention on some neutral object or merely looking into space. Looking gives way in a cycle to not looking, then back to looking after a respite, so that the infant does not become flooded with sensory stimulation. When the mother responds too much, the infant controls the degree of stimulation from her by attending to her for shorter periods and responding less. The infant learns to "turn off" the mother to reduce the amount of information from her to that which he can handle. The mother, on the other hand, if she is to communicate well with her baby, must learn the limits of his capacity to receive information.

Disharmony in a mother-infant interaction may have lasting effects on the infant's development. This was shown in a study done by Evelyn Thoman and colleagues at the University of Connecticut in which the development of infants whose interactions with their mothers had been observed at home was evaluated some months later.[15] Twenty mother-infant pairs were observed weekly for four seven-hour periods when the infants were 2, 3, 4, and 5 weeks of age. Although the observers who participated in the observations kept the infant's face continuously in view and followed the mother and infant around the house, they remained as unobtrusive as possible. Information on some 75 kinds of mother and infant behavior considered to be characteristic of mother-infant interaction were coded and recorded at 10-second intervals over the seven hours. In all, a total of 209,751 bits of behavioral data about the interactions were available for analysis.

At 7 and 12 months of age, the infants were given infant development tests, and at 2.5 years they were tested again. Thus, their development in later infancy and early childhood could be evaluated in terms of its possible relationship to mother-infant interaction in the first weeks.

The investigators were able to identify certain behavioral features of mother-infant interaction that were consistent for individual mother-infant pairs throughout the period of observation. These could then be compared with the average incidence of particular kinds of behavior in all the infant-mother pairs. In this way, a deviation from the norm could be detected that might be correlated with a developmental problem.

In three of the infants, subsequent testing revealed signs of retarded development, and all three had had less social interaction with their mothers during the home observations than the group as a whole. Their mothers looked at these infants less, and patted, caressed, and rocked them less, than did the average mother in the group. The infants did not fuss or cry, nor were they awake, for more than the average length of time, yet their mothers held or carried them for caretaking purposes only much more often than did the other mothers in the group. In other words, more of the infant's time while awake was used for caretaking than for social interaction.

A detailed analysis of interactions in one of the pairs showed that the infant had given the mother so many ambiguous signals that she was unsure how to respond to him, despite her seeming eagerness to do so. The investigators described a typical instance of this difficulty as follows:

> The episode began with the infant asleep in the crib. During the three minutes prior to the mother's intervention there were six epochs [10-second periods] during which open-eyed REM occurred. The mother picked the baby up, undressed him, and gave him an immersion bath which lasted for five minutes. Throughout the bath the infant's eyes did not open. As she talked to him, one of the mother's comments was that she did not understand why the infant kept his eyes closed. As she dressed her infant after the bath, he began to waken. She put him to the breast and after several efforts to get him to feed, she put him back into the crib and left the room. While in the crib alone, the infant remained awake and primarily alert for 15 minutes.[15]

Open-eyed REM sleep, which the mother interpreted as wakefulness, occurred more frequently in this infant than in any other infant in the study. This, in addition to his frequent changes from sleep to wakefulness, so confused the mother that she could not tell whether he was asleep or awake. Uncertain about what the baby needed, she kept picking him up and attempting to feed him—behavior to which the infant in turn had to adjust. The investigators described this infant-mother relationship as "a positive feedback system in which each individual accentuated the volatility of the other." The examiners who carried out the follow-up tests and a later assessment when the child was 33 months of age reported that none of the tests could be completed because of his changeability and on-and-off cooperation.

Although most developmental psychologists today view attachment to the mother as of central importance to the infant's emotional development, there are sharp differences of opinion as to the origins of this attachment and the mechanisms that set it in motion and maintain it. Depending on whether the researcher espouses the psychoanalytic, ethological, or social learning theory of attachment, the mother is seen respectively as the infant's love object, protector, and teacher.

According to psychoanalytic theory, the infant in the first year of life is in the oral stage of development, more recently called the "sensorimotor" stage by the contemporary child analyst Erik Erikson, using the term Piaget applies to intellectual development. The infant's principal release for the energy generated by the libido is through the mouth and lips. In *The First Year of Life,* René Spitz, a Freudian analyst who made careful observations of many infants, emphasized the importance of the mouth for the infant:

> ... The oral cavity ... is the first surface in life to be used for tactile perception and exploration. It is well suited for this purpose, for in it are represented the sense of touch, of taste, of temperature, of smell, of pain, and even of deep sensitivity.... It should not be forgotten that emotional qualities, namely, pleasure and unpleasure, partake in this perceptual experience.[16]

In the psychoanalytic view, the instincts that propel the psychic machinery must have a source, like the libido Freud postulated as the source of the sexual instinct, and an aim, like the libido's basic drive to propagate the species, as well as an agent or object through which the aim is achieved, or "cathected."[17] During the early weeks, the libidinal energy of infants is directed solely to the satisfaction of their needs. They make no distinction between themselves and the external world and experience only the tension produced by bodily needs and the release of tension that follows gratification of such needs.

In this first stage in the development of attachment, the infant's "object cathexis" is merely the pleasure associated with need gratification. In the second stage, as the infant becomes aware of the outside world, food becomes associated with the satisfaction of needs, and the breast or bottle becomes the love object. And in the third stage the infant has objectified the mother and identified her as the provider of food. It is at this point that the infant becomes attached to the mother as the primary love object. To a lesser degree, the mother's caring for the infant in other ways, stroking and holding him, also eases tension and contributes to attachment. This is called the stage of "true object relations," since attachment to the mother is now no longer dependent on her gratifying the infant's bodily needs, and the mother is now seen as the provider of love, affection, and approval. When the infant becomes attached to the mother for the purpose of being loved, he cannot readily transfer this attachment to others. It is at this stage that the infant, fearing the loss of the love object, becomes distressed when the mother departs.

The way in which object relations (or infant-mother attachment) develop in the infant can be exemplified by the changes in infant smiling during the first months, according to Spitz and other analysts. When the reflex smile has developed into a social smile, the infant first begins to smile selectively to human faces, and the basic form of the human face—two eyes set into an oval—appears to be the stimulus for these smiles. Then, by about the fourth month, and often before, as smiling becomes more frequent, the infant appears to recognize the mother's face and responds more positively to it than to other faces. The mother has now become the "libidinal object proper," as Spitz calls it.

Once the subjective language of infant psychoanalysis has been learned, it can be used to explain this and that condition of babies, particularly the abnormalities that may appear in the course of development. However, in the research climate of today, where the emphasis is on studies of behavior that can be measured and quantified, subjective terms such as "libido," "cathexis," and "love object," whose existence cannot be verified empirically, have an old-fashioned ring. Although Spitz and others have done psychoanalytically oriented behavioral studies, they have been criticized for disregarding evidence not in line with their preconception that attachment develops from need gratification and for depicting the infant as entirely passive when it is known that interaction with the environment is a necessity for the development of all living organisms.

Finally, analysts' concentration on the "oral cavity" has been questioned on the basis of animal experiments such as those of Harry and Margaret Harlow, who found that infant monkeys' urge to seek bodily contact with the mother was much stronger than their urge to satisfy their hunger.[18] Given a chance to cling to a terry cloth form shaped like a monkey mother and a wire-mesh monkey "mother" that provided milk, they overwhelmingly preferred to cling to the former. Such experiments have indicated that the mother's nutritive breast may not be the first "love object" nor the oral cavity the infant's principal source of gratification. As a result of these criticisms, enthusiasm for libidinal explanations of infant-mother attachment has diminished considerably.

The ethological theory of attachment, promoted especially by the work of the British psychoanalyst John Bowlby[19] and Mary D. Salter Ainsworth[20] in this country, emphasizes its biological utility in a species in which the young have a long period of dependency. Under these circumstances, survival required the development of behavior patterns that would keep the young in contact with or close to a protector and sheltered from the attacks of predators. Bowlby has proposed that the infant's attachment to the mother has its origin in these behavior patterns.

Bowlby identifies several kinds of infant behavior—some of which are apparent at once in the newborn, others of which emerge later as the infant matures—which give rise to infant-mother proximity and contact. Known collectively as attachment behavior, these include such things as signaling—crying, smiling, and vocalizing—which attracts the mother's attention at a distance and brings her to the infant's side. The active rooting, sucking, clinging, and embracing initiated by the infant also produce and maintain proximity, as do crawling and walking, which enable the infant to follow and approach the mother, thereby staying close to her. Infant orientation toward the mother, turning the head toward and looking at her and eventually turning the body in her direction, also facilitates attention and exchange. The infant oral cavity, then, plays only a partial role in seeking and maintaining the contacts that give rise to attachment, according to this theory.

Cuddling and clinging represent immediate contact between infant and mother, but this behavior has been more thoroughly investigated in nonhuman primates than in human infant-mother pairs. One study in which contacts between infant and mother bonnet macaque monkeys were observed was particularly revealing.[21] The purpose of the study was to determine how much of the contact was initiated by the mother and how much by the infant, and how this might vary as the infants grew older. In the bonnet macaque, ventro-ventral (or front to front) contact between infant and mother begins with birth. Occasionally, while still emerging from the birth canal, the baby macaque will grasp the mother's thigh and help to pull itself out! Once the baby is out, the mother simply pulls it against her belly while she tidies things up, meanwhile paying no attention to the new arrival. Thereafter, for four to five months, a great deal of the interaction between infant-mother bonnet macaque pairs involves their physical contact, particularly in the ventro-ventral position. After the fourth to fifth month, contact begins to diminish, with mothers pushing away their infants, who at the same time also begin to play with other young macaques.

Two groups were studied: mothers and their 6- to 7-month-old infants and mothers and their 16- to 19-month-old infants. To facilitate the observation of contacts, one member of each mother-infant pair was anesthetized, the mother at one time and the infant at another. The drug used was a general anesthetic, ketamine hydrochloride, in a dose that "knocked out" the monkey for about 30 minutes, but was followed by a quick recovery. (This procedure should be used sparingly, the researchers noted, since it might have long-term effects on the pair, as well as on other macaques in the group to which they belong.)

Observed under normal conditions, the infants and mothers of the younger age group made some form of contact 73 percent of the time, while in the older-age group, contacts occurred only 35 percent of the time. When the younger infant was anesthetized and returned to the pen, the mother frequently threatened the observer, dragged her infant to the back of the pen and sometimes up onto a shelf, and hovered over the infant, often holding it ventrally. She spent half the observation time contacting her infant. The older unconscious infant received much less attention from its mother (4 percent of the time). She might touch it briefly at first, but never held it ventrally.

On the return of the anesthetized mother to the pen, the younger infant rushed to her and contacted her in many ways over long periods, very often assuming the ventro-ventral position with her. Here, contacts were occurring 43 percent of the time. The older infant responded to its unconscious mother only half as much as did the younger infant, but spent about 50 percent of the contact time working its way into the ventral position vis-à-vis the mother.

On the basis of these observations, the researchers concluded that although infants and mothers seek contact about equally often, the normal decrease in contacts over time occurs more rapidly in the mothers.

Infant monkeys are mobile much earlier in life than are human infants and thus more capable of initiating physical contact with the mother. However, at birth, human infants have certain responses that help them to maintain contact, as has been mentioned. Newborns have a strong grasping reflex and will cling to things that touch their hands. They have the remnants of the embracing (Moro) reflex, in which they throw out their hands and then bring them together in a sort of holding gesture. And infants also have a "cuddling" response that researchers have suggested is similar to the ventro-ventral position of monkey infant-mother pairs.[20] When held high against the chest-breast-shoulder region of the mother, human infants will usually adjust their posture and relax their bodies into the typical cuddling position.

The cuddling response is not present in all infants, as has been noted. In one questionnaire study, it was found that perhaps as many as a quarter of an infant group were noncuddlers early in life and that the mother-infant attachment in these noncuddlers seemed to be less intense and slower to develop than in cuddlers. Some infants are constitutionally averse to cuddling, the researchers concluded. However, Ainsworth and her colleagues found in a behavioral study of infant cuddling that some infants who began as cuddlers became noncuddlers by 1 year of age, and there was clear evidence that maternal behavior had created an aversion to cuddling in these infants.

Crying and fussing, orienting with looking, smiling, vocalizing, and the behavior that promotes physical proximity, such as cuddling, all serve as precursors of infant-mother attachment, according to ethological theory.[20] Ainsworth has distinguished several stages in the development of this attachment. In the first, the infant displays a variety of innate, fixed-action patterns of behavior in signaling to and orienting toward other human beings indiscriminately. In the second stage, lasting until 6 or 7 months of age, infants continue to signal and orient, but now begin to respond differentially to the mother and one or two other persons. In a third stage, lasting from 7 months through approximately 2 years of age, infants take more and more initiative in maintaining proximity to the mother—clinging to her, following her, and climbing into her lap.

Silvia Bell of Johns Hopkins University, extending her previous work with Mary D. Salter Ainsworth, has explored the relationship between the development of the concept of object permanence and the development of infant attachment to the mother.[22]

Thirty-three babies (21 boys and 12 girls) were studied with their mothers in their homes at 8.5 and 11 months of age. Based on the step-by-step development of the concept of object permanence that Piaget has described, a scale containing 11 progressively more difficult tests was devised. For example, in the first test, the infant had to grasp and free a toy partly hidden behind a screen. In the second test, the infant had to search for and secure a toy entirely hidden behind the screen. In the fifth test, a toy was hidden behind a screen (A) and then moved behind another screen (B) as the infant watched. To pass the test, the infant was required to search first in A and then in B.

In the final test, the toy was transferred to a container for hiding behind three screens, one at a time, and the infant had to search directly behind the last screen from which the container emerged empty. This was a definitive test for object permanence, since to pass it, the infant had to know that an object can be moved to a variety of locations and still remain the same object. The same scale was used to test the infants' concept of the permanence of their mothers (person permanence) by having the mothers hide behind screens or couches.

A week after both object and person permanence tests at 11 months of age, the infants' reactions to a stranger were observed. The stranger came into a room where the infant and mother were present and interacted with the baby, from whom the mother gradually withdrew, finally leaving baby and stranger alone in the room together. Subsequently, the mother returned and the stranger left. This sequence was then repeated. The infants' behavior toward both the stranger and the mother, especially their responses to the mother on her return, were used to assess attachment, since the degree to which an infant seeks proximity to the mother in the presence of strangers is considered by many—but not all—developmental psychologists to reflect the degree of attachment.

At both 8.5 and 11 months of age, the infants clearly demonstrated that on the average their sense of person permanence was far in advance of their sense of object permanence. In only 7 of the 33 infants had the concept of object permanence progressed further than that for persons, and in 3 the development of both concepts was equally advanced. However, at both 8.5 and 11 months of age, the object permanence scores of the 23 babies who had tested higher on person permanence were significantly higher than the scores of the other 10 babies. The mastery of the object permanence concept is thus closely associated with the infants' concept of the mother as permanently existing.

On the basis of their reactions in the presence of strangers, the infants were placed in three groups: those who responded enthusiastically when the mother returned and frequently sought contact and interaction with her, preferring her to the stranger; those who were relatively indifferent to the mother in the reunion episodes or alternately approached and avoided her; and those who behaved ambivalently on the mother's return. It was found that the babies in the first group, considered by the investigators to be strongly attached to the mother, were significantly advanced over the babies in the other two groups in their concepts of both object and person permanence. The interviews with the mothers of the infants in the latter two groups revealed that they tended to reject their infants, rarely took them on outings, found open fault with them, and commented adversely on their temperaments. They expressed their disapproval by refusing to contact their babies, abruptly interfering with their activities, or even punishing them physically. On the other hand, the mothers of the babies who showed strong attachment often took them out, avoided even short separations from them, commented only on their favorable traits, and never strongly rejected or physically mistreated them. Insofar as environmental influences affect cognitive development, it appears, in the light of these findings, that the quality of an infant's interactions with the mother is of crucial importance.

By the age of 6 to 8 months,[20] when the infant-mother bond has become quite solid, infants may show two kinds of negative responses: fear at the approach of a stranger and anxiety when the mother is absent. Separation anxiety in its extreme form is seen in institutionalized infants. In these babies, the anxiety passes through three distinct phases. In the first phase, the protest phase, the infant becomes acutely distressed, crying and calling for the mother, searching for her insofar as he is capable of doing so, and watching anxiously for signs of her return. However, if his mother comes to visit him, he manifests his anger at being thus dispossessed by alternately seeking contact with her and pushing her away, or he may fail to recognize her or reject her altogether.

In the second phase, the infant shows signs of despair, becoming inactive and withdrawn, and crying monotonously. If the mother returns for a visit or a staff member attempts to interact with him, the ambivalent behavior of the protest phase recurs. The last phase, detachment, follows long-term separation. Although the infant may interact with staff members and adjust well enough to institutional life, his unresponsiveness to the mother when she visits him and his indifference when she departs are clear indications that the mother-infant tie has been finally severed.

In contrast to the ethological view, in which the infant's attachment to the mother is seen as biologically determined, the social-learning theorists regard attachment as a dependency relationship that is established by conditioning. Some regard the conditioning of basic drives as the key element in the development of this dependency. For example, the crying of the hungry infant is reinforced by the mother's nurturant behavior, and through the stimuli associated with the mother's presence, the infant acquires a drive to be close to the mother—a "dependency drive," as it is called. However, the consensus among social-learning theorists today is that dependency, or attachment, is shaped directly by instrumental conditioning of a variety of behavior patterns through positive reinforcement by the mother. Early in the infant's life, reinforcement of such behavior as crying is provided when the mother is physically close to the infant, soothing or feeding him. In time, closeness alone will become a reinforcing stimulus, so that behavior producing closeness will be strengthened.

Thus, rather than being a genetically determined behavior pattern as the ethologists believe, according to the social-learning theorists, the infant's "proximity behavior" has been conditioned to occur by the association of closeness to the mother with rewards such as food. The strength of attachment to the mother, in this view, lies in her having more reinforcement control over more of the infant's "behavioral systems" than any other person in his environment.

The proponents of the psychoanalytic, ethological, and social-learning theories of attachment lock horns on many fundamental issues, but on one point they are in complete agreement: that the infant's only significant relationship is to the mother. As a consequence, behavioral studies of emotional development have been based on the assumption that throughout infancy and whatever the social environment, the mother is the infant's major source of social stimulation. The results of a recent study have given only a modicum of support to this assumption.

An Israeli developmental psychologist, Rivka Landau, and her students observed groups of 2-, 4-, 7-, and 11-month-old male infants for the equivalent of one typical weekday.[23] She noted which familiar persons interacted in what ways with them, how frequently, and for how long. The infants, all of whom had one older sibling, were studied at home and in four different social environments: urban middle class; urban lower class; kibbutz, or communal group; and Bedouin. Bedouin families lived out in the desert, and because of the traveling this entailed, they were observed for somewhat briefer periods than were the other families.

"Familiar persons" interacting with the infants included the mother, father, grandparents, sister or brother, a neighbor's child, and, in the kibbutz, the nonparental caregivers. Their total social responses to the infant were recorded and divided by the number of minutes they were in the infant's vicinity. The resultant figure was designated the familiar people's rate of response. The mothers' rate of response was then calculated as a percentage of the responses of all familiar persons, including the mother. The social responses recorded included laughing, play behavior, and word and sentence utterances.

The observations revealed that infants in all these diverse environments received about the same amount of social attention from familiar persons, ranging on the average from three to five responses per minute during their waking hours. Responses to infants in the kibbutz averaged toward the lower end of this range, but not significantly so. Also, social responses to infants tended to decrease steadily, although slightly, with age, but again not significantly so. Infants in Bedouin homes tended to get the most attention, even though the families were poor and the Bedouin environment was thought to be unstimulating. Bedouin mothers or other female adults were always on hand to tend the babies, never leaving them alone or failing to relieve their distress. The infants were constantly at the center of their activities.

Mothers gave the infants the predominant amount of social stimulation, ranging from over four-fifths in the 2-month-old group to two-thirds in the 11-month-old group. The mothers also gave a major share of the responses in the kibbutz to 2- and 4-month-old infants, but well below half of the responses to the 7- and 11-month-old infants. In the lower-class and middle-class urban environments, the mothers gave the highest proportions of responses to their babies throughout all the age groups (84 percent), while this proportion was somewhat smaller in the Bedouin environment (76 percent) and much smaller in the kibbutz (54 percent).

Laughing, playing, and talking with the infants were analyzed in detail. Again, mothers laughed in response to the infants and talked to them far more than the familiar persons as a whole. Only in playing with the infants did familiar persons as a whole respond more than did the mothers, who engaged in only 45 percent of the play activity.

Thus, although the mothers provided the major share of their infants' total social stimulation during their first year, their contribution varied with the age of the infant, the type of social environment, and the kind of stimulation being measured. Landau therefore advised caution in relying on the mother's behavior alone to represent the infant's total social environment.

Although fathers were mentioned but once in Landau's report, their presence in the households she studied was at least acknowledged. But in most of the literature on attachment, the father is conspicuous only by his absence from consideration as a factor in an infant's development. Since the majority of infants are raised in a two-parent environment, and since a strong emotional bond between fathers and their children is a fact of human existence, is it so unreasonable to suppose that infants may also become attached to their fathers?

In a recent study done at Yale University, mothers and fathers were observed in their normal interactions at home with their infants.[24] A female "visitor" was also present at each observation session to give the infant a choice between interacting with her or with a parent. The observer remained as unobtrusive as possible while dictating *sotto voce* a narrative of the interactions onto a tape that was marked for 15-second intervals. The 20 babies observed were evenly divided as to sex and were visited at the ages of 7, 8, 12, and 13 months in two- to three-hour sessions, usually during evenings, weekends, or on some other day when both parents were at home. The six-month period from 7 to 13 months was selected to follow the development of attachment relations from their beginnings at about 7 months.

Four socioeconomic groups were represented: professionals, small-business owners, white collar workers, and skilled manual laborers. In four of the families the mother worked or studied part time, and while she was thus occupied, the father looked after the baby. Otherwise, the mothers and fathers played the traditional marital roles, with the mother the primary caregiver.

After the study was completed, the parents were asked what effect the presence of the observer and visitor had had on the spontaneity of their interactions with their babies. The parents of only two infants said they had felt inhibited. The rest considered their behavior during the observation period as representative of their normal interactions with the baby.

Two distinctive categories of infant behavior were observed: affiliative and attachment behavior. Affiliative behavior included infant smiling, vocalizing, looking, laughing, and proffering things to others—behavior that might well be used to express attachment but is also seen in infants' friendly interactions with others to whom they may not be attached. Attachment behavior was that resulting in physical proximity or demonstrating the desire for it, such as approaching another, staying in proximity, touching, reaching, seeking to be held, and fussing. The intensity of infants' positive, neutral, and negative reactions to others during the sessions was noted on a scale, particularly when the infant was being held or played with by one of the adults. Holding the infant was found to serve various functions, such as caretaking, discipline or control, playing, soothing, and simply expressing affection.

The analysis of the data revealed no sex or socioeconomic-class differences in the behavior of those who could crawl or move about and those who could not. Nor were there any significant differences in the behavior of the infants either at 7 and 8 months or at 12 and 13 months. Thus, all the data for 7 and 8 months, and all the data for 12 and 13 months, could be combined.

The infants directed significantly more attachment and affiliative behavior toward all the adults (mother, father, and visitor) when they were older than when younger, although when older and able to move about much more freely, they were less likely to remain close to any person. Also when older, they smiled less frequently at the mother and the visitor. With their rapidly developing language abilities, they vocalized much more frequently to all three adults when older than when younger.

The most important finding of this study is that although the infants, regardless of age, differentiated between the visitor and their parents by their display of attachment behavior, they showed no preference for the mother over the father. The older infants were more likely than the younger to focus attachment behavior exclusively on the parents. However, the infants directed significantly more affiliative behavior toward their fathers than their mothers, smiling, vocalizing, looking, and laughing more in the father's presence at both age levels. Some other studies have shown that when both parents are present in very stressful situations, year-old infants intensify their attachment behavior toward the mothers. In the relaxed home atmosphere of this investigation, however, the babies fussed to their fathers as much as their mothers, and their fathers soothed them as often as did their mothers.

Further analysis revealed that the fathers held the babies for very different reasons than did the mothers. This probably reflected the "division of labor" that is characteristic of conventional households, since the mothers were more likely to pick up the babies and hold them for caretaking, while the fathers did so in order to play with them. This may explain the greater frequency of affiliative responses to fathers than to mothers and the much more positive character of these responses. The fathers played more often and for longer periods with the babies than the mothers, and both parents played with the babies much more than did the visitor. And although the infants responded positively to play with both mother and visitor, their positive responses were most intense when playing with their fathers.

The findings of this study fail to support the assumption that the infant's primary bond is to the mother alone. From the very beginning of attachment relations, the infant appears to form attachments to both parents. However, as the investigator who carried out this investigation points out, if the father-infant bond were simply a replica of the mother-infant relationship, it would have little developmental significance. But it is not. The fathers in this study interacted with their infants in a qualitatively different way. The infants, then, must come to distinguish their parents not merely by their appearance but also by the differences in their behavior, as in caretaking and play. Thus, they are bound to learn different behavior patterns from each parent, with inevitable differential effects on their subsequent development.

Infants are usually thought of as egocentric and thus indifferent to their peers. But do they deserve this reputation? Back in 1933, the pioneering Katherine Bridges had noticed signs that babies interact with each other in early infancy.[25] A thorough study of "peer-oriented behavior" in infants was not reported until 1977, however, when Jacqueline Becker of the University of California at Berkeley published her observations of the social interactions of 16 pairs of 9-month-old infants playing together in 10 sessions and alternating between the homes of each pair.[26]

In these 50-minute social affairs, the infant pair was placed on the floor near each other and in the vicinity of toys. The mothers were present, but were asked to be only normally responsive to their babies and not to intervene unless it seemed essential. An unobtrusive observer recorded the behavior of the infants toward each other as well as toward the adults present, the toys, and other things in the room. The infant pairs were equally divided as to same or different sex, but, in fact, sex was not found to be a significant variable in the socializing of the pairs.

Far from completely disregarding each other, the two infants directed more of their behavior toward each other than toward the mothers, the observer, the toys, or anything else. Babies were more spontaneously sociable toward each other when in their own homes, showing more interest in the toys in the other infant's home. Over the 10 sessions, the pair paid more and more attention to each other, while each baby's attention to the other baby's mother and the observer decreased. Also, infant social behavior became more complex, with vocalizing, waving, crawling, and smiling toward and in response to each other significantly more often in each subsequent session. Furthermore, when introduced to a new baby in an eleventh session, the increased social reactions of the experienced babies as compared with a control group of "tyros" showed that a "social disposition" that generalized to other than their accustomed playmates had developed in the experimental group.

The increase in peer-oriented behavior was, for the most part, unrelated to whether or not a particular behavior evoked a response in the other member of the pair. Rather, it was significantly related to the total amount of spontaneous behavior directed toward the baby by the partner, whether or not it was in response to the baby's overtures. Thus, social behavior in these sessions, rather than being reinforced by obtaining a response from the partner, may simply have been "released" or "catalyzed" by the partner's peer-oriented behavior.

As they interact with their parents and others in a variety of social encounters, what do infants grasp, if anything, of the feelings being expressed by their partners in the interaction? This question can be approached in several ways: for example, by determining whether or not infants prefer some emotions to others. In a recent study, 4-month-old and 6-month-old infants, each group equally divided by sex, were individually shown 19 color slides when sitting in their mothers' laps.[27] The slides pictured carefully selected facial expressions assumed by an adult actor and representing anger, joy, and no emotion. Looking time was used as an index of preference.

The average infant looking time was 9.30 seconds for joy, 7.31 seconds for anger, and 6.36 seconds for neutral expressions. The infants, regardless of sex or age, looked at the joyful expressions significantly more than at angry or neutral expressions, but the slight difference between their responses to angry and neutral expressions was not significant. Under the conditions of this experiment, the infants seemed to be able to distinguish a joyful expression from the others and seemed to prefer it. The investigators suggested that infants 4 to 6 months of age may be able to discriminate joyful expressions because they have come to be associated with rewarding experiences by this time. On the other hand, they said, infants this young usually have not been faced with very much anger, and to cope with it would be beyond their capacity.

Infants' recognition of adult emotions can also be investigated via the habituation technique. This was done in a 1977 study in which 3-month-old infants were shown slide projections of still photographs of happy, sad, and surprised facial expressions posed by an adult male model.[28] A slide of one facial expression was repeatedly shown until the infant's fixation time decreased, signifying habituation. Another facial expression was then presented, and the infant's ability to discriminate between the two expressions was inferred if fixation time markedly increased.

The infants as a group reliably distinguished between happy and surprised facial expressions in the still photographs, and some infants were able to discriminate reliably between happiness and sadness. However, adults in preliterate cultures have a similar difficulty in distinguishing sad from happy facial expressions in photographs and are not always able to distinguish sadness from surprise. Thus, such distinctions of facial expressions in still photographs and in the absence of other cues such as postural attitudes or gestures are not easily made even by some adults.

Despite their failures in some respects, these 3-month-old infants were capable of distinguishing between the facial expressions of happiness and surprise and sometimes between sadness and surprise. These differences are subtle, and the finding that such young infants are able to detect them suggests that very early in life they may also be aware of subtle changes in the facial expressions of their parents.

By 3 to 4 months of age, then, infants are beginning to grasp the rudiments of the language of the emotions, perhaps far earlier than they are able to comprehend the spoken word.

CHAPTER 7

Discovery

Directly after birth, newborn rhesus monkeys begin to explore the mother.[1] As they cling to her, they go over her body with their eyes, hands, and mouths, familiarizing themselves with it. But within a day or two, their horizons have expanded. Despite the mother's attempts to restrain them, they venture a foot or so away to pick up, handle, and sniff at this and that. And the mother for her part must constantly retrieve them and pull them back within the circle of her protection. By 8 weeks of age, infant monkeys are nipping about at distances up to 30 feet from the mother, leaving her more often and for longer periods. They are frolicking with other infants, exploring and manipulating everything in sight.

Human infants take their whole first year to pass through the transitions achieved by infant monkeys within a month or two. Place-bound at birth, human infants explore by turning their heads. With the assistance of the rooting reflex, they find the nipple and savor the smell and taste of milk for the first time. The orientation reflex directs their attention to the changing sights and sounds in the flow of events around them. Soon, they are able to turn from back to side to stomach, hold up their heads, and look about without restraint. As their visual world expands, so does their capacity to explore it, and before long they begin to extend their arms toward objects that attract their visual attention.

In the newborn period, infants reach for objects of visual interest and sometimes grasp them when they are close enough. Between 1 and 4 months of age, however, grasping is directly initiated by anything that touches the infant's palm.[2] And though during this time they continue to reach for objects that they see, they rarely grasp them. Reaching and grasping, then, seem to go their separate ways in this period. This is the time infants discover their hands, study them for long periods, and investigate their possibilities, touching one hand with the other, and so on. At 4 to 5 months of age, infants can attend to their hands and an object at the same time. The eyes can follow the direction of reaching, and the infant can correct it if necessary. After this skill has been mastered, infants can reach for an object and grasp it successfully a good share of the time. And by 6 months of age, they rarely miss.

Soon after their capacities to grasp, hold, and manipulate things have matured, creeping, crawling, sitting, and standing vastly broaden the range of things that infants can investigate. In exercising these talents throughout the last six months of their first year, infants spend most of their time awake exploring and playing with things and persons. In infants and children these two activities are so closely related that they are often not distinguished and may be studied in the same experimental setting. Exploration and play can be thought of as two aspects of discovery: By exploring a person or object visually or manually infants find out what the person or object can do.[3] By playing with an object or person, they find out what they themselves can do with that object or person. Laughter and wariness of strangers and strange situations must also be included, since they are usually observed in the context of exploration and play.

One of the early experimental studies of exploratory behavior in infants was reported in 1961 by Harriet Rheingold, a developmental psychologist at the University of North Carolina.[4] Her observations were made during an assessment of the differential effects of stimulating and unstimulating environments on young infants. Accordingly, she observed and tested 3- to 4-month-old infants, half of whom were living in an institution and half of whom were firstborn children of well-to-do families.

The group of infants living at home were given more—and much longer—stimulation, were out of their cribs more often, and had many more toys than the group of institutional infants, who were lucky if they had as much as one rattle tied to the crib (often out of sight or reach). As a result, the "home" group of infants was accustomed to playing with toys, while the institution group played mainly with their hands, clothing, crib bars, bottle holder, or whatever was within reach. But although these infants played with different things, they played about the same amount.

Both groups of infants were given an object and an object-in-hand test in which they were presented with three rattles. Rattles were chosen over other toys because the babies had seemed most interested in them in a preliminary test. In the object test, the examiner held a rattle directly in front of the infant in the crib and shook it at 15-second intervals for a minute, watching the responses. In the object-in-hand test, she put the rattle into the infant's hand, moved back from the crib, and observed the infant's reactions until he dropped the rattle or had held it for a minute. Both tests were then repeated with second and third rattles, differing from the first only in color and the sounds they made. The infants' social responses during these tests, and in a separate "social test," were also noted.

The behavior observed in these tests included visual exploration, or regard (looking or gazing at the observer and the rattle); reaching for, grasping, and manipulating the rattle; and smiling or cooing, fussing or crying, moving arms or legs, or excited bursts of activity involving arching of the back and flurries of kicking. Manipulation included holding the rattle, bringing it to the mouth, mouthing it, shaking and waving it, fingering it, and passing it from one hand to the other.

On the whole, there were few differences between the responses of the "home" group and the institution group. In the object test, both groups of infants smiled and vocalized toward the rattles and the observer, but seldom reached out for the rattles, contacted them with their hands, or grasped them. The observer stimulated about as many smiles as vocalizations, but the rattles stimulated more vocalizations than smiles, as though these infants had already learned that smiles are more appropriate for people than for things. In the object-in-hand tests, both groups of infants looked at the rattles in their hands and held onto them for some time, but only rarely manipulated them. However, as compared with the "home" infants, the institution infants looked at them longer and manipulated them more.

Whether they had been raised in an institution or at home, quite clearly these 3- to 4-month-old infants explored things around them primarily with their eyes, and their responses to objects of interest were facial, vocal, and bodily activities. This was particularly the case when the "object" was a human being. Three to four months later, however, these infants would be banging two objects together to make an interesting noise.

It is not news to parents that banging is a prominent feature of early play. Few parents, however, are aware of its significance. But Piaget discovered long ago that when the ability to relate or combine two objects in play merges, the infant's cognitive development has moved one step forward.

In a recent experimental study of the developmental sequence in play, children 7, 9, 13, and 20 months of age were given a tea set to play with while their mothers sat in a chair at a distance and read a magazine.[5] The tea set consisted of two cups, two saucers, two spoons, and a pot with a removable lid. As the children played, the investigators watched them through a one-way mirror in an adjacent room, recording all their visual and manual contacts with the toys. Their expectation was that the children's behavior would reflect their stage of cognitive development.

In his observations of children, Piaget had found that at 6 months of age infants will play with one object at a time. A few months later, they will combine or relate two objects, putting one on top of the other or banging them together, for example. Still later, children will use two objects in appropriate ways—they will put a cup on a saucer, a spoon in a cup, and so on. In this way they indicate that they are aware of the functions of these objects. About this time, children will also begin to group things that are alike. And, as children begin to speak, they also begin to engage in symbolic play, that is, to "pretend."

As expected, the play of the 7-month-old infants consisted largely of banging two things together—a cup and a saucer, two spoons, and so on. None of these infants used the parts of the tea set appropriately. There was much more variety in the play of the 9-month-old infants, and they did less than half as much random banging. Almost all the infants performed simple "relational acts" other than banging, such as touching the pot with a spoon, which were rarely seen in the younger infants. And about a third demonstrated their awareness of the functions of the objects by placing cups on saucers or the lid on the pot. None of the younger infants had shown such awareness. Visual exploration and handling of the parts of the tea set were characteristic of both groups of infants, and they often put spoons, cups, and so on to their mouths and chewed on them.

Banging was observed in only a fourth of the 13-month-old children. Their play was largely devoted to appropriate use of the tea set—for example, putting the spoon in the cup or the cup on the saucer—and this kind of action was performed at some time or other by all the children in the group. Symbolic actions were observed in about three-fourths of the group: The children pretended to drink, pour, and stir with the spoon in the cup, for example. About a third of the children grouped things together (such as two cups or two saucers) and generally displayed an awareness of the connections between means and ends or cause and effect that Piaget found in the fifth sensorimotor stage.

All the 20-month-old children used the parts of the tea set appropriately and used them to "pretend." Grouping was observed in 80 percent of the children. Rarely seen in the younger children, sequential actions, such as putting the lid on the pot several times in succession, were prominent in this group, and banging had almost disappeared.

Exploration on hands and knees comes at about 10 months of age on the average. By this time, most infants have become expert creepers, skilled in the art of short-distance travel. When not asleep, creepers are usually found exploring every nook and cranny within their fields of view and touch. But creepers placed in an empty room containing toys will not explore it, nor will they play with the toys—they simply cry.[6] Infants venture forth into unknown territory only from the secure fortress-keeps of their mothers and only when they themselves decide to go. The factors that influence their decisions were revealed in an experimental study of 10-month-old creepers given the opportunity to explore with their mothers present.[7]

The creepers in this study, 10 boys and 10 girls, were brought to the laboratory at the time of day when their mothers judged them to be most alert. The experimental setting consisted of a large and a small room, bare of furniture or adornments, with off-white walls and an open doorway between them. Off-white draperies covered the windows in the large room. The mother sat on a cushion in the middle of the small room and put her baby on the floor beside her. Mothers were told that they could look and smile at their babies, but could make only brief, noncommittal remarks to them, leaving them free to do whatever they wished. The infants were seated so that they could see into the large room and had clear access to it. For 10 minutes, observers watched and recorded the explorers' safaris through one-way windows in both rooms. Toys were used as incentives to explore and included a pull toy containing colored marbles in a clear plastic ball, a chain of colored wooden beads, and a Donald Duck rolling toy.

In the first part of the experiment, the infants were divided into two groups, A and B. No toys were placed in the large room for group A infants, but group B could see the pull toy there on the floor. Whether or not the toy was present, all the infants crept into the large room almost immediately. However, both groups spent about half as much time there as they spent at "home base." Some infants shuttled back and forth between the two rooms—one baby entered the large room 13 times! As compared with the "toy" group, group A infants contacted their mothers more often and spent more time fingering things such as the draperies, the door hinges, and the wall in the large room. Group B infants sometimes vocalized and smiled at the mothers as they grasped the toy, as if to share their pleasure with her. They played with the toy for more than half the observation time on the average, but all but one infant brought the toy back to the small room to play with it.

In the second part of the experiment, also lasting 10 minutes, one toy was placed just beyond the door of the large room for half of both group A and group B infants. Three toys were set in place for the remaining half of both groups: one just beyond the door, one in the middle of the large room, and one in a far corner. Again, all the babies crept into the large room with dispatch. Those presented with three toys stayed there longer, crawled about for greater distances, and played with the toys longer than those given just one toy. However, as compared with group B, the infants from group A, who had a toy or toys for the first time, entered the large room sooner, stayed in it longer, and touched and played with the toy or toys sooner and longer.

With their mothers as a secure base, these infants did not hesitate to enter a strange room alone, with or without the lure of a toy. And they did so without fussing or crying. Signs of distress were observed very rarely, usually only toward the end of the 10-minute trials and then in the vicinity of the mother. With the incentive of three toys, as opposed to one, the babies explored faster and farther and stayed away from their mothers longer.

Since these infants explored the large room even when it was empty, it might be inferred that the novelty of a strange room was sufficient in itself to induce them to investigate it. On the other hand, three toys produced more—and more intensive—exploration than did one, suggesting that complexity added to the attractiveness of the novel environment.

As has been noted, young infants are attracted to and will attend longer to novel than to familiar stimuli, and longer to complex than to simple stimuli. A recent study was devoted to examining in greater detail how these factors affect exploratory behavior in infants capable of moving about.[8] The investigator also sought to determine whether or not the encounters with novel environments that mobility entails might produce fears and consequently inhibit exploration.

The investigation was carried out with 28 one-year-old infants, 13 of whom were female and 15 male, all capable of crawling about with alacrity from room to room in the laboratory at the University of North Carolina to which their mothers brought them. The procedure consisted of a 5-minute "familiarization" trial, followed shortly by a 10-minute experimental trial. In both trials, the infants' behavior was observed through a one-way window.

The experimental setting consisted of one large room (the "start" room) and three adjacent smaller rooms, toy rooms A, B, and C. In the familiarization trial, half the infants were tested with one toy (simple), the other half with four toys (complex). For half of each of these groups a toy was placed in either toy room A or B. Both A's and B's doors were left open, but the door to toy room C was closed. For the remaining half of each group, a toy or toys were placed in toy room C, and the doors to toy rooms A and B were closed.

Before the familiarization trial began, the mother carried her baby to the threshold of the room in which the toy or toys were present, and the experimenter moved a toy slightly to call the infant's attention to it and then left. The mother then sat down and placed the baby on the floor facing her, and the baby was free to explore. After the familiarization, the mother took her baby out in the hall for a few minutes while the experimental scenery was rearranged for the choice trial.

For the choice trial, the doors of toy rooms A and B were left open and toy room C's door was shut. This was a "familiar environment" for infants who had explored A or B in the familiarization trial. The toy or toys they had played with were in the same room as before, either A or B, but the other room contained a novel toy or toys. The setting of the choice trial was an "unfamiliar environment" for the infants who had explored toy room C in the familiarization trial. These infants also saw a familiar toy or toys in one room and a novel toy or toys in the other. In both "environmental" groups the number of toys, familiar or novel, remained the same as it had been in the previous trial—either one toy or four.

When the stage was set for the choice trial, the mother returned with her baby and sat down as before, with the baby in front of her and facing her. On this trial the examiner left without calling attention to the toys.

In the familiarization trial, despite the novelty of the rooms and toys the infants began to crawl away from their mothers within 11 seconds on the average, entering a toy room 9 seconds later, and contacting a toy or toys in another 9 seconds. In other words, they had a toy in hand within 30 seconds! All 28 of the infants left the vicinity of their mothers, 27 entered the toy room, and 26 contacted toys. They spent twice as much time in the toy room as they spent either near their mothers or somewhere else in the start room. On the average, they kept in manual contact with the toy for more than half the familiarization period. One infant fussed and cried briefly near the end of the period. Infants remained in four-toy rooms significantly longer than infants remained in one-toy rooms; they also played longer with the toys, but not significantly longer. The novelty of both the rooms and the toys was the obvious incentive for these infants to explore, while complexity influenced the time spent with the toys after contact.

In the choice trial, 22 of the 28 infants entered the room containing the novel toy or toys first. Later, 12 of these infants also contacted the familiar toys. Of the 6 infants who contacted the familiar toys first, 4 eventually contacted the novel toys as well.

For the entire group, the time spent with novel toys was significantly longer than that spent with familiar toys. As compared with the familiar-environment infants, infants for whom the toy rooms were novel spent significantly more time in the room containing the novel toy or toys and significantly less time with their mothers. There was no evidence that entering a strange environment produced anxiety. Only 7 infants fussed or cried during the choice trial, and only 2 of these infants were in the novel-environment group. As in the familiarization trial, infants with four toys available spent more time in the toy rooms than did infants given only one toy. But in this trial, they also played with the toys significantly longer.

Judging from this experiment, it appears that when given a choice between something familiar and something novel, year-old infants of this age will unerringly choose the novel. However, in an experiment with infants 6 and 12 months of age, two Scottish psychologists, H. R. Schaffer and M. H. Parry, found some wariness of novelty in the older infants.[9]

The infants in Schaffer and Parry's study were from day nurseries in Glasgow and came in the main from underprivileged families. Each infant was observed in his own nursery and was brought by a nurse to a room where the equipment to be used in the experiment had been set up. The nurse put the infant into a baby chair that directly faced the center panel of a three-panel, U-shaped screen. A shelf protruded from a rectangular opening in the center panel. A box was fitted into this opening, and the side of the box toward the infant was a sliding door.

When the door was opened, a funnel-shaped, plastic "nonsense" object fixed to a tray slid onto the shelf in front of the infant. The object was attached to a wooden base by a vertical rod through the object's center. It was shaped like an inverted funnel and had random protrusions (knobs) and depressions on its surface. Because of its vertical axis, the infant could turn the object but could not pick it up. Two such funnels were used in the experiment. One was bluish with green and black mottling, and the other was predominantly red, with yellow and black mottling.

As the experimenter watched the infants through one-way glass inserted in one of the screens, the infants were presented with either the red or the blue nonsense object for 30 seconds seven times in succession, with a 30-second interval between each presentation. During these trials, the gazing time of both groups of infants steadily diminished, indicating habituation. When the object of a different color was presented on the eighth trial, fixation time rose sharply in both age groups. And when, on the ninth trial, the object to which the infants had become habituated was presented again, fixation times in both groups dropped to the low levels of the seventh habituation trial. Thus, age was not a factor in the visual attention of these infants.

However, analysis of the infants' reaching, grasping, and manipulative behavior, also recorded, revealed a noteworthy difference. On all trials, the 6-month-old infants reached for the funnel within two seconds, but the 12-month-old infants hesitated for 9 or 10 seconds on the average before they touched the funnel on the first trial. Hesitation to manipulate the object took several forms. Some infants simply stared at it in a sober manner, some appeared "frozen" by it, and others looked afraid or made avoidance movements. And it took some infants several trials before they grasped the object. In the older group as a whole, hesitation diminished, but only slowly, over the habituation trials. Furthermore, the older infants' time to grasping did not increase significantly when the novel object was presented on the eighth trial, but neither did that of the 6-month-old infants.

In their discussion of these findings, the investigators noted that although the younger infants could recognize that an object was unfamiliar, this recognition did not control their behavior toward it. As they put it, "Knowledge and action" are "out of step" at this age. The year-old infants, on the other hand, because of their greater experience with objects, were able to react selectively to the familiar and the novel, appraising the novel object before approaching or avoiding it. "It is not until the second half-year," they concluded, "that inhibitory mechanisms develop and approach responses take place only after the sensory input has been appraised in relation to previous experience."

In a later study, using similar equipment and the same method, Schaffer and his colleagues attempted to pinpoint the age at which wariness of novelty first appears.[10] The experiments were conducted in the homes of infants from middle-class families during seven monthly sessions beginning when the infants were about 6 months old. Thus, by the last session, the infants were a year old. Again, regardless of age, habituation to one nonsense object was followed by increased visual attention when a novel object was presented. As before, the infants at 6 months of age happily reached out for the object within a few seconds, and this also occurred at 7 and at 8 months. However, at 9 months there was a sudden sharp increase in the time to manipulation, and although some avoidance reactions were observed, "temporary cessation of all overt activity" was the most common reaction as the infants appraised the object before reacting to it. At 10 and 11 months, the infants were slightly more hesitant to reach out for the object. At 12 months, the time to manipulation had decreased, perhaps because of the infants' lengthy acquaintance with the nonsense object.

Schaffer and his colleagues proposed that the sudden emergence of wariness at 9 months of age was the result of two processes: a "perceptual learning process," in which perceptual experience is acquired and the information is stored, and a "response selection process," in which responses are selected that are "suitable" in the light of the appraisal of the stored experience. Between 8 and 9 months, they suggested, the selective process begins to influence behavior. Noting that wariness at this age is usually discussed in relation to the fear of strangers, they pointed out that few of the infants they observed had shown fear of the nonsense object. Rather, wariness was usually manifested by the infant's stopping all activity to gaze at the object, appraise it, and select an appropriate response.

The good ship loaded with Schaffer's conclusions soon ran into stormy weather however. In her studies of 6-month-old infants' responses to familiar and novel stimuli, Judith Rubenstein, of the Tufts University School of Medicine, was forced to contrary conclusions.[11] In her most recent experiment, 6-month-old infants equally divided by sex were tested while seated in their mothers' laps at the kitchen table in their homes. Eleven odd and presumably novel objects were used, including, for example, a gold change purse, a piece of leather with a silver buckle, three deflated balloons tied together, one with a Mickey Mouse face and ears, a small bell, three plastic interlocking disks, and so on. An infant was first presented with one of these objects on the table and permitted to familiarize himself with it for 10 minutes. Then this now familiar object was presented to the infants paired with 10 different novel objects for one minute each and the infant's gazing and manipulation times observed.

Gazing time when the novel objects were presented was four times the length of gazing at the familiar object. On the average, the infants manipulated the novel objects three times longer than the familiar objects. All the infants looked at novel objects significantly longer than at familiar ones, and most of them manipulated the novel objects significantly more.

Thus these infants made selective manipulatory responses based on visual information far earlier than the infants in the Schaffer studies. However, it has been suggested that differences in the experimental conditions, as well as in the times measured (time *to* manipulation versus time *of* manipulation), may account for the failure of the Schaffer and Rubenstein studies to agree, so the matter is by no means settled.

The hesitation and occasional avoidance reactions in response to the unfamiliar documented by Schaffer and his colleagues would not come as a surprise to those who believe that fear of strangers inevitably appears during the last half or fourth of an infant's first year, and that it is a sign that development is proceeding normally. Many, perhaps most, parents, pediatricians, and developmental psychologists sub-scribe to this widespread belief.[12] In a survey report on the subject, Harriet Rheingold and Carol Eckerman quoted the following flat statements from the 1969 edition of the pamphlet *Infant Care,* published by the Children's Bureau of the U.S. Department of Health, Education, and Welfare: "Fear of strangers begins around 7 to 8 months, or soon thereafter."[13] Similar statements appear in most recently published developmental psychology textbooks.

The terms of the ubiquitous phrase, "fear of strangers," may be varied, with "wariness," "anxiety," "dread," or "negative reactions" substituted for fear, for example. But whatever the terminology, the onset of fear of strangers is commonly regarded as a developmental milestone by which all infants must normally pass toward the end of their first year. Thus, it appears in many developmental tests for infants. Sometimes it is regarded as a sign of infant-mother attach-ment, sometimes taken as a pathological symptom, particularly by psychiatrists and clinicians who tend to call it "anxiety" and view it anxiously as well. With more carefully designed and broadly based research in recent years, however, "fear of strangers" has been cut down to its actual unterrifying size. It appears to be an occasional phenomenon of infanthood, which, rarely, may be extreme under stress.

Two long-term investigations of wariness of unfamiliar persons and objects in infants are representative of some of the work now being done in this area. (The term "wariness" is used here as more descriptive of the actual phenomenon than "fear," which connotes an extreme reaction.) One was carried out by Gordon Bronson, working in Honolulu, and the other by Everett Waters and colleagues at the University of Minnesota, Minneapolis. Bronson's study involved 32 infants, equally divided by sex, observed in their homes over the age period from 3 to 9 months.[14] Half the infants were of Caucasian ancestry and half of Chinese, Japanese, Filipino, Hawaiian, or combined descent. Everett Waters and his colleagues studied 26 five-month-old and 11 seven-month-old infants for a period of four months, thereby observing them to the ages of 8 to 10 months.[15] They obtained additional data by one or two observations of other groups of 9- and 10-month-olds. All their infants were males and all were studied in the laboratory. In both projects, the parents were mainly from the middle class.

Videotapes were made of the infants' responses in both investigations, and the Waters groups also recorded the infants' heart-rate changes. Both studies used rating scales devised to record a series of degrees or intensities of positive and negative reactions in encounters with unfamiliar persons or novel objects.

Bronson's rating scale involved five stages: (1) smiled with delight (accompanied by wiggling or vocalizing at 3 and 4 months; repeated broad smiling with cooing at 6.5 and 9 months); (2) smiled (more than once, but not broadly); (3) neutral (blank expression and no vocalization); (4) uneasy (severe frowning or puckering of the chin at 3, 4, and 9 months, or crawling to mother, squirming, or turning the body away on pickup at 9 months); and (5) cried (whimpering or crying at any age).

The rating scale of the Waters groups covered the following kinds of behavior: (1) positive responses (active, broad smile with wiggling or simple broad smile); (2) neutral response (a relaxed, open expression with mouth open or closed and sobering gaze, or inattention, or doing something else); and (3) negative responses (a wary and wrinkled brow [mouth closed or turned down at the corners and lower lip protruding], wary, averted gaze [eyes narrowing and face turned down and away], avoidance [stiffening as a stranger reaches, pushing the hands away, with fretting, averted gaze, or looking toward the mother], a "cry" face, with eyes narrowed, eyebrows lowered, and mouth puckered or turned down, and audible crying).

In the Bronson study, infants were tested and videotaped in their homes at the ages of 3, 4, 6.5, and 9 months, with tests adapted to the capacities of the infants at these ages. In the tests at 3 and 4 months, the mother put her baby in a crib, spoke to him briefly, and then withdrew from sight. A beardless, Caucasian male stranger then bent over the baby, smiled, called his name, and asked for a smile, until the baby gave broad smiles, cried, or a minute was up. The same episode was repeated after a series of novel objects had been presented to the infant.

At 6.5 months, the infant was placed in an infant seat on the floor with the mother seated in view 4 feet away. After the baby was presented with a novel object, which was a large, beeping, red and white box, the stranger came into the room, squatted beside him, and smiled and spoke until the baby smiled, cried, or a minute was up. This stranger episode was repeated twice, and each time a different novel object was presented to the infant before the stranger entered. In the second episode, the mother said good-bye and left the room for about a half-minute if the baby had not cried. In the third episode, if the baby had not cried, the stranger picked him up and set him face to face on his knee until the baby began to smile, cry, or one minute was up.

At 9 months, the baby was seated on the floor beside a toy dog with the mother in view 4 feet away. After the beeping novel box had been presented to the infant, the stranger entered the room and greeted the infant as before, meanwhile covering the novel object with a cloth and moving it away from the infant. This episode was repeated during the stranger's third visit. On his second visit the stranger uncovered the box, turned on the sound, and moved it close to the infant. On his final visit, the last episode of the 6.5-month procedure was repeated.

In the Waters group study, the 5- to 10-month-old infants were tested and videotaped in the laboratory at monthly intervals, and the same basic procedure was used throughout. The mother was seated 4 feet from her baby, who was in a high chair. An unsmiling female stranger entered the room in the first episode, paused, and called the baby's name. Then she walked closer and called the infant's name again. She extended her arms in a pickup gesture, paused a moment, and slowly picked the infant up and held him briefly 2 to 3 inches above the high chair, maintaining eye-to-eye contact with him. Then she put the infant down, turned, and left the room. The whole episode took about half a minute. In the second episode, another female stranger entered and approached the baby in the same manner, but this time the mother left the room, and the infant was alone with the stranger for 20 seconds. In an additional test, the mother approached the infant in the high chair in the same manner as the strangers had, to see how the infant's reactions to the mother might differ from those to a stranger.

Although the series of episodes in these two experiments vary in details, both involved the approach of a stranger and his or her interactions with the babies in a relatively brief time, and both included brief separations from the mother. Similar episodes probably occur quite frequently in the normal day-to-day lives of the babies.

Wariness of strangers was observed in both studies. However, it was found to develop gradually, and a sudden emergence of full-fledged wariness during the last quarter or half of the first year was not observed. In Bronson's study, at 3 and 4 months of age, infants in the crib showed signs of uneasiness (frowns) or cried in about 20 percent of the brief confrontations with the stranger. These signs appeared in 30 percent of the episodes at 6.5 months with the infants in an infant seat, and there was considerably more crying than at 3 to 4 months. At 9 months, with the infant on the floor, the infants in about half of the episodes showed uneasiness or cried, primarily the former. At both 6.5 and 9 months, being held by the stranger elicited the greatest amount of infant wariness. However, definite smiling expressions, along with a lesser number of neutral expressions, made up the bulk of the infants' reactions to the stranger at 3, 4, and 6.5 months, and in the remaining half of the 9-month-olds.

The proportion of neutral expressions increased progressively, so that it was highest at 9 months. This neutrality included periods of staring at the stranger intently, which decreased in duration with age. Apparently, as the infants became more capable of discriminating the stranger from the mother, they took less time in inspection and thus reacted more quickly, whether positively or negatively.

Bronson also observed a considerable number of ambivalent responses. In 5 percent of the episodes at 6.5 months and 11 percent at 9 months, the infants would, for example, appear both pleased with and wary of the stranger. Therefore, the increase in neutral responses with age can be interpreted as partly a manifestation that a conflict has developed between wariness and a desire to affiliate with a stranger.

Bronson found no statistically significant relationships between either sex, birth order (first or later born), or ancestry and infants' reactions to strangers. Nor was wariness at an early age always predictive of wariness later, although there was some consistency in individual infants.

In reporting the results of their study, Waters and his colleagues commented that "The age of onset of negative responses to the stranger can be seen to vary according to the behavioral criteria of fearful or negative responses." When crying was taken as the criterion for wariness, they found, wariness was not significant until 10 months, but when any and all negative responses on their scale were combined, wariness was present in a significant proportion of infants at 8, 9, and 10 months—23, 35, and 59 percent respectively. On the other hand, only 10 to 15 percent of infants 5 to 7 months of age showed negative reactions to strangers, less than half of which involved crying.

Thus, these investigators found the same gradual development of wariness that Bronson had observed. Extreme distress reactions occurred in only about 14 percent of the 10-month-olds. As in the Bronson study, positive responses were common. The "strong affiliative tendencies" of the infants in their study, they said, were apparent in "the high proportion of infants smiling during the approaches." And they, too, occasionally observed ambivalence in the presence of a stranger, suggesting that infants are sometimes both wary of and attracted to new people.

Bronson found that the mother's departure had no consistent significant effect on wariness until the age of 9 months, when some infants showed increased uneasiness when the mother left the room. The wariness of infants aged 6.5 months decreased when they were held by their mothers, and this also was true at 9 months, when the infants often went to their mothers when the stranger appeared. As opposed to wariness of strangers, novel objects elicited very few signs of wariness. The infants tended to gaze at them at 3 months, reach for them at 4 and 6 months, and crawl to them at 9 months of age. None of the 9-month-old infants crawled away from the box that bleeped, and only 5 percent cried. Half the infants, however, hesitated before beginning to crawl toward the box. This appears to be the same phenomenon that Schaffer observed in older infants presented with a nonsense object on a sliding tray.

Harriet Rheingold and Carol Eckerman obtained quite different results in their investigation of infants' reactions to strangers.[12] The 24 infants (12 girls, 12 boys) they studied were divided into three groups of eight—8, 10, and 12 months of age. The infants were given a series of tests in the laboratory with the mother and a female stranger present. The tests lasted much longer and the test conditions were more free and easy than those in the Bronson and Waters studies.

The first stranger greeted the mother and infant in the reception room, and the mother's role in the tests was discussed. They then went into a small test room, the mother placed her infant in a high chair where a toy was available, and for 10 minutes the stranger faced the infant, played peek-a-boo with him, and joined him in play with the toy, meanwhile chatting with both infant and mother. In three following tests, in a larger room furnished with a mobile and wall posters, a second stranger sat down beside the infant and mother on the floor, with a toy on the floor in front of each one. The adults chatted together and looked and smiled at the infant, but did not play with or call to him. Then, after five minutes, a single toy between the mother and the stranger was substituted for the two toys and the situation continued for five minutes. Finally, the stranger picked up the infant and held him for two minutes (or until he fussed or cried), talking with him and walking about showing him the posters and mobile. A test was added for 13 of the infants, in which the mother left the room, closing the door behind her, while the stranger held the infant for another two minutes.

None of the infants fussed or cried on the first test. Fussing or crying in the second test was minimal and occurred toward the end of the test. Five infants fussed or cried briefly during the third test. Only 4 of the 24 infants protested when, on the fourth test, they were picked up and held by the stranger for two minutes. And in the fifth test, none of the infants protested or struggled to get down when the mothers left the room.

The investigators conceded that their infant-stranger tests provided conditions that might be expected to encourage positive responses: The test periods were longer than usual in such experiments; both strangers were female; mother and stranger talked with each other; and the infants were picked up slowly, not abruptly. Expressing this reservation, they described their findings in the following terms:

> The infants of this study, whether 8, 10, or 12 months old, did not show fear of a stranger. Instead they accepted the strangers and, what is more, made friendly overtures. Although only a few feet from a

stranger, they played freely with toys, left the mother's side, and vocalized in a relaxed manner; further, they looked and smiled repeatedly at the strangers, actively participated in a game of peek-a-boo, and most allowed a stranger to hold them both in the presence and in the absence of the mother.

Studies of wariness in infants are still going on, but the weight of the evidence so far suggests that wariness is not universal in infants of any age, but is quantitatively related to age, and that its appearance may be dependent on the conditions prevailing when the infant encounters a stranger.

The negative responses of infants to strangers should not be emphasized at the expense of their positive, affiliative responses, commonly expressed in smiling, laughing, and friendly approaches to people. Some work has been done recently on laughter in infants and its development over the first year, but a look backward into the scanty history of studies of laughter reveals how little attention has been given to investigating its roots in infancy.[16]

Charles Darwin not only provided a good behavioral description of laughter, but also reported some observations of it in his children.[17] His description in *The Expression of the Emotions in Man and Animals* (1872) tells it all:

> The sound of laughter is produced by a deep inspiration followed by short, interrupted, spasmodic contractions of the chest, and especially of the diaphragm. Hence we hear of "laughter holding both his sides." From the shaking of the body, the head nods to and fro. The lower jaw often quivers up and down, as is likewise the case with some species of baboons, when they are much pleased. During laughter the mouth is opened more or less widely, with the corners drawn much backwards, as well as a little upwards; and the upper lip is somewhat raised.

At the age of 113 days, Darwin's firstborn son made "a little bleating noise," which he thought was "certainly incipient laughter." His second child, in whom smiling developed more rapidly than in the first, "uttered noises very like laughter" at the age of 65 days. It is now believed that laughter develops at about 4 months of age, considerably later than the full-fledged smile of social recognition.

Darwin's brief references to infant laughter failed to stimulate any interest, and for over a half-century nothing of moment was published on the subject. The first experimental study of infant laughter was reported in 1929 by Ruth Washburn, who had used various laugh-provoking stimuli with infants 16 to 52 weeks old and observed their reactions.[18] She found no evidence of any changes in laughter over the first year nor in the kind of stimuli that provoked it. However, she used very intense visual and auditory stimuli, such as a "threatening head" and "rhythmic hand clapping," which probably would elicit laughter in infants of any age, obscuring any age differences. It was not until 1972, in a study carried out by L. Alan Sroufe and Jane Piccard Wunsch of the University of Minnesota, that evidence of developmental changes in laughter was obtained.[19]

Sroufe and Wunsch studied the laughter of infants at home as elicited by their mothers with a series of laughter-provoking actions. Seventy infants, ranging in age from 4 to 12 months, were tested in this manner. In a second study, 26 infants 7 to 8 and 11 to 12 months of age were similarly observed. And in a third study, 10 infants were followed monthly from the age of 4 months to 12 months. About half the infants in the second study were observed in the laboratory; otherwise, all the observations were made in the infants' homes. It is noteworthy that when the laughter-provoking actions were more carefully delineated and controlled more consistently in the second and third studies, the infants laughed much less. Apparently, the infants found the spontaneity and variability of the earlier episodes more amusing.

The investigators selected some 30-odd laughter-provoking actions, some of which were basically auditory, others tactile, visual, or social in character, although many combined stimuli for several senses. One auditory stimulus was lip-popping: starting with cheeks full and lips pursed, the mother gave several lip pops in a row, then paused. Another consisted of saying "Boom, boom, boom" at one-second intervals in a loud, deep voice, another of saying "Hi, baby, how are you?" in a squeaky, falsetto, Mickey-Mouse voice. Still another auditory laugh-producer consisted of blowing out through loose, relaxed lips like a "tired horse."

Tactile laugh-elicitors included four quick pecks of the lips on the infant's bare abdomen, blowing gently at his hair for a few seconds, tickling the baby under the chin gently, placing him on the knees facing away and bouncing him vigorously, and mouthing the back of his neck (with suction) several times. Visual items included shaking the head vigorously about a foot from the baby's face, waddling like a penguin, crawling on the floor across the baby's field of view, pretending to suck on the baby's bottle (when he was not hungry), and holding up a white cloth or mask where he could see it, covering the face with it and leaning toward him, slowly leaning back, and then removing the covering. So-called social laugh-instigators included walking fingers toward the baby and giving him a poke in the ribs, playing tug with the baby, allowing him to grasp yarn and then tugging on it, and saying "I'm gonna get you" while leaning toward the baby with hands out to grab, then grasping him around the stomach.

Infant laughter in response to these actions markedly increased with age. In the first study, laughter was produced in 10 percent of the episodes in infants 4 to 6 months of age, in 37 percent in the 7- to 9-month-old group, and in 43 percent in the 10- to 12-month-old group, increasing from quarter to quarter, with the greatest increase in the third quarter.

The types of actions causing laughter also reflected developmental changes over the period studied. Not so the basically auditory episodes, which the infants found relatively unfunny throughout the study period. Tactile actions became less effective in arousing laughter in the third and fourth quarters. The researchers called tactile and auditory actions "intrusive," more directly physical, and perhaps intensely stimulating to the infants. Opposed to these were the more subtle, perhaps less intense, visual-social actions with which infants are stimulated from a distance and which may usually require more interpretation. Most visual actions and some social actions became increasingly effective from quarter to quarter.

The strongest laugh-producers from 9 to 12 months were visual or social, while the tactile and auditory actions were most effective during the fifth and sixth months—4-month-old babies laughed most at "kissing stomach" and "gonna get you." Actions that made the greatest cognitive demands on the infants, requiring that they be interpreted and identified, became more potent in eliciting laughter with the older infants. During the second half-year, infants noticeably joined more and more in the interactions and began to laugh more at what they themselves were doing in the episodes—behavior that becomes even more pronounced in the second year of life.

CHAPTER 8
Roger and Over

One day in 1972, in a laboratory room of the lying-in division of a Boston hospital, two men in white looked down at a crib in which a small infant lay, clad only in diapers. A flood lamp cast a pool of light over and around the crib. A television camera on a tripod stood nearby, its lens facing the crib. A nurse sat on one side of the room, quietly watching the proceedings. Having noted that the infant responded alertly when they spoke, the men walked away. One took up a position behind the camera, pointing it down toward the baby. The other moved to a spot in the corner of the room and, as the camera began to whirr, said casually, "Come over an' see who's over here..." and went on talking. The baby turned his head slightly toward the sound, wiggled a shoulder, and made other slight movements as the talking continued. When the baby closed his eyes and appeared to be drifting off to sleep, the cameraman signaled the speaker and stopped the filming. The nurse wheeled the baby out and returned with another. But this time, it was she who went to a corner of the room and talked as the baby's reactions were filmed. This procedure was repeated until a total of five hours of high-speed sound film had been obtained, recording the responses of 16 infants—two 2 weeks old and the others ranging in age from 12 hours to 2 days.

The two men in white were Drs. William Condon and Louis Sander of the Child Development Unit of Boston University Medical Center.[1] The purpose of their study was to follow up a chance observation that Dr. Condon had made some five years before.

Back in 1967, Dr. Condon and a colleague, while reviewing some high-speed sound films, had noticed what appeared to be synchronization between adult speech and the body movements of a 3-month-old and a 6-month-old infant. This observation was only incidentally made in the course of some adult research in kinesics, which is the systematic study of expressive body postures and movements related to communication—called microkinesics when the movements are imperceptible to the naked eye and must be recorded by a high-speed camera. The body postures and motions of head, arms, and hands when one person talks to another can disclose, for example, how friendly the speaker is toward the listener, and at the same time can provide information about the listener's receptiveness.

Microkinesic studies of conversing adults have revealed discrete, almost imperceptible, body movements of both speaker and listener. As Condon has expressed it, ". . . the body of the listener dances in rhythm with that of the speaker."[2] Microkinesics has opened up wholly new vistas in the study of language, analogous to the advent of the radio telescope in astronomy, when new kinds of stars and galaxies were discovered of which there had been no inkling before.

What Condon and Sander found when they analyzed their film record of infant responses to adult speech compels reexamination of current theories about the way language is acquired. Their high-speed precision camera took 30 frames a second, or one frame every three-hundredths of a second, far exceeding the capacity of the human eye to record events. Painstaking analysis of this film, frame by frame, revealed that as the adults spoke, the infants, who appeared virtually motionless to the unaided eye, made constant slight and changing movements of the head, eyes, shoulders, arms, hips, legs, fingers, and toes. Remarkably, these movements started, changed, or stopped in almost perfect synchrony with the speech. But it was not just the words to which the infants responded. Nor was it the syllables into which words are customarily divided—the *oh* and *ver* of *over,* for example. Instead, the babies' reactions varied with each distinctive sound of articulated speech. Thus, their responses to the three speech sounds in *over*—the *ooo, vv,* and *irir*—could be distinguished. Since these movements often started and stopped within less than a tenth of a second, only a very few could be detected by the unaided eye.

Was this synchronization of infant movements and adult speech merely a chance phenomenon? The study demonstrated in many ways that this was not the case. Infant micromotions filmed during silence had patterns different from those made in response to speech. Speech from tape recorders elicited similar infant movements, ruling out the possibility that the speaker was adapting his or her speech rhythms to that of the babies' activities. Further, newborns responded in the same synchronous manner to taped Chinese speech. But synchronization diminished markedly when tapes of disconnected vowels or simple tapping sounds were played. Clearly, it was normal adult speech to which the infants responded—so precisely that they often changed motions already in progress when a speech sound changed. Most striking were the synchronous reactions of two infants only 2 days old to speech sequences of 89 and 125 words.

Thousands of times before they learn to talk, infants must participate in these shared rhythms of speech and movement. Thus, they may already have laid down the rhythmic forms of language even before they start to babble. The acquisition of language, that uniquely human ability, begins, it seems, with the micromotions of 12-hour-old newborns.

Condon and Sander's discovery that the bodily movements of newborns are synchronized with speech sounds adds a new dimension to earlier findings that infants are highly sensitive to differences between these sounds. The foundation for infant studies in this area was laid by more than a decade of research into the characteristics of articulation that enable the adult to distinguish one speech sound from another. These "just distinguishable" sounds are called phonemes, the basic sounds of speech. A brief description of some of the articulatory features that permit such distinctions will provide background for the infant studies.

To produce a speech sound, or phoneme, air is expired from the lungs, passes through the vocal cords into the throat and mouth, and then exits through the lips or nose. The kind of phoneme that is produced depends on whether or not the airstream is obstructed in its passage, as well as on the manner of the obstruction. Vowel phonemes, such as hate, bat, and palm, are produced without any major obstructions to the airstream. To produce the consonant phonemes, on the other hand, either partial or complete obstruction of the airstream is necessary, and consonants are classified according to the nature of the obstruction.

The close approximation of articulators, such as the teeth and lips, produces fricative consonants—the upper teeth and lower lip must be closely approximated to produce f, for example. In stop consonants, on the other hand, the obstruction is complete—the lips must be pressed together to produce a *b* and a *p,* for example—so that the airstream is momentarily prevented from leaving the mouth. In nasal stops, the airstream leaves via the nose. In plosive stops, its release from the mouth has a plosive quality. Much of the research in speech-sound perception has focused on perception of the sounds of the plosive stop consonants, which are *b, d, g, p, t,* and *k.*

The phonemes *b, d,* and *g* are referred to as voiced, while *p, t,* and *k* are called voiceless. Voicing (vibration of the vocal cords) is, of course, involved in both groups, the major difference being the later onset time of voicing following the release of the airstream in the voiceless consonants. Voiced and voiceless stop consonants are used in nearly all the world's languages. In a very few, such as Spanish, Thai, and Kikuyu (a Bantu language of Kenya), there is also a prevoicing of consonants, that is, the vibration of the vocal cords comes *before* the release of the airstream.

What enables a listener to distinguish between the voiced-voiceless pairs *b-p, d-t,* and *g-k,* since each pair is articulated in the same place (*b* and *p* at the lips, for example)? In the voiced *b, g,* and *d,* voicing follows the release of the airstream by less than 30 milliseconds. With the voiceless *p, t,* and *k,* however, the voicing onset time is more than 30 milliseconds. Listeners are able to detect this minute difference and thereby distinguish the voiced *b* from the voiceless *p, d* from *t,* and *g* from *k.*

Investigation has revealed a remarkable feature in the perception of voiced and voiceless consonants.[3] Somewhat as people categorize a color as blue if it falls within a certain span of wavelengths in the spectrum, they identify voicing onset times within a certain range of milliseconds as *p* and onset times within another range as *b.* The same is true for *d* and *t* and *g* and *k.* Listeners are not able to distinguish differences in sounds made *within* the range—they all sound like *p*'s or *b*'s, as colors are seen as blues through a range of wavelengths. Such categorical auditory perception does not occur with nonspeech sounds, in which a whole series of finely shaded sounds can be distinguished.

This acute differential perception of phonemes led investigators to the view that there must be some very precise perceptual-motor mechanism in the human auditory apparatus that is specifically tuned to enable human beings to hear and articulate the phonemes in this categorical fashion. And they suggested that such a finely tuned, universal capacity is probably species-specific in man and thus innate.

If an inborn mechanism for hearing and producing speech is present in human beings, then it might be found in infants. Peter Eimas and his colleagues at Brown University proceeded to investigate this possibility, working with two groups of infants: 26 who were 1 month old and 26 who were 4 months old, each group evenly divided as to sex.[4] The general plan of the experiment was as follows: The infants were given non-nutritive (no milk) nipples or pacifiers to suck. When they sucked, they heard a taped speech sound produced by an electronic speech synthesizer. With any given sound, their sucking rate increased at first, apparently because they wanted to produce more sounds, since they received no other reward. Then as they became habituated to the repeated sound, their sucking rate diminished. If the same sound was then continued, the sucking rate decreased steadily, but if a sound that the infants could perceive as a new one was presented, the sucking rate reverted to its original high level.

The electronic speech synthesizer was used because it can produce exactly the same sound time after time. However, whether or not the synthesizer accurately replicates the sounds of human speech is a matter of controversy. Some linguists believe that recorded synthesizer speech is hard to distinguish from good recordings of natural speech. Others refer to the "speechlessness of synthetic stimuli" and judge that they sound "more like telephone busy signals than fluent English."[5] At any rate, synthetic speech sounds do contain precise voice onset times, a necessary condition for this experiment.

The infants in each age group were placed in three subgroups, each of which was tested under different speech-sound conditions. Infants in the first subgroup were presented with the sound of the voiced consonant b with a voice onset time of 20 milliseconds until they became habituated to this sound. Then they heard three repetitions of the voiceless consonant p with a voice onset time of 40 milliseconds. Infants in the second subgroup were given two sounds differing by voice onset times of 20 milliseconds within the onset-time range for b, or two sounds within the onset-time range for p, also differing by 20 milliseconds. The second group also heard one sound until habituation and then heard the other sound. The third subgroup, which was a control, listened first to one of the sounds given to the other groups until habituation, then heard the same sound repeated. All the sounds presented to the other groups were tested with the control group infants in this manner.

Only the first group of babies showed by their significantly increased sucking rates after habituation that they clearly distinguished the *b* and *p* phoneme sounds across these phoneme boundaries, separating the sounds precisely although their voice onset times differed by only 20 milliseconds, or two-hundredths of a second. The second group of infants, presented with two sounds from *within* the same phoneme category but also differing by 20 milliseconds in voice onset time, gave scarcely any indication that they perceived the differences between these sounds—their sucking rates kept right on diminishing, nearly as much as did those of control-group infants.

Eimas and his associates concluded that infants as young as 1 month are able to make fine discriminations between speech sounds and to perceive them in the same perceptual categories used by adults.[4] Such infant capacities, they say, imply that "the means by which the categorical perception of speech . . . is accomplished may well be part of the biological makeup of the organism and, moreover, that these means must be operative at an unexpectedly early age." This capacity seems to be all of a piece with the newborn responses to natural human speech sounds observed by Condon and Sander and implied as well in a Netherlands investigation[6] of the reactions of newborns to human speech and synthetic sounds varying in their similarity to speech.

A later study of Kenyan infants 2 months of age tended to confirm the work of Eimas and his colleagues, although the study also raised a further question.[7] The infants were all from Kenyan homes in which only Kikuyu, a Bantu language, was spoken. As noted, this language uses a number of prevoiced consonants, including a prevoiced *b*, in which voicing onset time *precedes* the release of the airstream by about 60 milliseconds. Kikuyu also uses voiced consonants, in which the voice onset time is delayed by less than 30 milliseconds, but has no voiceless consonants with the substantial voicing delays of the English *p, t,* and *k*. Thus, speakers of Kikuyu do not have to make the voiced-voiceless distinction.

The technique of measuring non-nutritive sucking to establish habituation was also used in this investigation, and the 2-month-old Kenyan infants proved themselves entirely adequate to the task of distinguishing between speech sounds that do not occur in their language: a prevoiced *p* from one in which the voice onset time was simultaneous with the release of air (0 milliseconds). They also recognized the difference between a voiced *p* and a voiceless *b* as these occur in the English language. However, they could not discriminate between two *p*'s separated by the same voice onset time as the other consonants they distinguished, but all within the onset-time range for the phoneme *p*. That is, like American infants and adults, they could distinguish between phonemes but not within phonemes.

Eimas and his colleagues have reported that American infants were unable to make the prevoiced distinction unless the voicing onset time difference was extremely large.[8] Unlike the Kikuyu infants, who hear a number of prevoiced consonants, American infants do not hear prevoicing in their language environment. However, the Kikuyu infants are not exposed to the voiced-voiceless distinction that they made so readily. Thus, it may be that the perceptual processes that enable such distinctions are inborn and universal in some instances and culturally acquired in others.

Recent investigations have demonstrated that infants reliably perceive the difference between the sounds of the syllables *bah* and *gah* (pronounced as in "*father*"). The initial consonants *b* and *g* of these syllables are both voiced and thus do not differ from each other in voice onset time. They are articulated in different places, however: the *b* at the lips, the *g* at the back of the tongue and soft palate. Also, they vary slightly in the second group of sound frequencies, called the second "formant," that is emitted during the voicing. In *gah,* this formant is high in pitch at first and then falls, but in *bah* it starts low and gradually rises.

In one experiment, 5-month-old infants indicated by the slowing of their heartbeats (cardiac deceleration) with the shift from one syllable to the other that they were able to distinguish between synthetic *bah* and *gah* syllables.[9] In another test, based on shifts in rates of infant sucking, it was shown that even infants 40 to 54 days old could discriminate *bah* from *gah*.[10] Furthermore, they could distinguish whether the *bah* was pronounced with a rising intonation, like that used in a question, or a falling intonation, like that used in a simple declarative sentence.

A suggestive, although by no means definitive, study of cardiac deceleration in an anencephalic infant in response to various sound stimuli must be mentioned.[11] This infant, whose brain weight was only 9 percent of normal, had minute cerebral hemispheres and a very malformed midbrain. However, his lower brain was normal, though underdeveloped. Yet when the infant was given sound stimulation during active sleep at 19, 20, 25, and 40 days of age, his heart rate strikingly decelerated. Furthermore, deceleration was much greater to speech syllables and other pulsed sounds than to continuous sounds, suggesting that the effectiveness of speech extends also to the lower brain.

It has now been well established by these studies, as well as by others, that young infants can discriminate voiced and voiceless differences in consonants, differences in speech sounds articulated at different places in the vocal passage (b and g, for example), and varying intonations of speech sounds. Previous experience with speech is in most instances apparently neither a necessity nor a major factor in this infant capability. In consequence, as the results of these experiments came in, many developmental psychologists and psycholinguists began to conclude that, for example, "The production of speech is a species-specific trait, characteristic of man alone" and that man "may possess special perceptual mechanisms that are structured in terms of his species-specific vocal repertoire."[10]

Then, out of the blue, came a report that made short work of speculations that speech perception is controlled by a mechanism unique to man.

The basic auditory capabilities of chinchillas are similar in many respects to those of human beings. Two investigators, working with four chinchillas in an elaborate series of experiments employing a less than gentle avoidance conditioning technique involving shocks, found that chinchillas, too, are perfectly capable of perceiving the difference between voiced and voiceless consonant phonemes.[12] First, they found that the chinchillas could be trained to respond differentially to the syllable da (with the voiced initial d) and to the syllable ta (with the voiceless initial t). The syllables used for some of the animals in this first training had been recorded on tape by two men and two women. Others were trained with synthesizer-produced syllables. After this training, and regardless of which group they were in, the animals responded correctly to these syllables spoken by different speakers, to syllables with different vowels (such as *to* as opposed to *ta*), and to syllables produced by a synthesizer. Furthermore, the animals then proved that they could distinguish *da* from *ta* in a series of synthesizer-produced syllables that shifted gradually from *ta* to *da*, whether they had been originally trained on natural speech or computer-synthesized speech.

The researchers compared the chinchillas' performance with that of human subjects who had heard the same series of tapes and found no noteworthy differences. Thus, human beings do not have some kind of unique phonetic perception mechanism, since the distinctions involved can be made by at least one other mammal—and perhaps many more—with no capacity to speak and no experience with language. The uniqueness of human beings in this respect is their use of this fine discriminatory capacity to create language.

Speculating about the original biological function of speech as the human species evolved, a linguist at the University of Connecticut, Ignatius Mattingly, suggested that there is an analogy between the basic elements of language, that is, the acoustic cues of the phonemes such as voicing onset time, and the characteristics of sign stimuli, the cues that release various adaptive activities in animal species.[18] Thus, in the gull, the red spot on the bill of the parent gull is a sign stimulus for the chick gull to peck, and its pecking at the red spot produces disgorgement of food from the parent's bill. Or the bright plumage (visual) of male birds and their mating songs (auditory) serve to attract the female and ensure the reproduction of the species. Sign stimuli, then, "release" behavior of great survival value for a species.

To strengthen his argument by analogy, Mattingly set out to examine the essential features that jointly characterize human language and sign stimuli. He observed that sign stimuli can be effective even when drastically simplified, as long as they retain certain essential features. Thus, the dummy red spot at which baby gulls will peck can be of various sizes and shapes on a variety of bill shapes, and still the babies will peck. Similarly, "dummy" speech synthesized by a computer can still be understood though greatly simplified, as long as it retains certain basic features such as the voicing onset time of stop consonants. A sign stimulus will be effective even though just one of its features is present. For example, either the contrast of the patch with the bill of the parent gull alone, or its red color alone, will release the chick's pecking. Similarly, in human language, Mattingly observes, although multiple cues are given by phonemes, such as the voicing onset time, the various formants, and the places in which the phonemes are articulated in the vocal passage, some can be defective or merged with other cues in the ongoing flow of speaking, and yet the speaker will be understood.

Finally, sign stimuli appear to operate through some form of admittedly hypothetical neural releasing mechanism in the brain, and a similar mechanism has been proposed to explain why speech perception alone among auditory stimuli is categorical, while in other sounds, each and every fine change is distinguishable.

Mattingly speculates that in early man, speech sounds functioned as sign stimuli for mutual recognition between infants and parents, for the protection of infants from predators and other dangers, for communicating the approach of a predator to others, and even for expressing threats of aggression and thereby avoiding the lethal possibilities of physical combat, and for distinguishing between the sexes and encouraging reproductive behavior. Human speech has, of course, gone far beyond its possible original source in the cries and babbling of infants, primeval danger signals, and threat and mating cues. It can now convey infinite shades of meaning and emotion expressed through complex syntax and an endless variety of words, based on the original phonemes that may have served only as vocal sign stimuli to our remote ancestors.

Whatever its biological significance, the aptitude for speech-sound discrimination these pioneering studies have discovered in infants has received very little research attention compared with that devoted to the development of expressive language, or speaking. Concerned about the dearth of studies of infant listening to speech, Bernard Friedlander, of the University of Wisconsin, made the following observations in 1970:

> I know of no serious contemporary study of early language growth that gives lengthy, systematic attention to receptive language organization . . . as a significant area for developmental research. Except among audiologists concerned with problems of hearing acuity, investigators have focused their attention almost exclusively on the young child as a speaker and little attention has been paid to him as a listener.[14]

Signs are appearing, however, that receptive language development is beginning to interest researchers, and the results of a few recent investigations indicate that infants are very selective listeners, with subtle preferences all their own.

One recent study explored the speech preferences of infants in three age groups averaging 4, 7, and 12 months of age.[15] Based on what is known about infants' visual preferences at various ages, it was predicted that the infants in the youngest group, just developing their speech schemata, would prefer the normally inflected speech with which they were becoming familiar. The 7-month-old age group would prefer the moderate discrepancy of flat monotone speech, without expression, and the older infants, with more thoroughly developed speech schemata, should prefer speech with scrambled word order because of its great discrepancy from well-established schemata.

To test this hypothesis, the infants were first instrumentally conditioned. If they gazed steadily for at least two seconds at either one of two small screens in a wall about a foot in front of them, a screen was removed, revealing either a 1-square or a 16-square checkerboard pattern, the reward for their sustained attention. After the infants were thoroughly conditioned, loudspeakers were substituted for the visual stimuli, giving the infants the opportunity to listen to a brief recorded speech when they looked for two seconds at either screen. Three recordings produced a female voice saying "Hello, baby," "Can you smile?" and "Let's see a smile," either in a normally inflected manner at 88 words per minute, a monotone at 55 words per minute, or in a scrambled word order at 62 words per minute. The scrambled speech—"A see smile let's," and so on—was spoken with a normal inflection. During each of six three-minute trials, the infants were given a choice between two of these three recordings, randomly paired, to see which preferences they would express, determined by the length of time they spent visually orienting toward the sources of the three different kinds of speech.

A consistent preference was defined as one expressed in two or more trials. By this criterion, three-quarters of the babies showed a consistent preference for one or another of the three types of speaking: that is, listening longer to monotone speech than to inflected speech in both trial one and two, for example. However, there was no significant relationship between age and type of preference as had been predicted. For the group as a whole, the order of preference was first monotone, second normal speech, and third scrambled word order.

The infants' preferences seemed to be influenced in some measure by word order, which was normal in both the inflected and the monotone speech that they preferred over the scrambled word order, despite the novelty of the latter. Conceivably, the apparent significance of word order might indicate that these infants had already developed some awareness of meaning or of syntax, the rules by which words are put together to make sentences. This is unlikely in view of what is known at present about language acquisition. The rate of speaking may have influenced their preferences, for the monotone speech, their first choice, was delivered at the slowest rate and over half of them preferred it. Babies may like slowed speech simply because it is often used in addressing them.

The investigator concluded that the speech preferences of infants may be influenced by many variables—word order, inflection, speech rate, or possibly the reality of the speech, that is, how close it is to normal speech—but that further research is needed to determine the bases for their preferences.

Bernard Friedlander made a small-scale attempt at studying the speech preferences of a few infants in their natural environment—at home.[16] Three infants, 11 to 13 months of age and all male, were given their choice of recordings to listen to when placed in their playpens in the normal course of the day's activities. Two knobs at the side of the playpen each turned on a different recording when it was pushed or pulled in any direction. The infants were trained in a series of preliminary sessions with nonspeech recordings, so that they were well versed in the use of the knobs when the experiment began.

A 13-month-old baby was given a choice, for example, between listening to a lively Bach organ piece or to his mother's voice speaking phrases familiar to him in a bright, inflected voice. After he had tried out both tapes for a few minutes, his preference for hearing his mother's voice began to emerge strongly. In fact, he preferred his mother's voice in a total of 15 of 17 sessions in the playpen over a period of 10 days. But such a clear preference did not simply mean that he preferred speech to music. In a previous series of seven sessions, he had shown a slight preference for organ music over a stranger's bright voice reading a happy story. In the first session of a following series, he preferred a female stranger's voice to his mother's. However, this time his mother spoke of impersonal matters in a flat monotone, while the stranger spoke in a sprightly manner and used phrases familiar to the baby. In subsequent sessions with the same choice of recordings, the baby's responses to the sound knobs trailed off, and no clear preference for either voice was discernible.

At 15 months of age, another baby showed a definite preference for his mother's brightly inflected voice using familiar phrases to a stranger's flatly inflected voice using unfamiliar phrases over a series of nine playpen sessions. (Given a similar choice, the 13-month-old infant had shown no preference.) When the stranger's and mother's manners of speaking were reversed, the baby became very cautious, sampling both voices for equally long times. Then he began to show a slight preference for his mother's disguised voice consistently, and by the eleventh session he had virtually stopped listening to the stranger's voice. More advanced in language development than the first infant, he had apparently been able, after careful listening, to identify the specific characteristics of his mother's voice, despite its disguise, while the younger infant had been "taken in" by the attractiveness of the stranger's voice.

A year-old baby was presented with a choice between hearing his mother's flat and monotonous voice (reading the regulations of the municipal skating rink) and her normal voice, brightly inflected and speaking phrases familiar to him. At the first session, the baby displayed a slight preference for his mother's normal voice and then shifted more and more decisively to her monotonous voice, maintaining this strong preference over 10 sessions. Friedlander noted the preference for discrepancy shown by this infant, which is also typical of visual preferences. He suggested that such a "listening appetite" for something novel would make it possible for babies to become familiar with a variety of vocal models—a necessary condition for the development of speech.

A similar explanation might be given of the same infant's response when given a choice between a 4-minute tape of a lively family conversation, including the voices of his father, mother, and a family friend, and a short excerpt from the same conversation repeated every 20 seconds. At first, after sampling both a number of times, he listened almost exclusively to the frequently repeated short conversation. This had been predicted, on the ground that it would be easier for him to assimilate. In the next series of sessions, his interest flagged and his responses were sparse and equivocal. However, in the series that followed the low-output, no-preference sessions, there was a radical shift to an overwhelming preference for the long conversation. This same pattern also was evident in his reaction to a 40-second versus a 12-second tape of a family conversation. Here he devoted 4000 seconds to listening to the longer tape, giving the greatest number of listening responses in the entire experiment.

Since the possibility of selection on the basis of the speaker's identity, inflection of the voice, or familiarity with the vocabulary had been ruled out, Friedlander was convinced that this infant's choice had been based on a preference for the *content* of the conversation. In arriving at this conclusion, he was not implying that the baby had grasped the meaning of the two conversations, but merely that he had been listening carefully enough to detect differences in their "fine inner structure," and apparently preferred the structure of the longer conversation.

Virtually nothing is known about infants' language comprehension, for this is an area of research to which investigators have yet to apply their remarkable talent for probing the "inner infant." Writing in 1974, Lois Bloom, of Columbia University, noted that developmental psychologists have paid little or no attention to the relationship between understanding and speaking, focusing almost entirely on early speech and ignoring what children understand of what they hear.[17] This, she said, is primarily attributable to the difficulty of measuring comprehension, not to any lack of interest. She added, however, that comprehension has been too much taken for granted, in view of the scarcity of evidence, either anecdotal or experimental, that has been presented. In fact, anecdotes about individual infants' language comprehension are about all the evidence we have. Two century-old reports illustrate the anecdotal approach to this subject.

In 1876, a French philosopher, Hippolyte Taine, contributed to *Revue Philosophique* a series of observations he had made on "the development of language in a young child . . . a little girl whose development was ordinary, neither precocious nor slow."[18] After discussing the manner in which this infant's babbling, which he called "a sort of very distinct twittering," appeared and gradually changed, Taine reported on her first comprehension of the meaning of words:

As yet she attaches no meaning to any word she utters, but there are
two or three words to which she attaches meaning when she hears
them. She sees her grandfather every day, and a chalk portrait of
him . . . has been often shown to her. From about ten months when
asked "Where is grandfather?" she turns to this portrait and laughs.
. . . From eleven months when asked "Where is mama?" she turns
towards her mother, and she does the same for her father.

Taine noted that such a specific association between a sound
("mama") and a particular individual could be made by a dog as well
as a little girl! But then at 12 months, the little girl seemed to have
acquired a general concept of *bébé:*

This winter she was carried every day to her grandmother's, who often
showed her a . . . picture of the infant Jesus naked, saying at the same
time "There's bébé." A week ago in another room when she was asked
"Where's bébé?" meaning herself, she turned at once to the pictures . . . that happened to be there. *Bébé* has then a general significance for her, namely whatever she thinks is common to all pictures
and engravings of figures and landscapes, that is to say, if I am not
mistaken, *something variegated in a shining frame.* . . . This is her first
general word.[18]

These observations by Taine stimulated Charles Darwin to report
in his "Biographical Sketch of an Infant" some observations he had
made of his own children:

When exactly seven months old, he [one of Darwin's six sons] made the
great step of associating his nurse with her name, so that if I called it
out he would look around for her. Another infant used to amuse
himself by shaking his head laterally. We praised and imitated him,
saying "Shake your head"; and when he was seven months old, he
would sometimes do so. During the next four months the former infant
associated many things and actions with words; thus when asked for a
kiss he would protrude his lips and keep still. . . . I may add that when
a few days under nine months old he associated his own name with his
image in a locking-glass, and when called by name would turn towards
the glass even when at some distance from it.[19]

A century later, Lois Bloom, in discussing a few reported observations
of infant language comprehension, was herself forced to turn to the
anecdotal method:

Some time toward the end of their 1st year, then, children may indicate recognition of an association between an acoustic event and an object by a shift in gaze toward the object, or an arrest of attention. . . . My daughter, Allison, first recognized the word *birds* in association with the mobile above her dressing table and then, shortly after, the word *music* in association with the record player in her room, before her 1st birthday. Unfortunately, the information that exists about emerging comprehension as children begin to associate sounds and referents is anecdotal in just this way.[17]

And here the matter rests. Although occasional allusions to ongoing research in infant language comprehension appear in the literature, for the moment the anecdote still holds the floor.

Although the word "infant" derives from the Latin word *infans,* meaning "not speaking," babies produce many sounds that foreshadow the eventual development of speech during their first 12 months. And, as opposed to the ways in which infants listen to and begin to comprehend speech, their sound production, or vocalization, from birth onward is a relatively straightforward phenomenon to observe. Consequently, it has been well researched.

In general, in studies of infant vocalization, researchers have concentrated on the various functions that vocalization plays in an infant's overall development. One recent investigation, however, explored the relationship between sounds made by infants in the first eight weeks and later speech development.[20] The vocalizations of two female infants were studied in their homes in a half hour immediately before and during feeding and while the mother was playing with them after feeding. They were recorded on tape in three sessions, when the infants were 1 to 2, 3 to 4, and 8 weeks old. The mothers were asked not to talk while the infants were vocalizing, but otherwise to behave normally.

The sounds the infants made were classified independently by three listeners as "cry," "discomfort," and "vegetative." Crying was defined as the series of sounds that occurred when the infant was distressed because of hunger, pain, or absence of the mother. Discomfort sounds were produced when the infants were merely frustrated or needed to protest—the sounds usually called fussing or fretting. Vegetative sounds were those involved in various bodily functions, such as coughing, burping, sucking, snorting, sneezing, or hiccuping. Researchers have variously suggested in the past that speech develops from vegetative sounds, or that none of these early sounds is related to the later cooing and babbling from which speech emerges, or that noncrying vocalizations (cooing, babbling, and speech) emerge from fussing sounds.

Five typical 7- to 10-minute samples of each infant's cry, discomfort, and vegetative vocalizing from each of the three sessions were used for the analysis. The researchers first listened to a number of the taped infant utterances to determine what features would be used to detect differences between the three types of sounds. Among the features selected were those related to breath direction (inward or outward), voicing and pitch, and features involved in making vowel-like and consonantlike sounds—all of which would eventually be used in speaking. The frequency with which the various features occurred did not change significantly over the eight-week period studied, although the two infants differed sufficiently from each other in the frequency of particular features so that a trained observer could reliably tell them apart. Detailed differences were found between the cry and discomfort sounds on the one hand and the vegetative sounds on the other. Vegetative sounds, for example, were typically consonantlike and voiceless, whereas cry and discomfort sounds were vowel-like 95 to 100 percent of the time and typically voiced. Speech elements, then, were found in all three types of sounds.

The researchers concluded that these features must enter into new combinations with each other and new features must be added as infants acquire speech-production skills. They suggested that the first such combination may be represented by cooing, which begins after 8 weeks of age and had formerly been regarded as a discontinuity in vocal development. At this age, infants are still making vegetative sounds, and cooing may emerge from a combination of their consonantlike features and the voicing and other features of discomfort sounds, which cooing most closely resembles.

Infants become adept at cooing in their second to third months, and then at around 4 to 6 months of age, they begin to babble. Babbling is a more complex kind of vocalization than cooing, often consisting of syllables strung together and repeated over and over. There is some evidence that it tends to diminish in frequency a month or two before the onset of meaningful speech.[21]

Cooing and babbling might not be possible, however, without the reshaping of the back of the mouth and the pharynx (upper throat) that occurs about this time. The hyoid bone, a roughly U-shaped bone around the upper throat, is situated at the root of the tongue and serves to anchor it. The bone functions both in swallowing and in voice production. When food is swallowed, muscles raise the hyoid bone and the floor of the mouth at the same time, the tongue presses upward against the roof of the mouth, and food is forced backward and down the throat. Motions of the hyoid bone also raise or lower the back of the tongue in vocalizing, changing the shape of the voice cavity. In neonates, the hyoid bone is high up in the throat, so that the root of the tongue is mostly within the mouth. This kind of structure is found in nonhuman primates as well.[22] By 6 months of age, the descent of the hyoid bone has occurred to a great extent, although the pharynx will not develop its final shape until the age of 2 years.[23] The root of the tongue then lies below the mouth, and the voice passage is adequate for the full range of vocalization.

For many years it has been accepted doctrine, originally promulgated by linguistic authorities, that the babbling of infants merely reflects the entire range of possible human voice sounds and has no relationship to language development. However, the contention that infant babbling is simply a meaningless exercise of the vocal mechanism with no relevance to speech production has been called into question by the findings of a recent study.[24]

Researchers at the University of Washington made audiotapes of the babbling of over 50 infants brought into their laboratory in Seattle. The infants ranged from 4 to 13 months of age, but only the tapes of five infants 6 to 8 months old and five 12 to 13 months old were finally analyzed. These tapes were selected on the basis of their clarity and the frequency with which babbled utterances occurred in them. For the purpose of the study, the researchers defined a babbled utterance as an utterance that consisted of at least one vowel and one consonant—that is, a syllable. After determining the frequencies of particular phonetic elements in these utterances, the investigators were in a position to compare them with the frequencies with which the same elements occur in meaningful children's speech as it develops in the next year or two.

Over 90 percent of the consonants the infants babbled were single, rather than grouped with other consonants in clusters. By comparison, it has been reported for a number of languages that meaningful children's speech contains many more single consonants than the double consonant used in the adult speech of these languages. Rather than saying "stop," for example, children will say "top." Also, when syllables have both an initial and a final consonant, like the syllable *dad,* it has been found that children commonly drop the final consonant but rarely the initial one. This was also true for the infants' babbled syllables, with initial consonants outnumbering the final consonants by a ratio of three to one. In early meaningful speech, children tend to substitute voiceless for voiced initial stop consonants in syllables, saying "Peppy," for example, rather than "Peggy," and all 10 infants revealed a strong preference for initial voiceless consonants. They also overwhelmingly preferred voiceless final consonants to voiced final consonants in their syllables, which has also been found typical of children's meaningful speech in several languages. In these and many other respects, the speechlike sounds made in babbling were similar to the speech utterances of children who are beginning to speak their native language.

On the basis of their analysis, the investigators felt justified in questioning the claims of the traditionalists that babbling is mere random vocalization without relevance to meaningful speech. Rather, they said, there is a continuity between the two, "and, by implication, between babbling and phonological universals," that is, adult speech.

Although the researchers were not clear as to their significance, many examples of utterances that are common neither in early children's speech nor in the world's languages were also found in the babbling data. Among these were trills made with both lips and nasal syllables. However, these unusual utterances did not occur with the high frequency characteristic of the phonetic elements that resemble children's early speech.

Cooing and babbling sometimes appear to be spontaneous vocal exercises, done simply for the fun of it. Or, by cooing and babbling, infants may seem to be greeting others and attempting to establish a social interchange.

Vocalization and other "prespeech" behavior as manifestations of the infant's attempts to communicate are the focus of a study done by Colwyn Trevarthen at the University of Edinburgh after preliminary work with Martin Richards and Jerome Bruner at Harvard.[25, 26] The infants, some as young as 3 to 6 weeks of age, were placed partly reclining in infant chairs, so that their heads and limbs were free to move. Their mothers, seated close by, were simply told to chat with them, and infant-mother interactions were filmed for later detailed analysis.

Trevarthen and his colleagues have found that as early as three weeks after birth, infants respond differentially to objects and people. Babies attend to nearby moving objects, track them visually, and move their arms and hands in "prereaching" gestures. Embryonic communication is displayed in their interactions with their mothers, however. Some of the baby's prespeech is unvoiced, consisting of mouth movements and tonguing, with the tongue extended through pouted or pursed lips; some is vocalized, with the mouth open and small, and rapid lip and tongue movements. Unvoiced prespeech is often accompanied by waving of the hands, finger gesticulations, and arm movements, the latter becoming much more vigorous when the infant vocalizes. Signs of pleasure and joy frequently accompany vocalization. All this is strongly reminiscent of animated adult conversation. Trevarthen suggests that

> Human social intelligence is the result of development of an innate human mode of psychological function that requires transactions with other persons. This function includes rudiments of the quite unique human activity of speech, which becomes the chief medium of individual human mental growth and the essential ingredient of civilised society.[26]

Trevarthen notes that infants communicate long before they are able to manipulate objects, and that this embryonic communication is by far the most complex behavior they manifest in their first six months. Infants appear to use certain symbols (mouthing, tonguing, and gesturing) and follow certain rules (like the grammar of speech itself), of which the mothers become aware and follow, so that a reciprocal exchange of "messages" is created.

By about 20 weeks of age, a time when infants are able to reach for objects, their full concentration on the interchange with the mother diminishes, and they become increasingly inclined to shift her attention from themselves to an object that has caught their fancy, apparently hoping to make it an object of mutual interest. Thus, they now use objects as a means of communication, which implies to

Trevarthen that social interchange is primary to the infant, "dealings with the physical world being to a great extent based upon it."[25]

Since vocalization is regarded by developmental psychologists as one way in which infants socialize with others, considerable research has been devoted to determining what environmental factors, if any, produce and increase vocalization. Infant vocalization has proved to be easily modified by social influences, but exactly how these influences operate—whether by conditioning or some other mechanism—is still a matter of debate.

A pioneer effort to condition infant vocalization was made in 1959 by Harriet Rheingold, Jacob Gewirtz, and Helen Ross at the National Institute of Mental Health with 3-month-old institutionalized infants.[27] Their method was similar to that used by Brackbill in her study of infant smiling. On two successive days the babies' average "baseline" rates of vocalizations were recorded as an experimenter leaned over the crib and looked at the baby with an expressionless face. Then, on the next two days, the experimenter, standing in the same position, immediately reinforced each vocalization by smiling broadly, saying "Tsk, tsk, tsk," and lightly touching the baby's stomach with one hand. By the second day the rate of vocalization had doubled on the average, showing a marked and consistent increase. On the two days following—the extinction trials—the experimenter again assumed her "deadpan" expression, and vocalization diminished, almost reaching the baseline level by the second day.

Since adult attention following these infants' vocalizations greatly increased their frequency, and extinction of the response followed the usual pattern, Rheingold and her associates felt reasonably sure that they had succeeded in instrumentally conditioning vocalization. However, they were careful to suggest an alternative explanation: that the social stimulation provided by the experimental setting might have caused the infants to vocalize more, that they might have done so even if the stimulation had been given at random times and not simply as a reward for vocalizing. In that event, the stimulation would be serving as a releaser, rather than a reinforcer, of social responses, and they raised the possibility that some aspect of the stimulation—perhaps the experimenter's smile—might be functioning as a social releaser. Although they strongly favored the conditioning explanation the researchers suggested that an experiment be done in which stimulation was given with the same frequency as in their study but never directly after a vocalization.

In response to this suggestion, another investigator, Paul Weisberg, devised an experiment to compare the effect of stimulation contingent on vocalization with the effect of random stimulation unrelated to vocalization.[28] And by using sound stimulation, as well as social stimulation, in the experiment, Weisberg also explored the possibility that vocalizing might increase when the infant discovered that it produced the sound of a chime. Weisberg's subjects were 3-month-old institutionalized infants, 38 in all, whom he divided into four groups. In one group, the experimenter rubbed the infants' chins with thumb and forefinger, smiled broadly, and said "Yeah" immediately following their vocalizations. This group was the only one in which vocalizations significantly increased, indicating that they had been reinforced by the stimulation and thus conditioned. Another group received the same social stimulation presented randomly four times a minute and independent of vocalization. This produced no significant change in vocalization rate, and thus no evidence that the stimulation functioned as a social releaser. Vocalization also failed to increase in two other groups who heard the sound of a door chime either immediately following their vocalizations or presented randomly four times a minute. This merely established that the chime used in the experiment neither reinforced nor elicited vocalization in infants of this age, but did not imply that nonsocial stimuli have no conditioning potential under any circumstances.

The stimulation that was used in both the Rheingold and the Weisberg experiments provided composite reinforcement: a smiling face, a voice speaking to the infant, and a light touch. Which element of this constellation of stimuli has the most reinforcing value? Some investigators have suggested that the voice is the most potent reinforcer of infant vocalizations; others have claimed that it is the face. Two researchers, working with 16 infants averaging 3 months of age, attempted to resolve this controversy.[29]

Placed in a crib, the infants were given immediate tape-recorded auditory reinforcement through a loudspeaker whenever they vocalized. The reinforcement consisted of an adult female voice slowly repeating the phrases "Hello, baby," "pretty baby," and "nice baby." Half the infants were given this reinforcement alone, and half received it while an expressionless adult stood at the head of the crib.

Vocalization rates in the group who had an adult in view increased significantly more than those of the group without the adult presence, although vocalization in the latter was significantly reinforced just by the voice. The investigators felt that they had settled the matter. The human presence, they said, is not essential for conditioning infant vocalization, but "it functions to increase the reinforcing effectiveness of the human voice." Thus, it may serve as a catalyst, or setting event, as eye contact has been found to do.

The results of all these studies weigh heavily in favor of reinforcement as a key factor in the development of infant vocalizations. However, this is not the end of the story.

Experiments done by Kathleen Bloom, of Dalhousie University, Halifax, Nova Scotia, and an associate failed to substantiate Weisberg's contention that infant vocalization increases only when reinforced.[30] (Bloom's work in showing the catalytic effect of direct eye-to-eye gaze between infant and adult on infant learning has already been described.) She had questioned the conclusion that random social stimulation independent of vocalization did not elicit it directly, for her informal observations of adults attending to babies seemed to indicate that the babies naturally responded in a social way to adult attention. So she compared the effects on the vocalization rates of 16 infants, 3 months of age, when an adult smiled, said "Tsk, tsk, tsk," touched the infant, and maintained eye-to-eye contact following every vocalization with the effects of identical stimulation given with no relation to vocalizations. The social stimulation succeeded in almost tripling the infants' vocalizations in both groups. Thus, stimulation given as reinforcement was no more effective than that given independent of vocalization, and Weisberg's finding was not replicated.

All this casts a rather dark shadow of doubt on the role of instrumental conditioning in such situations. And additional Bloom experiments increasing the doubt were to come, although fewer subjects were involved.[31] In one, four infants were observed in four consecutive daily sessions, each of which consisted of 12 minutes of experimental study. After obtaining their baseline vocalization rates while the experimenter was socially unresponsive, half the infants, directly after they vocalized, received social stimulation with direct eye-to-eye contact from an experimenter who wore glasses with clear lenses. The other infants received the same treatment while the experimenter looked at them through tiny holes in opaque lenses, so that the babies could not see her eyes. Under these conditions only the infants in eye-to-eye contact showed a significant spurt in their vocalization rate. The same results were also obtained in infants given social stimulation with eye contact or no-eye contact independent of their vocalizations. Bloom concluded that this experiment "showed that a responsive adult was effective as a social stimulus, a 'releaser' of infant vocal sounds, only when the infant could see the adult's eyes." Thus, she has changed her original position, based on her earlier study, that eye-to-eye contact facilitates *learning* and now emphasizes its role as a catalyst in the infant's social expressiveness.

Whether it is ultimately decided that social stimulation increases an infant's responsiveness by reinforcing it or merely by creating a socially stimulating atmosphere, all of these vocalization studies show conclusively that the attention of adults is a key factor in the social development of infants insofar as vocalization reflects such development.

Although speech production in the service of communication (and thereby socialization) may be the principal function of vocalization in infants, another role that it also seems to play late in the first year of life, the expression of excitement or its contrary, boredom, has been explored in considerable detail.[32, 33] The studies have been made primarily by cognitive psychologists, who, though they agree that vocalization can be produced by reinforcement, believe that it can also signify cognitive processing of sensory information by the infant. They suggest that vocalization, as well as other expressive reactions like smiling, may follow a successful cognitive effort to assimilate a new event into an established Piagetian schema. On the other hand, an infant may express boredom with a frequently repeated event by vocalizing.

A number of studies have been made of infant vocalizations of the cognitive sort in response to events of varying discrepancy, particularly by Philip Zelazo, Jerome Kagan, and Rebecca Hartmann and their colleagues at Harvard University.[34] In one of their investigations, the vocalizations of 144 infants equally divided as to sex and age (9.5 and 11.5 months) were studied in the laboratory. Seated in their mothers' laps, they were presented with a series of events in an apparatus that resembled the stage of a puppet theater, complete with curtains. An experimenter behind the curtains reached a hand between them, took an object out of a box, moved it across the stage in a path tracing a broad **N** in the air, and then returned it to the box. Three objects were used: a 2-inch orange cube as the standard stimulus, repeated and familiar; a 1.5-inch orange cube as a moderately different or discrepant stimulus; and a 1.5-inch yellow plastic cylinder as a very discrepant stimulus.

The infants were divided evenly into two experimental groups and a control group, equally represented as to sex. After the repetition of six trials with the standard stimulus, the 2-inch cube, one experimental group was shown the moderately different smaller orange cube for three trials, then the standard cube for three more trials. The second experimental group had three trials of the novel plastic cylinder after six standard cube trials, then three more trials of the standard cube. The control group had the same total number of trials, all viewing the familiar standard cube alone.

The mothers were told to look away from the stage and not to react to their infants' responses. Observers recorded the fixation times of the infants on the stimuli and their vocalizations to it.

Vocalizations to the stimuli showed up more clearly between the trials than during presentations of the stimuli, although some occurred in both intervals. It was as if the infants concentrated on attending to the objects and processing the information and then "commented" on them after their removal. When the familiar standard stimulus of the large orange cube was repeated for the control group, both the 11.5-month-old boys and the 9.5-month-old girls tended to vocalize more, probably because they became bored with this repetition. However, the moderately discrepant stimulus of the smaller cube evoked increasing vocalization, particularly among the 11.5-month-old girls. Furthermore, the girls continued the high level of vocalization when the small cube changed back again to the larger, standard cube to which they had become accustomed in the earlier trials.

The researchers suggested that the girls particularly were expressing the excitement and effort accompanying attempts to understand the changes, assimilating them to their familiar schemata as Piaget would say, and that perhaps this indicated that the girls were "developmentally precocious." And vocalization to the yellow plastic cylinder, which was extremely discrepant, was lowest in the older girls.

This experiment, as well as prior studies by the same investigators and others, appears to identify a fairly reliable and significant sex difference between the infants, at least by 1 year of age, although it has been noted in younger infants during the last half-year of infancy. The researchers suggested with caution:

> It cannot be determined ... whether the disposition of infant girls to vocalize following examination of a moderately discrepant stimulus is a basic and perhaps universal sex difference, a product of different child rearing differences, or a manifestation of their relative precocity at these ages.[34]

The existence or nonexistence of sex differences in infants is a thorny issue, full of inconsistencies in experimental results and a source of controversy among developmental psychologists. It is fair to say that most investigations of infant behavior have failed to demonstrate any significant differences between male and female infants. And for those few investigations that have revealed such differences, the question whether they are attributable to differential handling by caregivers, to the more precocious behavioral development of one sex as opposed to the other, or to an inborn sex difference has remained largely unresolved.

The women's liberation movement seems to have produced a backlash effort to marshal every scrap of evidence for innate sex differences in behavior, whether the evidence is solid and statistically significant or merely suggestive, replicated in other experiments or not. In a thorough review of the issue, the psychologist Beverly Birns remarks on the tenuousness of this evidence:

> Clearly neither the presence nor absence of early sex differences can be claimed with great conviction. *Nonetheless,* what happens is that the few studies demonstrating sex differences are widely quoted and cited as evidence for "biological" determination of sex differences. (The failure to replicate, or studies demonstrating no sex differences, are often ascribed to methodological shortcomings or tests that are insensitive to subtle differences.) However, on the basis of evidence cited above it appears that behavioral sex differences, like beauty, might exist primarily in the eye of the beholder.[35]

Two studies of infant vocalization exemplify the inconsistent results that even frustrate attempts to investigate differential handling of male and female infants.

In *Change and Continuity in Infancy*,[33] Kagan reports briefly on observations of about 90 mother-infant pairs in the home when the infants were 4 months of age—a part of a much more extensive, long-term study of infant development. Recording normal mother-infant interactions every five seconds for a period of four hours, he found that upper-middle-class mothers vocalized about twice as much to their infant daughters in face-to-face situations as did lower-middle-class mothers. This class difference, however, did not hold for infant sons. Such immediate stimulation by vocalization, often responded to in kind by infants, as has been seen, could strongly affect the daughters' vocalizations over the long run.

In another, more recent study, this time of 18 male and 18 female infants, maternal language directed toward the infants was observed and recorded in their homes when they were 1, 3, and 8 months of age.[36] The frequency of infant vocalizations increased significantly with age, although maternal vocalization concomitantly decreased, becoming significantly less to the infants at 8 months than at 1 and 3 months. Furthermore, face-to-face talking reached a peak at 3 months and then tended to diminish. The more educated mothers did significantly more talking to their infants than did less educated mothers, and in both groups, firstborns were talked to more than later-born infants. However, the investigators reported with respect to sex differences that maternal language behavior toward infant sons and daughters "was not different and does not suggest any early input reason for language precocity in girls."

Class differences in maternal vocalization to infants were further explored in a study of the interactions of some 56 mothers with their firstborn 10-month-old baby girls made by Steven Tulkin and Jerome Kagan.[37] The general purpose of the study was to specify how, if at all, working-class and middle-class mother-infant interactions might differ. To this end, 26 of the mothers were working class, with either one or both of the parents having dropped out of high school and neither having attended college, or with the father an unskilled or semiskilled worker. Thirty of the mothers were middle class, with one or both parents having completed college and the father working in a professional job. The mothers' interactions with their babies were recorded in two-hour visits to their homes on two separate days.

Significant differences between the groups in nonverbal behavior were few and far between. Physical contact, kissing or holding of infants, prohibitions or restraints on the infants, and physical closeness of mothers and infants did not vary significantly between the classes. The middle-class mothers were face to face with their infants twice as often as were the working-class mothers and responded oftener to their infants' fretting. However, the infants responded as positively to working-class mothers as to middle-class mothers, touching their mothers or offering things to them almost equally in the two classes. Thus, the emotional climate was similar in both groups.

However, verbal behavior in the two groups of mothers was strikingly different. Middle-class mothers as a group offered their babies much more verbal fare than did working-class mothers, although there were individual differences within classes and thus no pattern of "deprivation" in working-class infants. Total middle-class maternal vocalizations to infants were over twice those of working-class mothers, as were face-to-face and reciprocal vocalizations— vocalizing back and forth with each other—even though the infants themselves showed no significant differences in their spontaneous vocalization rates. Every kind of vocalizing response was given significantly more by middle-class mothers, and they provided their infants with more stimulation of other kinds as well, entertaining their infants more often with play and games such as peek-a-boo and more frequently giving them things to keep them busy.

Informal interviews with the mothers after observations had been completed disclosed some of the reasons for the lesser cognitive stimulation provided the working-class infants. Some working-class mothers regarded their babies as incapable of communicating much with others or of expressing adultlike emotions. These mothers vocalized less to infants because they thought it a waste of time. Also, some were inhibited by the attitude prevailing at this socioeconomic level that it is ridiculous to talk to an infant. Many working-class mothers were fatalistic: A baby is born with a particular set of characteristics that a mother can do nothing to change. This feeling of powerlessness to influence their infants' development perhaps derived from a fatalism about being able to change anything in their own lives.

A number of investigators have looked into the differences between ordinary conversation and the ways in which adults talk to infants and young children. Utterances to infants are simple, containing very few subordinate clauses. The pitch of the voice is often higher than usual, and many greetings are given and questions are asked the babies by their caregivers.

In a recent study, Catherine Snow at the University of Amsterdam analyzed videotapes and audiotapes of the vocalizations of two infant-mother pairs at about six-week intervals from the age of 3 months onward.[38] She found that even when the babies were only 3 months old, their mothers were attempting to carry on conversations with them, although the babies' responses were limited to coos, cries, or grunts, or smiles, laughs, coughs, head turning, and so on. Even if the babies were obviously not paying attention, the mothers tended to interpret anything the baby did as a response.

To their 3-month-old infants the mothers talked primarily about the baby's behavior, needs, or intentions. The simplicity, brevity, and repetitiveness of the mothers' conversation appeared to derive from their efforts to produce a conversational back-and-forth with an immature conversational partner. Greetings and questions by the mothers enabled them to treat any of the babies' behavior as communicative responses, or to take the baby's conversational turns themselves when no infant response was forthcoming.

By 7 months of age, however, infants became more active partners in the conversations, listening to their mothers' comments and responding more appropriately. The mothers more often talked about objects or events to which they were jointly attending with their infants, rather than about the infants themselves. With babies of this age, mothers began to restrict their responses to the more speechlike vocalizations of their infants. This tendency increased as the babies developed, with mothers often repeating and expanding or infant babblings. By carrying on conversations with their babies in this manner, mothers gradually stimulated, shaped, and strengthened their babies' communicative capacities, the investigator said.

Adults, particularly caregivers, often respond to infant babbling and later speech utterances with baby talk—"itty-bitty" or "teenie" for little or tiny, "choo-choo" for train, "bye-bye" for going out, or "bow-wow" for dog, for instance. Called a "sublanguage system," baby talk is a part of almost every language. Its vocabulary is not a spur-of-the-moment creation, but is relatively stable, sometimes persisting for centuries. For example, the Roman grammarian Varro, in the second century B.C., cited the Latin words *bua, pappa,* and *naenia* as baby talk for "drink," "food," and "lullaby," and these terms, or variations thereof, are still prevalent in the baby talk of Mediterranean languages—Italian, Spanish, and Moroccan-Arabic—some 2000 years later.

Adult attitudes toward baby talk vary. Americans are often apologetic about it and may feel somewhat embarrassed in using it—even reluctant to give examples of it. Many feel it is inappropriate for men to use baby talk, and the opinion that it may actually hinder infants in learning to talk is widespread, even appearing in many books on child development. However, baby talk is used freely and without embarrassment in many other cultures, where it is believed to help infants acquire language. This was shown in an investigation of baby talk in six varied languages, Arabic, Marathi (Bombay Indian), Comanche (American Indian), Gilyak (Siberian), English (American), and Spanish.[39]

The study, which was carried out by Charles Ferguson at the Center for Applied Linguistics, Arlington, Virginia, revealed a surprising number of similar features in these six baby-talk sublanguages. Thus, complex clusters of consonants are often simplified in baby talk, as in "tummy" for "stomach." The rather difficult *r* is often replaced by another consonant, as "wabbit" for "rabbit." Consonants formed by the back of the tongue and soft palate are replaced by tip-of-the-tongue consonants, as in "tum on" for "come on." Other sounds are also simplified or substitutions are made for them, as in "oou" for "you" or "soos" for "shoes." And it is not only pronunciations that are simplified or made easier in baby talk; the grammar is simplified as well. Verbs are often dropped entirely, as in "dollie pretty" for "the doll is pretty," and nouns are used much more than verbs or pronouns. When a language has masculine and feminine forms, the gender may be reversed in expressing affection, using the feminine form for a male baby, for example.

While the speech variations of baby talk can be applied to any words, the study of the six languages showed that the baby-talk vocabulary is usually limited to anywhere from 25 to 60 words. The most common references are to kin (mother, father, baby), to body functions (food, drink, sleep, urination, defecation, bath, hurt, foot, breast, and genitals), to basic qualities of things (nice, bad, dirty, hot, cold, little), and to animals or games (dog, cat, bird, peek-a-boo, carry on back). However limited the vocabulary, it is adequate to cover most things that directly affect an infant.

Baby talk is usually uttered slowly, with marked emphases and frequent changes in inflection and intonation, with the voice rising or falling dramatically in pitch and much use of the lips. Part of words or whole words are often repeated ("din-din," "itty-bitty"). Grammar is made very simple, with certain parts of speech, such as prepositions, omitted altogether. Babies are thus presented with the bare bones of a language with only a basic vocabulary.

Observing that the features of baby talk in the six languages were also characteristic of children's speech before they begin to use sentences, Ferguson speculated that baby talk provides infants with a simple set of speech utterances that they can readily imitate as they begin to speak themselves. Baby talk seems calculated not to interfere with the learning of the standard vocabulary and can be discarded once the child learns the words of the language. And in fact, when adults are asked why they use baby talk, they will often reply that it is easier for the baby to understand than normal conversation. However, noting that in all six cultures adults used baby talk with infants long before they begin to speak—and to pets as well—Ferguson suggested that baby talk also serves to express feelings of protectiveness and affection.

CHAPTER 9
Nature and Nurture

Mothers and fathers, nurses, pediatricians, and developmental psychologists all agree that babies differ widely in their personal combinations of behavioral characteristics, though they have many characteristics in common. Babies manifest individuality as well as uniformity. In the few days that most newborns remain in the hospital nursery, nurses become familiar with the individual differences in the reactions of the babies in their care. And it takes only a week or so for parents to tell that this baby is "just like" or "not a bit like" one or another of their children.

Right after birth, differences in temperament are apparent in infants' reactions to sensory stimulation. This was shown in an experiment with 30 newborns whose responses to a soft and a loud tone, a cold metal disk pressed against the thigh, and a pacifier dipped in sugar were observed on the second, third, and fourth or fifth days of life.[1] The intensity with which the infants reacted to these stimuli was determined by observing the changes in the infant's bodily movements and rated on a scale from 0 (no observable response) to 5 (hard crying plus any activity, or intense overall activity). Responses to the pacifier were measured by the intensity of sucking, also on a five-point scale. Each newborn was tested three times with each stimulus on four occasions, and a median "intensity of response" to each of the stimuli was calculated from the total of 12 ratings.

When the data for all the infants were compared, consistent individual differences were found in the intensities of response to stimulation. Some infants would, for example, jump at a soft tone, while others would not move a muscle. In response to a loud tone, some infants would just wiggle a toe, but others would startle and cry loudly. Furthermore, infants tended to maintain their relative rankings no matter what the stimulus. For example, if infant A's intensity of response to the pacifier was the fourth highest in the group, he would be likely to be fourth in his response to the loud tone. Thus, the fourth highest rating could be identified a priori as infant A's. Finally, the infants' median ratings remained relatively stable from the first through the fourth sessions—infants who responded vigorously on their second day of life were still responding vigorously on their fourth or fifth day.

The characteristic intensity of response is one feature of infant behavior that enables us to distinguish infant temperaments, one from another, so that we regard some babies as easygoing and placid and others as "live wires." But the placid baby and the live wire are not distinguishable only because one is imperturbable and the other "jumpy." Additional features of behavior that express an infant's temperament have been identified in a long-term study carried out by two child psychiatrists in New York City, Alexander Thomas and Stella Chess, with several colleagues.[2,3]

In preliminary observations of young infants, Thomas and Chess had found nine distinct features of behavior, or characteristics as they called them, which when evaluated in individual infants, sharply differentiated one infant's from another's. Then, using parents' answers to a series of standard questions relating to these characteristics in their own infants, together with observations in the home, Thomas, Chess, and their colleagues followed a group of some 130 individuals from the age of 2 to 3 months through high school—and now even through college, for the study is still going on. The overall objective of their study has been to determine whether or not infant temperaments persist into adult life.

These nine characteristics can be briefly described and exemplified: *Activity level,* rated as high, medium, or low, refers to the vigor of an infant's movements while being dressed, handled, bathed and fed (and later, when reaching, crawling, and walking), as well as to the relative proportions of active and inactive periods as in the sleep-awake cycle. A parent would indicate a high level of activity with such statements as "She's impossible to dress, she squirms so," and a low activity level, "In the bath he lies quietly and doesn't kick." *Rhythmicity* of behavior covers the degree of regularity of repeated functions, such as feeding and sleeping, rated as very regular, varying, or irregular. A baby who falls asleep at about the same time each night and wakes up about the same time every morning would be described as very regular, for example.

Approach or *withdrawal* relates to the baby's reactions to anything new, such as a new toy, food he has never eaten before, or the approach of a stranger. It is rated as positive approach, partial withdrawal, or withdrawal. A parent's statement that "He always smiles at strangers" would be rated positive approach, and "It takes him a long time to warm up to a new toy," as withdrawal. *Adaptability* is the ease with which infant behavior in new or changed situations can be successfully modified in desired directions. The infant is rated as very adaptable, slowly adaptable, or nonadaptable. The infant of a parent who says "He used to spit out cereal whenever I gave it to him, but now he takes it fairly well" shows adaptability. Infants are assessed as nonadaptable on the basis of such parental statements as "Whenever I put her snowsuit on she screams and struggles."

Intensity of reaction is equivalent to the intensity of response studied in newborns and is rated as low, mild, or intense and characterized as negative or positive. An intense positive reaction is exemplified by "Whenever she hears music she begins to laugh and to jump up and down in time to it," and an intense negative reaction by "He cries whenever the sun shines in his eyes." On the other hand, *threshold of responsiveness,* rated as high or low, refers to the intensity of sensory stimulation required to elicit a discernible reaction. A high threshold for visual stimuli and a low threshold for auditory stimuli would be indicated by a parent's saying, "You can shine a bright light in his eyes and he doesn't even blink, but if a door closes he startles and looks up."

Distractibility is again related to response to stimulation. The behavior of a distractible infant can be altered or interfered with easily, but that of a nondistractible infant is difficult to change. An infant who stops crying when picked up is distractible, for example, but nondistractible if he keeps on crying when picked up or given a toy.

Quality of mood refers to the general emotional quality of an infant's behavior. Moods are rated as positive, slightly negative, or negative. A parent's statement that "Whenever we put him to bed he cries for about 5 to 10 minutes before falling asleep" would be assessed as negative, but "Whenever he sees me begin to warm his bottle he begins to smile and coo" as positive.

Finally, *attention span* and *persistence* distinguish babies' temperaments. The attention span is the length of time an infant continues with a particular activity; persistence is the length of time the infant will continue when faced with obstacles. Both are rated high or low. If an infant continues pouring water from a glass into the tub for a long time, his attention span would be judged high, and if he continues despite his mother's saying "No," his persistence would rate high as well. Some infants will struggle to make a toy work, for example, and have a high tolerance for frustration, while others will give up at the slightest difficulty.

When Thomas and Chess looked for any natural groupings of these temperamental characteristics, they found certain clusters that seemed to differentiate three types of infant temperaments: the "easy" baby, the "slow-to-warm-up" baby, and the "difficult" baby. Easy babies are very regular and predictable, approach rather than withdraw from new situations, are very adaptable, have a moderate or low intensity of reaction, and are positive in mood. An easy baby soon settles into regular feeding and sleeping schedules, is cheerful and good-natured, and quickly adapts to new persons, foods, situations, and routines.

Infants with difficult temperaments, on the other hand, are irregular in rhythmicity, tend to withdraw when first encountering new situations, adapt only slowly to changes in their environments, are usually intense in their responses, and are generally negative in mood. They vary in activity level, threshold of responsiveness, distractibility, and attention span and persistence. Such babies may often be irregular in their feeding and sleeping habits, slow to accept new foods, toys, or persons, and adjust to new routines only very gradually. They cry quite often, their laughter tends to be louder than normal, and their low tolerance for frustration often sends them into a tantrum.

In between the easy and the difficult babies are those slow to warm up. They have a low to moderate activity level, tend to withdraw when first faced with a new situation, are slow to adapt, have mildly intense reactions, and are slightly negative in their moods. Their rhythmicity varies, as does their distractibility and attention span, and their threshold of responsiveness may be either high or low.

In this sizable group of infants followed over long periods of time, the researchers identified the easy temperaments in some 40 percent of the babies, the slow-to-warm-up temperaments in 15 percent, and the difficult temperaments in some 10 percent. The remaining third of the babies were not readily classifiable, and the investigators did not attempt to squeeze these infants into the Procrustean bed of their types. And, of course, even difficult babies are not always difficult, nor easy babies always easy. Furthermore, the temperamental characteristics of individual babies sometimes change, the investigators discovered as they followed the infants into childhood. Even basic traits of temperament may not be immutable. And they foresee the possibility that they may find that "inconsistency in temperament is itself a basic characteristic in some children." But, on the whole they found that temperaments remain stable and that difficulties in infancy are predictive of later difficulties. Thus, problems requiring psychiatric attention developed later in life in some 70 percent of the difficult babies, but in only 18 percent of the easy babies.

Easy babies respond favorably to various kinds of handling because of their adaptability.[4] However, their ability to adapt to a variety of caregiver routines may lead to later stresses because they have absorbed these routines so thoroughly that they find it difficult to adjust to different routines outside the home, say in day-care situations or in schools. Finding routines to which difficult babies will adapt requires great patience, effort, and tolerance on the part of the parents. If parents are impatient, inconsistent, or punitive, difficult infants are likely to react negatively. Since easy infants quickly fall into regular sleeping and feeding routines, they will work out very well on a self-demand feeding schedule, but difficult babies, whose crying may express negative feelings more than hunger, are most effectively fed on a set and consistent schedule. Similarly, easy infants will turn from breast or bottle feeding to cup and spoon feeding with equanimity, but difficult babies may require many repeated trials before they adapt to weaning. Slow-to-warm-up babies, on the other hand, need to be permitted—and encouraged—to approach weaning or any new situations at their own pace. Otherwise, they may withdraw or become extremely negative.

Summing up their experience with these infants, the investigators concluded that there is no one formula that can be applied to the rearing of every child. "The individual temperament of the child and the suitability of the practice applied must always be considered." [4]

In 1975, Stella Chess told a *New York Times* reporter that she and her associates were still following up the people they had observed in infancy.[5] Seventy of them, then of college age, had been interviewed, and it was apparent that their characteristic ways of behaving had not changed. Some had turned out "magnificently"; others had turned out "very, very sadly." The parents' job, Dr. Chess observed, "is to understand the child's temperament and learn to deal with it sensibly."

The focus of their observations and their conclusions may appear to put Thomas, Chess, and their colleagues on the "nature" side of the nature versus nurture controversy. But they firmly reject both extremes, believing that the development of a personality is a complex process in which temperament and environment constantly interact.

Of all the environmental influences that shape an infant's development, perhaps the most pervasive are the folkways and mores of the culture into which the infant is born. This was revealed very clearly in a comparative study of the child-rearing practices in 30 Japanese and 30 American middle-class urban families.[6] Most of the families were nuclear, consisting of father, mother, and baby, their firstborn. The babies ranged in age from 3 to 4 months, and the ratio of male to female infants was 15:15 in the American group and 18:12 in the Japanese group. The American families, who were at least second-generation, of European ancestry, and all white, lived in the greater metropolitan area of Washington, D.C., and the Japanese families in the rather traditional city of Kyoto or the more modern Tokyo.

The mothers were told that the researchers were interested in the everyday lives of infants in different countries and were asked to carry on their normal activities in their homes during observation. The observers, both married women of their respective cultures, recorded the activities of mother and infant at four-minute intervals during two four-hour observation periods on two successive days. If mothers went outdoors with their babies, the observers followed, always merging into the background and remaining as unobtrusive as possible.

The investigators found that the behavior of female and male infants within each group was remarkably similar. In neither group did the sex of the baby produce differential infant behavior or differential handling on the part of the mothers. The American male infants played with toys slightly more than the girls, and American mothers were slightly more affectionate with their male than with their female babies, but the correlations were not high.

In caring for their infants' physical needs, Japanese and American mothers treated their babies similarly—there were no significant differences in the frequency of feeding, diapering, or dressing the infants. The mothers in the two groups were as affectionate—patting, kissing, talking to, and playing with their babies with equal frequency. It was in the style rather than the amount of mothering that major differences were observed.

Japanese mothers typically spent more time with their babies than did the American mothers, and soothed their babies more, carrying them in their arms and rocking them more. Their approach to communication with their babies was more physical than verbal. The mothers' interventions appeared to be directed toward keeping the babies content and quiet. The Japanese value reticence: "One treats one's mouth like a guarded jar," a Japanese proverb advises. American mothers, on the other hand, seemed to want their babies to be active and vocal. They gave them more stimulation than the Japanese mothers provided their babies. They adjusted or positioned their infants' bodies more, looked at them more, and spent less time in soothing them.

Furthermore, the infants' behavior seemed to fit the styles and expectations of their mothers. As compared with the Japanese babies, the American babies were more active physically, more happily vocal, and explored their bodies and the things around them more often. American babies sucked their fingers more or brought other things to their mouths more and played more with toys and other objects. Japanese babies were generally passive, more active than American babies only in their unhappy vocalizations.

American mothers' chatting with their babies was correlated significantly with the babies' happy vocalizations, but not so for Japanese mothers, who chatted when their babies were vocalizing unhappily—the Japanese mothers used vocalization for soothing their infants, the American mothers for stimulating and responding to theirs. This difference in the functions of vocalization exemplifies the contrast in the child-rearing styles of the two groups—a contrast that had its counterpart in the infants: Japanese infants were more unhappily vocal when alone, while American infants left alone tended to be playful and to vocalize happily.

In concluding their report, the investigators did not hesitate to attribute the ethnic differences they had found in their study to cultural influences:

> We feel that the most parsimonious explanation of our findings is that a great deal of cultural learning has taken place by three-to-four months of age, and that our babies have learned by this time to be Japanese and American babies in relation to the expectations of their mothers concerning their behavior. . . . If these distinctive patterns of behavior are well on the way to being learned by three-to-four months of age, and if they continue over the life span of the person, then there are likely to be important areas of difference in emotional response in people in one culture when compared with those in another.

The statistical relationships between caretaking styles and infant behavior found in this study do not necessarily exclude the possible effect of inborn factors. The similarities in the behavior of mothers and infants might also derive from their similar genetic background. If this hypothesis is correct, ethnic differences in behavior might be apparent at birth.

Some evidence that these differences are in fact present was obtained in an investigation of 24 Chinese-American and 24 American infants of European ancestry tested with the Brazelton Assessment Scale shortly after birth.[7] The average age of these infants was 34 hours (range, 5 to 75 hours), and their average five-minute Apgar scores were comparable and high. The European-American infants had a somewhat higher average birth weight, but it was determined by a statistical procedure that this would not bias the findings. There were 11 male and 13 female infants in each ethnic group.

The infants' scores on the Brazelton scale were essentially equivalent on tests for neurological status, sensory development, central nervous system maturity, motor development, and social responsiveness. However, on certain tests that are indicative of temperament, the group averages differed significantly.

The temperamental differences between the groups can be generally expressed in terms of excitability versus imperturbability. Thus, as compared with the Chinese-American group, the European-American infants tended to cycle back and forth more rapidly between upset or excitement and contentment or placidity. Again, when a cloth was placed over the infants' faces as they lay on their backs and was held there, the European-American babies immediately tried to remove it by swiping toward it with their hands and by lifting their heads or turning them to the side. The Chinese-American babies typically lay still and, when placed supine, would lie impassively with their faces to the bedding, although infants in both groups had been shown to be equally capable of holding their heads steadily upright when they were pulled to a sitting position.

The Chinese-American infants became habituated to a flashlight repeatedly shone at their closed eyes when sleeping more rapidly than did the European-American infants. Both groups of babies cried an equal amount of time on the average, but the Chinese-American babies stopped crying almost immediately on being picked up and talked to and also tended to stop crying sooner without soothing. Thus, they were more easily consolable and better at self-comforting than the European-American infants. All in all, the European-American infants were more changeable, active, and excitable; the Chinese-American infants more predictable, imperturbable, and passive.

The findings of these cross-cultural studies must be viewed as preliminary, for they leave many questions unanswered. For example, would Chinese infants born, say, in Canton, China, have the same kind of temperaments as Chinese-American newborns? If Japanese infants were studied at birth, would their behavior have the same characteristics as it does at 3 or 4 months of age? Are there temperamental differences between infants of other ethnic groups?

One other variable that may be involved in these ethnic differences is the kind or amount of physical activity that is characteristic of pregnant women in different cultures. It has been suggested that "the placidity of the Chinese baby at birth ... may be at least partly a response to the gait and movement patterns of Oriental women."[8] In the industrialized West, women on the whole engage in much less strenuous physical labor than do women in preliterate and in traditional societies. This may provide the fetus with quite a different prenatal environment and adapt it to quite a different level of stimulation, which may explain in part why Chinese-American and Japanese babies are often unresponsive to levels of stimulation that arouse or excite infants of Western origin.

During the late 1950s, a group of American anthropologists lived for six months to a year in villages in a number of preliterate or "undeveloped" societies with the explicit aim of exploring relationships between cultural child-rearing patterns and subsequent differences in temperaments.[9] Some of their observations will be described here.

The Gusii, a dark-brown Negroid tribe living near the equator in western Kenya, Africa, practice polygyny (in which a man may have more than one wife), with four wives considered the ideal. The Gusii economy is agricultural. Gusii men concentrate on clearing the bush for fields, plowing, building fences and houses, and looking after the cattle. The women plant, weed, harvest the crops (largely millet and maize), and do the cooking. Each married woman lives in her own thatched hut with her children, while husbands divide their time between (or among) co-wives.

Several older women serve as midwives at births, and mothers go back to full-time work in the fields within a month. Mothers breast-feed their infants on demand, usually responding to their cries within a few minutes. Infants sleep with their mothers and lie on a cloth in the hut during the day. The cloth also serves for wrapping and carrying the infants, who are not diapered but wiped off with soft leaves. When mothers are away, in the fields or at market, infants are cared for by child-nurses (usually their older sisters) 6 to 10 years old. Nurses may feed the infants a thin gruel or carry the baby to the fields for the mother to nurse. Infants used to be force-fed the gruel by holding their noses and pushing the gruel into their mouths. But missionaries have discouraged this practice, and it is now rarely seen.

Beyond feeding their babies, mothers give them very little attention. They tend to nurse their infants rather mechanically, while talking with others or busying themselves with their many tasks. The child-nurses are a little more attentive: When an infant has a long crying spell, nurses may shake or jostle him up and down, sometimes tapping his body. Fathers rarely hold their babies or pay any attention to them. Mothers and child-nurses are the principal caregivers, although co-wives will occasionally look out for older infants when the mother is away.

Minimal as it is, infants receive the greatest amount of attention in the period from birth to weaning. They are not trained, for they are believed incapable of learning. (A similar belief is held by some lower-class mothers in the United States.) Parents worry a lot about their infants' health and survival because infant mortality is so high. Medicine men may be called in to treat diarrhea or other illnesses with potions or with small incisions in the infants' bodies. Babies are born with light brown skins that gradually darken. Until this happens, they are believed to be especially sensitive to the "evil eye." After a glance from the evil eye, bits of things like grain, feathers, or flowers are thought to stick to the babies' light skins and penetrate their viscera, killing them. When such bits are found on infants, they are rubbed with clarified butter, and even the smallest bits are meticulously removed. Infants have hot blood, it is believed, and this makes them weak and fearful of the cold. To harden them, infants are exposed to the cold and rarely wear even a shirt. Boys and girls are treated much alike in infancy, but girls, not boys, may have a string of beads around the abdomen.

Infants are pacified whenever they cry by nursing, feeding of gruel, or shaking. Toward the end of infancy, they may also be quieted or controlled by fear. Mothers or nurses may tell babies that a dog, cow, chicken, or even an insect is about to eat them up, or that strangers will take them away. These mothers, the observers said, make "a determined attempt . . . to frighten their children with animals and strangers in order to make them more subject to parental control." And they noted that this "fear training" begins before the children can speak and "is one of the first kinds of verbal cues learned by the infant."

Infants are encouraged to stand and begin to walk by about 12 months of age, since they must become more independent of their mothers and child-nurses before the next baby is born. However, mothers try to avoid conception until the baby is walking. If they become pregnant, they soon wean their babies in preparation for the next one.

Adults of the tribe are afraid of the dark and the animals abroad at night, so they stay close to or in their huts after dark. But the results of fear training are evident much earlier. The child that emerges from infancy, the observers said, is "a dependent, fearful individual," who, although he is able to demand food or protection from his mother and other caregivers, is "unaggressive, quiet, and timid in his approach to the physical environment and to strange things."

Quite different conditions and treatment are encountered by infants born into a farming community in the state of Oaxaca in southern Mexico, a mountainous region bordering on the Pacific. The Mixtecan Indian language is used in this community, although most adults speak some Spanish as occasional contacts in town demand it. The extended families live around a courtyard in one-room adobe houses, windowless and with only one door, although women have their own preserve in the cook shacks where food is prepared. Man and wife form cooperative monogamous units with their children, with the husband's brothers and parents in other houses around the courtyard, or other families, as the case may be. Husbands work in the fields raising corn, beans, and squash, and tending the farm animals. Equality of husband and wife in energy for work and in dominance is the ideal. There is little open bickering or fighting, for the expression of strong emotions is avoided or controlled insofar as possible. Strong emotion is believed to cause illness and even death, in which sorcerers, improper diets, and the evil eye are also implicated. Thus, it is considered essential to keep infants from becoming frightened or angry.

Midwives preside over births, after which mothers must rest in bed for about 40 days, or at least stay in the house and do no hard work. For the first eight days, newborns are held by their mothers, although they may be placed briefly in cradles to sleep during the day. They are always covered with a cloth, usually the rebozo (shawl) worn by the women and also used for carrying babies. For about 10 months, infants at all times are swaddled lightly in a square of cloth from the neck down.

Only members of the immediate household can look at the baby, since visitors might possess the evil eye. Particularly during the infant's first month or two, parents watch him for signs of fever or vomiting, which may indicate that the evil eye has cast its spell. To ward off the evil eye, older infants are entirely covered while sleeping, or completely wrapped in the rebozo when taken out. Later, they may wear a brief shirt and a diaper. For the first year, infants are wrapped and carried prone in the rebozo, with no part of their bodies exposed to the air or the view of others. Babies are believed to be very weak, especially in the neck and backbone, so they are not put to the shoulder until they can hold up their heads steadily. They are "like a tender flower—you might break the stem," mothers say.

The mother is the infant's primary caregiver for the first four to five months. Later, older sisters, cousins, or a grandmother may help to care for him. During the first 40 days, newborns sleep with the mother and father. Mothers give infants the breast at the slightest cry, cuddle and rock them, and give them sponge baths on occasion. Mothers, and nurses as well, are demonstrative and express their affection for the infants openly and often. Fathers are generally affectionate with their babies, but they are away most of the day and are not considered responsible for their care. They may pick up and jounce their babies a little in the evening, but otherwise, females are the caregivers. Male and female infants are treated much the same.

The Mixtecan word for infant translates as "darkness," its antonym, "awareness," as "This child now knows." Since "awareness" is a consequence of weaning, no attempt is made to teach babies anything until they are weaned at the age of 1 or 2 years. To wean their babies, mothers put bitter herbs or dirt on their breasts and otherwise try to hurry the process along. The Mixtecans believe that the "awareness," as well as the ability to reason, develops slowly and naturally, without assistance from adults. Children are considered incapable of reasoning until they reach the age of 7, and until then, their behavior is not considered subject to moral judgment. After the onset of "awareness," infants are occasionally scolded, ridiculed, or even hit to control their behavior, but for the most part, training and discipline are postponed until children have arrived at the "age of reason."

The goal of infant care in this society, the observers said, is "[adjustment] without friction . . . and if this proves to be impossible, withdrawal rather than domination is the answer." Reared in this atmosphere, infants have even, cheerful temperaments, are placid, have no extreme mood swings, and are free of emotional disturbances.

The Mixtecan infants receive considerably more care and affection than do infants whose present reincarnation takes place in the Hindu Rājpūt Indians, farmers who live in the village of Khalapur, which is north of New Delhi and close to the Himalayas. There is considerable separation of the sexes in this group, since the men spend much of their time with their cattle, and the women remain in their brick or adobe houses surrounding courtyards. Women cover their faces in the presence of men, including their husbands, and hold a largely subordinate position, preparing food, weaving cloth, feeding their babies, and performing countless other household tasks. People in the village are viewed more as members of the group than as individuals in their own right, for in terms of their religion, Hinduism, the individual life is just one of countless reincarnations through which the soul passes, always governed by Karma, the fate that determines everyone's destiny. The same beliefs are predominant in their treatment of their infants.

The Rājpūt Indians think of their newborn infants as pure and holy. Since they cannot learn, they cannot distinguish good from evil and so can commit no sins. Infants are not considered teachable until they learn to speak. Mothers breast-feed, wash, dress, and otherwise care for their own babies, although children or elderly men too feeble for field work occasionally serve as nurses. Babies sleep with their mothers for several years or until a new baby comes along. Their health is a matter of great concern, since infant mortality is high. Babies are believed especially open to the evil eye and to "ghost sickness," an affliction caused by ghosts sticking to the babies' skins and possessing them. To ward off the evil eye for their first few weeks, infants wear a black dot on the forehead or foot, but it is often worn for years. For further protection from the evil eye, infants are covered with cloths or blankets when placed in their cots and wrapped in the sari when they are carried.

Babies are given little attention until they cry, when their mothers nurse them or otherwise try to pacify them. Mothers occasionally give their babies opium to quiet them, but most mothers realize that opium is not suitable for a baby and do so only as a last resort. Babies are not diapered, and mothers are casual about their urination; it will dry, they say. However, they try to anticipate the infants' bowel movements and clean them up afterward. Mothers or nurses attend to the babies' needs, but largely to keep them quiet, and they give babies little stimulation or affection—and the babies have few toys. The lives of babies are peaceful and largely free of stress, but they are never the center of attention, and mothers would not think of showing them off for fear of arousing envy. A jealous person is particularly likely to cast the evil eye on an infant. For this reason, people in general avoid looking at infants.

Infants are weaned by the age of 1 or 2 years and may be started on gruel or bits of bread from the age of 6 months on. As they grow, they tend to behave in the passive manner with which they are treated, dependent on others and merging in with the family group rather than standing out as individuals in their own right. They learn to crawl and walk without pressure or encouragement from adults. Mothers or nurses carry them on their hips as they work with others in their courtyards, but babies are observers, not active participants, in the busy life going on around them. They are not cuddled and played with. Adults display little affection for children of any age. So infants can always feel secure members of their group, their physical needs satisfied when they fuss or cry, but they are never treated as individuals.

Lack of attention and affection is far from the norm for babies born into native Philippine farming families in the country north of Manila on the island of Luzon. The people speak Ilocano, one of the Malayo-Polynesian family of languages. Rice is their staple crop and food, although they also raise fruits and vegetables, keep pigs and chickens, and raise native tobacco. Each household has its own papaya tree. Homes are grass-thatched huts with bamboo walls and are raised several feet above the ground. Women grow the rice plants from seeds and transplant them to the rice paddies, care for the pigs and chickens, and prepare the meals, which keeps them constantly busy. Marriage is monogamous and families are stable.

After birth, mother and child must stay in bed for from 11 to 30 days, with the mother getting up only for elimination. Babies can be touched with nothing cold and are wrapped and capped and kept covered with a blanket. During this period and later, visitors come in to see, pat, and fondle the baby. If other women are busy with planting or harvesting, the husband takes care of his wife, builds the fires, cooks, and washes as necessary. Mothers must follow strict dietary regimens for five months to be sure of an adequate milk supply.

Babies must be watched carefully to be sure they are not bewitched by ancestral or other evil spirits. When babies cry, they are always fed and often cuddled. These babies, the observers said, "are helpless, irresponsible, charming little creatures, hence they are quickly nurtured, carefully protected, and smothered with affection" by one and all. Unless asleep, they are held, rocked, bounced, patted, and crooned to. They sleep with their parents until the next baby is born, usually after about 2 years. As babies grow older, other women in the household or child-nurses may look after them when mothers are busy.

Fathers are as affectionate with their babies as are mothers or other women. Fathers may hold their babies, bathe them, change their clothes, feed them tidbits, and play with them. Infants are fully weaned usually at the age of 2 to 3 years. They are not particularly urged to crawl, walk, or talk. Parents and others are very indulgent of and affectionate toward them, giving them constant attention and making few demands. The prevailing attitude toward babies seems to be that "They do what they will. It is of no use to press them. They do not yet understand what is wanted. This is a time for parents to be patient. Their turn will come later when there is more understanding."

Sociability is perhaps the key characteristic of these Filipino infants, a result of their many interactions with others. Young children often play peek-a-boo with the babies, holding a cloth, or just their hands, before the face. Although toys are rare, the babies are constantly attended to, cared for, and played with. The observers noted that the Filipino infant is more passive than the average American infant, but exhibits a "far greater pleasure in sociable interaction with others of any age." These babies respond with delight to large numbers of people with whom they are familiar and are "socialized" very rapidly. Their interest is in people, not in things.

However, weaning, at 2 to 3 years of age, is an unhappy experience for these infants. Their mothers strictly follow a custom of stopping their nursing all at once, and this "cold-turkey" treatment results in intense crying and unhappiness for a few days, followed by a sullen, whining period lasting several weeks more as the babies gradually adapt to the catastrophe that has befallen them. When the babies are weaned, mothers will no longer hold them in their laps, driving the babies away with scolding and threats. The babies may be soothed by child-nurses or other women in the family, and gradually they join with other children in play and settle down.

Giving little affection and little more than perfunctory attention, using fear as a disciplinary measure, the Gusii rear infants who tend to be passive, dependent, and fearful. The Mixtecans keep their infants "under wraps," restricting their activity, but protect them against strong emotions such as fear and anger and offer them much affection. Their infants, like themselves, are even-tempered and emotionally restrained. The Rājpūts treat their infants as members of a group and in an offhand manner, caring only for their physical needs. They show their infants little affection and are indifferent to their development as individuals. The infants they raise are passive, dependent, and lacking in individuality. The Filipino natives rear their infants with permissiveness, affection, and constant attention, and their every need is instantly satisfied. Although very sociable and outgoing, their infants are overly dependent on others.

Certain broad similarities are evident when these child-rearing practices are compared with one another. Because of the ubiquitous evil eye and other malevolent influences, parents in all these societies are constantly anxious about their infants' health. As a result, warding off evil spirits is an important ingredient of infant care. Where nothing is known about what causes disease, attributing it to a supernatural agency is a natural impulse. From "The baby was fine until so-and-so came in and looked at him," it is not so unreasonable to infer that the evil eye has done its work.

In all these cultures, the basic needs of the infants for food and protection are largely satisfied, and mothers customarily breast-feed their babies. However, mothers are very casual about hygiene, and diapers are in short supply. All the infants sleep with the mother or both parents, although affectionate interactions with them vary. In most of these societies, fathers and other males hold themselves aloof from babies, leaving infant care up to the mothers or their female assistants. However, there is little differential handling of male and female infants. Mothers soon turn over some of the responsibility for infant care to child-nurses or other women in their widely extended families. Thus, girls in these societies have experience in caring for infants before they become mothers, which rarely happens in industrialized societies.

Infants who have few toys, no mobiles over their cribs (or no cribs), no music boxes, no picture books, and illiterate parents who do not teach them anything might justifiably be said to be "culturally deprived." Yet evidence has been accumulating over the past two decades that infant development in undeveloped societies is, for a period at least, advanced over infant development in the "civilized" societies of the industrial West. This precocity has also been observed in mixed cultures, such as that of the Kikuyus, in which Westernized and tribal life-styles exist side by side.

The Kikuyu people live some 25 miles from Nairobi, the capital city of Kenya, in a predominantly agricultural community. Some Kikuyu follow traditional tribal ways, which may include the practice of polygamy. Others, much influenced by their contacts with the large urban center of Nairobi, have been educated to varying degrees and work at skilled jobs or farm their own land, sometimes consisting of two acres or more.

To explore the possible effects of these socioeconomic differences on infant development in this community, a group of investigators tested 65 Kikuyu infants at two-month intervals with the Bayley Scales of Infant Development.[10] The Bayley Scales have been thoroughly standardized with large populations of infants in the United States and have been used extensively in Europe and other countries around the world to study intercultural differences in infant development. They consist of two parts: a mental scale, which assesses perceptual and sensory functions, and a motor scale, which tests neuromuscular function. Since the study group consisted of infants born in the six-month period before testing began, the infants had their first test either at birth or when they were approximately 1 to 6 months old. Thereafter, they were tested every two months on four to eight occasions. Thus, scores were available for the first through the fifteenth months.

On both the mental and the motor tests, the Kikuyu infants were precocious, scoring significantly higher than would be expected for American infants of the same ages. As compared with the standard score of 100 that American infants average on these tests, the average Kikuyu mental score was 108, and their average motor score, 129. The Kikuyu infants bettered the standard score on 33 mental-scale items and on 20 motor-test items. They were lower than the standard on only seven of the mental-test items and two of the motor-test items. However, the researchers were under the impression that these items involved implements that are familiar to American infants but not familiar to Kikuyus. When Kikuyu infant test scores month by month were compared with month-by-month scores for white infants in the

United States and the United Kingdom, and black infants in the United States, the Kikuyu infants performed better on both mental and motor tests throughout the 15-month period of observation than did any of these other groups. However, the superiority of their performance tapered off somewhat toward the end of the period.

A number of reports have suggested that subequatorial African infants are precocious in their motor development and possibly also in their mental development, and this study appears to confirm these reports. However, the major objective of this study was to determine whether or not differences in psychological development—and effects on precocity, if any—were related to socioeconomic factors. Such a relationship was found when indicators of socioeconomic status such as income, educational level of the father, and modern amenities in the home were compared with the infants' test scores. Higher scores, both on the mental and motor scales, were found among infants from families with greater economic resources, more educated fathers, and amenities in the home, such as clocks, calendars, and books.

Higher motor scores were also correlated with the number of people 40 to 60 years of age in the household. Infants from homes with two or more people in this age group had the highest scores, and those with no one in this age group in their homes had the lowest. The investigators suggested that an older person in the home would supplement the mother's caregiving activities and would thus give the infant a further opportunity for motor development.

Although the investigators were able to conclude that socioeconomic class, even in this transitional community, influenced test scores, they had no definitive explanation for the overall precocity of Kikuyu infants, nor could they explain why the degree of precocity is affected by environmental factors.

Investigators have found developmental precocity in literally dozens of cultures around the world—in other tribes in Africa and in many societies in Latin America and Asia.[11] In preindustrial communities in these regions, the infants are more advanced than Caucasian infants both in mental and motor development. This precocity is most marked at birth and for the first six months of life. At birth, the sensory-perceptual and motor development of these infants is equal to that of American and European infants 3 to 4 weeks of age. In Africa and Latin America motor development in premature infants weighing less than 5.5 pounds has been found equivalent to that in a full-term Caucasian infant. And the brain waves of newborn African infants suggest a more mature central nervous system than that found in Caucasian infants.

A number of common features in the first year of life of all these precocious infants have been identified: many caregivers, usually in extended families; breast feeding on demand; fairly constant contact with caregivers either in sleeping or in being held and carried; lack of restrictive clothing and of set routines for feeding, elimination, and sleeping; and frequent stimulation from adult activities carried on in the infant's presence. Some or all of these features, along with genetic factors, may contribute to the precocity of these infants.

During the last six months of their first year, however, the precocity of many of these infants begins to diminish. This may be related to the introduction of solid food to supplement breast milk, with greater probable exposure to bacteria and a reduction in the quality of the diet. By 2 years of age—and probably accentuated by the completion of weaning, which is sometimes abrupt—scores of these infants have usually dropped below those of infants reared in the industrialized West.

Infants in preliterate or traditional cultures are not always precocious, nor is precocity unknown in the West. In Japan and Mexico, for example, where infants are reared quite passively and are kept bundled up, motor development in the early months of life is about equal to—or may be less than—that of Western infants at the same period. Similarly, upper-middle-class infants in some Westernized urban cultures in Africa are less precocious during the first year of life than are traditionally reared infants. And, as in Western infants, their development accelerates during their second year. As compared with infants in traditional or preliterate societies, they are breast-fed less frequently and for shorter periods, live in smaller and nuclear families, and usually sleep alone in their cribs rather than with the mother and father.

During the first year, the mental development of American black infants is equal to that of white infants, but their motor development is precocious. After the first year, their motor development begins to fall below that of white infants. Black infants reared in permissive families are even more precocious. In Israel, infants in the kibbutz are precocious until they are weaned at the age of 10 to 15 months. Precocity found in ethnic groups in developed countries, however, is not as great as that in rural, preindustrial societies.

Overall, the greatest precocity has been found in black infants, both in Africa and in the United States, followed by Indian infants in Latin America and infants in Asia. Caucasian infants rate lowest on the precocity scale. Within each ethnic group, infants reared in a permissive manner typical of preindustrial societies, with many caregivers, had higher developmental scores than those reared by the more restrictive Western methods, although their scores sharply declined after weaning. This decline seems to be related to the termination of breast feeding, which may occur suddenly, and the simultaneous reduction in stimulation provided by physical closeness to the mother. However, the root causes of these declines in precocity have not yet been determined. Nor is it clear whether genetic or environmental factors, or combinations of both, account for precocity.

Between 1969 and 1971, Melvin Konner of Harvard University observed infants of !Kung hunter-gatherer bands who live in the Kalahari Desert in southern Africa.[12] These seminomads may provide hints of the adaptations our ancestors made over 99 percent of the period of human evolution. The !Kung mothers, carriers of their young like most higher primates, usually held their babies upright on the hip in slings. There the babies can nurse whenever they please, play with dangling beads, or watch the activities of the many children and adults around them. Under such conditions, the !Kung infants were clearly precocious in both neuromuscular and cognitive development when compared with infants of "advanced" cultures.

Although "the child plays and teaches himself" naturally as he matures, !Kung parents believe, they teach their infants to sit up, crawl, stand, and walk. The precocity may derive in part from this training and in part from the infants' constant physical contact with their mothers, their upright posture, and the stimulation provided by the crowd around them. In view of the special environment of these infants, Konner believes that the burden of proof falls on those who speculate that such precocity is genetically based. And he points out that infant caregiving practices in the isolated nuclear families of developed cultures may possibly have diverged too far from the natural conditions provided by hunter-gatherers like the !Kung, whose babies have the sling—and indulgence, stimulation, and nonrestriction.

Like the Mixtecan babies of Mexico, Guatemalan Indian infants, for a good share of their first year, are kept indoors in small, dark, windowless huts. Only when they can walk are they allowed outdoors. Guatemalan women do not work in the fields but spend their days at home preparing meals, weaving, and looking after their babies. They usually keep the baby in their laps, or in a cloth on their backs, or close to them on a floor mat or in a hammock. Mothers believe sun, air, and dust are harmful for their babies, so keep them inside, but rarely talk or play with them or permit them to crawl. However, these mothers are not intentionally neglecting their babies. They are simply rearing them in the manner customary in their culture. Whenever their infants cry, their mothers nurse them. This is their method for dealing with any signs of infant distress, and crying is minimal as a result. Thus, these infants are raised in a very limited, unstimulating environment, and it might be expected that this would be reflected in their development. Jerome Kagan and Robert Klein, who assessed the cognitive development of these infants, described them as follows:

> These infants are distinguished from American infants of the same age by their extreme motor passivity, fearfulness, minimal smiling, and, above all, extraordinary quietness. A few with pale cheeks and vacant stares had the quality of tiny ghosts.[13]

In cognitive tests of duration of attention, attainment of a sense of object permanence, and onset of stranger wariness or anxiety given at several intervals during their first year, these infants were far behind middle-class American infants tested at the same ages, sometimes by several months. Their unstimulating environment and lack of interactions with others had strongly affected their cognitive growth. However, when tests of cognitive development were given to 11-year-old Guatemalan children reared under the same conditions, their performance was comparable in all respects to that of middle-class American children of the same age. And, Kagan and Klein report, Guatemalan children at the age of 11 are "active," "gay," and "intellectually competent."

If it is assumed that the adverse effects of certain environments can never be overcome, the retardation seen in Guatemalan infants would be presumed to be irreversible. This would also be assumed by those who hold that an infant is born with a certain level of general intelligence that does not change. Since the normal cognitive development of the 11-year-old Guatemalan children refutes both of these assumptions, an alternative assumption is required. Noting that at each stage of cognitive development particular abilities emerge, Kagan and Klein propose that the cognitive abilities of preadolescence may emerge at the normal time no matter how early or late the cognitive abilities peculiar to infancy appeared. The time that these cognitive capacities emerge is influenced by environmental factors. Once Guatemalan infants are freed from the restrictive environment considered proper for infants in their culture, their cognitive development proceeds normally.

In the same report, the investigators tell the story of two American sisters who were given psychological tests on a number of occasions when they were between the ages of 4 and 9 years and tested again when they were 14 and 15 years old. The sisters had been restricted to a crib in a small bedroom from shortly after birth, since their mother, who had three older children, felt that she was unable to cope with two more. The infants were fed by their 8-year-old sister, but for 23 of the 24 hours of each day, they were left alone in the barren crib without toys or attention.

When the girls were 2.5 and 3.5 years old, their plight was discovered. Malnourished and severely retarded, they were removed from their home and admitted to a hospital. After a month there, they were placed with a middle-class couple who had several young children and lived in a rural area in Ohio. The younger sister responded with a steadily rising IQ and reached nearly normal scores on other psychological tests, but the older child did not recover to the same degree. However, at 14 and 15 years of age, the girls seemed much like any average rural Ohio adolescents in their behavior with others, despite their isolation in infancy and their consequent retardation.

Infants, then, are more resilient, more competent, more discriminative, and far more interested in us than we have assumed them to be. But they are also far more complex than we have imagined. And so, as snapshots of a gull sailing in the wind do not give a full picture of gull flight, the bits and pieces of knowledge gathered about infants cannot tell the whole story of their behavior as it develops during the first year. Still, even this fragmentary picture, so at variance with our preconceptions, cannot help but change the way we look at infants.

The tangled web woven by the interplay of environment and natural endowment has not been finally unraveled, but the conditions that stimulate or constrain an infant's psychological growth are gradually coming into focus. And we have discovered that respect for persons must begin at birth, for in the behavior of the newborn infant, the stamp of individuality is already apparent.

References

Preface

1. White, B. L. *Human Infants: Experience and Psychological Development.* Englewood Cliffs, N.J.: Prentice-Hall, 1971, p. 38.

Chapter 1: The Infant Reassessed

1. Steiner, J. E. The gustofacial response: Observation on normal and anencephalic newborn infants. In J. F. Bosma (Ed.), *Fourth Symposium on Oral Sensation and Perception: Development in the Fetus and Infant.* DHEW Publication No. (NIH) 73–546. Bethesda, Md.: U.S. Department of Health, Education, and Welfare, National Institutes of Health, 1973, pp. 254–310.

2. Steiner, J. E. Discussion paper: Innate discriminative human facial expressions to taste and smell stimulation. *Annals of the New York Academy of Sciences 237:* 229–233, 1974.

3. Eibl-Eibesfeldt, I. The Ethology of Man. In *Ethology: The Biology of Behavior.* New York: Holt, Rinehart and Winston, 1970.

4. Sternglanz, S. H., Gray, J. L., and Murakami, M. Adult preferences for infantile facial features: An ethological approach. *Animal Behaviour 25:* 108–115, 1977.

5. Fullard, W., and Reiling, A. M. An investigation of Lorenz's "Babyness." *Child Development 47:* 1191–1193, 1976.

6. Berman, P. W. Social context as a determinant of sex differences in adults' attraction to infants. *Developmental Psychology 12:* 365–366, 1976.

7. Haskins, R. Effect of kitten vocalizations on maternal behavior. *Journal of Comparative and Physiological Psychology 91:* 830–838, 1977.

8. Hall, G. S. Notes on the study of infants. *Pedagogical Seminar 1:* 127–138, 1891.

9. James, W. *The Principles of Psychology.* New York: Holt, 1890, p. 488.

10. Demany, L., McKenzie, B., and Vurpillot, E. Rhythm perception in early infancy. *Nature 266:* 718–719, 1977.

Chapter 2: Enter Infant

1. Avery, M. E. Some effects of altered environments—Relationships between space medicine and adaptations at birth. *Pediatrics 35:* 345–354, Feb. 1965.

2. Carmichael, L. The onset and early development of behavior. In P. H. Mussen (Ed.), *Carmichael's Manual of Child Psychology.* New York: John Wiley & Sons, 3d ed., 1970, pp. 447–563.

3. Boddy, K., and Robinson, J. S. External method for detection of fetal breathing in utero. *The Lancet 2:* 1231–1233, 1971.

4. Boddy, K. and Mantell, C. D. Observations of fetal breathing movements transmitted through maternal abdominal wall. *The Lancet 2:* 1219–1220, 1972.

5. Rudolph, A. M., and Heymann, M. A. Fetal and neonatal circulation and respiration. In J. H. Comroe, Jr. (Ed.), *Annual Review of Physiology.* Palo Alto, Ca.: Annual Reviews, Inc., 1974, pp. 187–207.

6. Humphrey, T. Postnatal repetition of human prenatal activity sequences with some suggestions of their neuroanatomical bases. In R. J. Robinson (Ed.), *Brain and Early Behaviour: Development in the Fetus and Infant.* New York: Academic Press, 1969, pp. 43–84.

7. Humphrey, T. Human prenatal activity sequences in the facial region and their relationship to postnatal developments. In R. T. Wertz (Ed.), *American Speech and Hearing Association (ASHA) Report No. 6, Patterns of Orofacial Growth and Development.* Washington, D.C.: American Speech and Hearing Association, 1971, pp. 19–37.

8. Freud, S. *General Introduction to Psychoanalysis.* New York: Liveright Publishing Corp., 1935, p. 344.

9. Karpf, F. B. *The Psychology and Psychotherapy of Otto Rank.* New York: Philosophical Library, 1953.

10. Leboyer, F. *Birth Without Violence.* New York: Alfred A. Knopf, 1975, pp. 6 and 20.

11. Spitz, R. A. *The First Year of Life: Psychoanalytic Study of Normal and Deviant Development of Object Relations.* New York: International Universities Press, 1965, pp. 38–39.

12. Apgar, V., Holaday, D. A., James, L. S., Weisbrot, I. M., and Berrien, C. Evaluation of the newborn infant—second report. *Journal of the American Medical Association 168:* 1985–1988, 1958.

13. Drage, J. S., Kennedy, C., and Schwarz, B. K. The Apgar score as an index of neonatal mortality—a report from the collaborative study of cerebral palsy. *Obstetrics and Gynecology 24:* 222–230, 1964.

14. Yang, R. K., Zweig, A. R., Douthitt, T. C., and Federman, E. J. Successive relationships between maternal attitudes during pregnancy, analgesic medication during labor and delivery, and newborn behavior. *Developmental Psychology 12:* 6–14, 1976.

15. Desmond, M. M., et al. The clinical behavior of the newly born: I. The term baby. *Journal of Pediatrics 62:* 307–325, 1963.

16. Murphy, W. F., and Langley, A. L. Common bullous lesions—presumably self-inflicted—occurring in utero in the newborn infant. *Pediatrics 32:* 1099–1101, 1963.

17. Brazelton, T. B. *Neonatal Behavioral Assessment Scale, Clinics in Developmental Medicine No. 50.* Spastic International Medical Publication. Philadelphia: J. B. Lippincott, 1973.

Chapter 3: Opening Moves

1. Ashton, R. The state variable in neonatal research: A review. *Merrill-Palmer Quarterly 19:* 4–20, 1973.

2. Thoman, E. B. Sleep and wake behaviors in neonates: consistencies and consequences. *Merrill-Palmer Quarterly 21:* 295–314, 1975.

3. Prechtl, H. F. R. Problems of behavioral studies in the newborn infant. In D. S. Lehrman, R. A. Hinde, and E. Shaw (Eds.) *Advances in the Study of Behavior 1.* New York: Academic Press, 1965, pp. 75–98.

4. Ashton, R. Behavioral sleep cycles in the human newborn. *Child Development 42:* 2098–2100, 1971.

5. Brackbill, Y., and Fitzgerald, H. E. Development of the sensory analyzers during infancy. In L. P. Lipsitt and H. W. Reese (Eds.), *Advances in Child Development and Behavior 4.* New York: Academic Press, 1969, pp. 173–208.

6. Roffwarg, H. P., Muzio, J. N., and Dement, W. C. Ontogenetic development of the human sleep-dream cycle. *Science 152:* 604–619, 1966.

7. Koulack, D. Rapid eye movements and visual imagery during sleep. *Psychological Bulletin 78:* 155–158, 1972.

8. Dobbing, J., and Sands, J. Timing of neuroblast multiplication in developing human brain. *Nature 226:* 639–640, 1970.

9. Boismier, J. D. Visual stimulation and wake-sleep behavior in human neonates. *Developmental Psychobiology 10:* 219–227, 1977.

10. Thoman, E. B. Early development of sleeping behaviors in infants. In N. R. Ellis (Ed.), *Aberrant Development in Infancy: Human and Animal Studies.* New York: John Wiley and Sons, 1975, pp. 123–138.

11. Peiper, A. *Cerebral Function in Infancy and Childhood.* Tr. by B. Nagler and H. Nagler. New York: Consultants Bureau, 1963.

12. Bench, J., Collyer, Y., Langford, C., and Toms, R. A comparison between the neonatal sound-evoked startle response and the head-drop

(Moro) reflex. *Developmental Medicine and Child Neurology 14:* 308–317, 1972.

13. Korner, A. F. Neonatal startles, smiles, erections, and reflex sucks as related to state, sex, and individuality. *Child Development 40:* 1039–1053, 1969.

14. Birns, B. The emergence and socialization of sex differences in the earliest years. *Merrill-Palmer Quarterly 22:* 229–254, 1976.

15. Halverson, H. M. Genital and sphincter behavior of the male infant. *The Journal of Genetic Psychology 56:* 95–136, 1940.

16. Richards, M. P. M., Bernal, J. F., and Brackbill, Y. Early behavioral differences: Gender or circumcision? *Developmental Psychobiology 9:* 89–95, 1976.

17. Eibl-Eibesfeldt, I. *Ethology: The Biology of Behavior.* New York: Holt, Rinehart and Winston, 1970.

18. Simner, M. L. Newborn's response to the cry of another infant. *Developmental Psychology 5:* 136–150, 1971.

19. Darwin, C. *The Expression of the Emotions in Man and Animals.* London: Murray, 1872, and New York: Philosophical Library, 1955, p. 147.

20. Brackbill, Y., Adams, G., Crowell, D. H., and Gray, M. L. Arousal level in neonates and preschool children under continuous auditory stimulation. *Journal of Experimental Child Psychology 4:* 178–188, 1966.

21. Salk, L. Mothers' heartbeat as an imprinting stimulus. *Transactions of the New York Academy of Sciences 24:* 753–763, 1962.

22. Smith, C. R., and Steinschneider, A. Differential effects of prenatal rhythmic stimulation on neonatal arousal states. *Child Development 46:* 574–577, 1975.

23. Brackbill, Y. Cumulative effects of continuous stimulation on arousal level in infants. *Child Development 42:* 17–26, 1971.

24. Brackbill, Y. Continuous stimulation and arousal level in infancy: Effects of stimulus intensity and stress. *Child Development 46:* 364–369, 1975.

25. Bell, S. M., and Ainsworth, M. D. S. Infant crying and maternal responsiveness. *Child Development 43:* 1171–1190, 1972.

26. U.S. Children's Bureau. *Infant Care.* Care of Children Series No. 2. Bureau Publication No. 8 (rev.), 1924, p. 44.

27. Muller, E., Hollien, H., and Murry, T. Perceptual responses to infant crying: Identification of cry types. *Journal of Child Language 1:* 89–95, 1974.

28. Mills, M., and Melhuish, E. Recognition of mother's voice in early infancy. *Nature 252:* 123–124, 1974.

29. Korner, A. F., and Thoman, E. B. Visual alertness in neonates as

evoked by maternal care. *Journal of Experimental Child Psychology 10:* 67–78, 1970.

30. Scarr-Salapatek, S., and Williams, M. L. The effects of early stimulation on low-birth-weight infants. *Child Development 44:* 94–101, 1973.

31. White, J. L., and Labarba, R. C. The effects of tactile and kinesthetic stimulation on neonatal development in the premature infant. *Developmental Psychobiology 9:* 569–577, 1976.

32. Zelazo, P. R., Zelazo, N. A., and Kolb, S. "Walking" in the newborn. *Science 176:* 314–315, 1972.

Chapter 4: First Impressions

1. Peiper, A. *Cerebral Function in Infancy and Childhood.* Tr. by B. Nagler and H. Nagler. New York: Consultants Bureau, 1963.

2. Nowlis, G. H., and Kessen, W. Human newborns differentiate differing concentrations of sucrose and glucose. *Science 191:* 865–866, 1976.

3. Engen, T., Lipsitt, L. P., and Peck, M. B. Ability of newborn infants to discriminate sapid substances. *Developmental Psychology 10:* 741–744, 1974.

4. Lipsitt, L. P., Engen, T., and Kaye, H. Developmental changes in the olfactory threshold of the neonate. *Child Development 34:* 371–376, 1963.

5. Engen, T. Psychophysical analysis of the odor intensity of homologous alcohols. *Developmental Psychology 70:* 611–616, 1965.

6. Rovee, C. K. Psychophysical scaling of olfactory response to the aliphatic alcohols in human neonates. *Journal of Experimental Child Psychology 7:* 245–254, 1969.

7. Russell, M. J. Human olfactory communication. *Nature 260:* 520–522, 1976.

8. Gallup, G. Cancer, blindness top fear listing. *The Hartford Courant,* Dec. 2, 1976.

9. Bornstein, M. Infants are trichromats. *Journal of Experimental Child Psychology 21:* 425–445, 1976.

10. Fantz, R. L. Pattern vision in newborn infants. *Science 140:* 296–297, 1963.

11. Fagan, J. F. III. Infant color perception. *Science 183:* 973–975, 1974.

12. Wooten, B. R. Infant hue discrimination? *Science 187:* 275–277, 1975.

13. Fagan, J. F. III. Infant hue discrimination? *Science 187:* 277, 1975.

14. Peeples, D. R., and Teller, D. Y. Color vision and brightness discrimination in two-month-old human infants. *Science 189:* 1102–1103, 1975.

15. Bornstein, M. H. Qualities of color vision in infancy. *Journal of Experimental Child Psychology 19:* 401–419, 1975.

16. Humphrey, N. Colour and brightness preferences in monkeys. *Nature 229:* 615–617, 1971.

17. Bornstein, M. H. Hue is an absolute code for young children. *Nature 256:* 309–310, 1975.

18. Bornstein, M. H., Kessen, W., and Weiskopf, S. The categories of hue in infancy. *Science 191:* 201–202, 1976.

19. Bornstein, M. H. The influence of visual perception on culture. *American Anthropologist 77:* 774–798, 1975.

20. Bornstein, M. H., Infants' recognition memory for hue. *Developmental Psychology 12:* 185–191, 1976.

21. Milner, A. D., and Bryant, P. E. Cross-modal matching by young children. *Journal of Comparative and Physiological Psychology 71:* 453–458, 1970.

22. Blank, M., and Bridger, W. H. Cross-modal transfer in nursery-school children. *Journal of Comparative and Physiological Psychology 58:* 277–282, 1964.

23. Davenport, R. K., and Rogers, C. M. Intermodal equivalence of stimuli in apes. *Science 168:* 279–280, 1970.

24. Rogers, C. M., and Davenport, R. K. Capacities of nonhuman primates for perceptual integration across sensory modalities. In R. H. Tuttle (Ed.), *Socioecology and Psychology of Primates.* The Hague: Mouton Publishers, 1975, pp. 343–352.

25. Bryant, P. E., Jones, P., Claxton, V., and Perkins, G. M. Recognition of shapes across modalities by infants. *Nature 240:* 303–304, 1972.

26. Gottfried, A. W., Rose, S. A., and Bridger, W. H. Cross-modal transfer in human infants. *Child Development 48:* 118–123, 1977.

27. Allen, T. W., Walker, K., Symonds, L., and Marcell, M. Intra-sensory and intersensory perception of temporal sequences during infancy. *Developmental Psychology 13:* 225–229, 1977.

28. Bower, T. G. R., Broughton, J. M., and Moore, M. K. The coordination of visual and tactual input in infants. *Perception and Psychophysics 8:* 51–53, 1970.

29. Bower, T. G. R. The object in the world of the infant. *Scientific American 225:* 30–38, 1971.

30. Ball, W., and Tronick, E. Infant responses to impending collision: Optical and real. *Science 171:* 818–820, 1971.

31. Bower, T. G. R. *Development in Infancy*. San Francisco: W. H. Freeman and Company, 1974.

32. McKenzie, B. E., and Day, R. H. Object distance as a determinant of visual fixation in early infancy. *Science 178:* 1108–1110, 1972.

33. Kagan, J. The determinants of attention in the infant. *American Scientist 58:* 298–306, 1970.

34. Schaffer, H. R., and Parry, M. H. Perceptual-motor behaviour in infancy as a function of age and stimulus familiarity. *British Journal of Psychology 60:* 1–9, 1969.

35. Miranda, S. B. Visual abilities and pattern preferences of premature infants and full-term neonates. *Journal of Experimental Child Psychology 10:* 189–205, 1970.

36. Salapatek, P., and Kessen, W. Prolonged investigation of a plane geometric triangle by the human newborn. *Journal of Experimental Child Psychology 15:* 22–29, 1973.

37. Salapatek, P. Pattern perception in early infancy. In L. B. Cohen and P. Salapatek (Eds.), *Infant Perception—From Sensation to Cognition;* Vol. I, *Basic Visual Processes*. New York: Academic Press, 1975.

38. Haith, M. M., Bergman, T., and Moore, M. J. Eye contact and face scanning in early infancy. *Science 198:* 853–855, 1977.

39. Fantz, R. L. The origin of form perception. *Scientific American 204:* 66–72, 1961.

40. Wilcox, B. M. Visual preferences of human infants for representations of the human face. *Journal of Experimental Child Psychology 7:* 10–20, 1969.

41. Haaf, R. A., and Brown, C. J. Infants' response to facelike patterns: Developmental changes between 10 and 15 weeks of age. *Journal of Experimental Child Psychology 22:* 155–160, 1976.

42. Thomas, H., and Jones-Molfese, V. Infants and I scales: Inferring change from the ordinal stimulus selections of infants for configural stimuli. *Journal of Experimental Child Psychology 23:* 329–339, 1977.

43. Carpenter, G. C., Tecce, J. J., Stechler, G., and Friedman, S. Differential visual behavior to human and humanoid faces in early infancy. *Merrill-Palmer Quarterly 16:* 91–107, 1970.

44. Kinney, D. K., and Kagan, J. Infant attention to auditory discrepancy. *Child Development 47:* 155–164, 1976.

45. Scaife, M., and Bruner, J. S. The capacity for joint visual attention in the infant. *Nature 253:* 265–266, 1975.

Chapter 5: Learning

1. Watson, J. B. *Psychological Care of Infant and Child*. New York: W. W. Norton, 1928, pp. 45–46.

2. Garrett, H. E. *Great Experiments in Psychology.* New York: D. Appleton-Century, 1941.

3. Fitzgerald, H. E., and Brackbill, Y. Classical conditioning in infancy: Development and constraints. *Psychological Bulletin 83:* 353–376, 1976.

4. Kasatkin, N. I. First conditioned responses and the beginning of the learning process in the human infant. In G. Newton and A. H. Riesen (Eds.), *Advances in Psychobiology.* New York: John Wiley & Sons, 1972, p. 251.

5. Spelt, D. K. The conditioning of the human fetus in utero. *Journal of Experimental Psychology 38:* 338–346, 1948.

6. Lipsitt, L. P. Learning in the first year of life. In L. P. Lipsitt (Ed.), *Advances in Child Development and Behavior 1.* New York: Academic Press, 1963, pp. 147–191, 1963.

7. Marquis, D. P. Can conditioned responses be established in the newborn infant? *Journal of Genetic Psychology 39:* 479–492, 1931.

8. Marquis, D. P. Learning in the neonate: The modification of behavior under three feeding schedules. *Journal of Experimental Psychology 29:* 263–282, 1941.

9. Sostek, A. M., Sameroff, A. J., and Sostek, A. J. Evidence for the unconditionability of the Babkin reflex in newborns. *Child Development 43:* 509–519, 1972.

10. Fitzgerald, H. E., Lintz, L. M., Brackbill, Y., and Adams, G. Time perception and conditioning an autonomic response in human infants. *Perceptual and Motor Skills 24:* 479–487, 1967.

11. Siqueland, E. R., and Lipsitt, L. P. Conditioned head turning in human newborns. *Journal of Experimental Child Psychology 3:* 356–376, 1966.

12. Bower, T. G. R. *Development in Infancy.* San Francisco: W. H. Freeman and Company, 1974.

13. Watson, J. S. The development and generalization of "contingency awareness" in early infancy: Some hypotheses. *Merrill-Palmer Quarterly 12:* 123–135, 1966.

14. Koch, J. Conditioned orienting reactions in two-month-old infants. *British Journal of Psychology 58:* 105–110, 1967.

15. Wahler, R. G. Infant social attachments: A reinforcement theory interpretation and investigation. *Child Development 38:* 1079–1088, 1967.

16. Brackbill, Y. Extinction of the smiling response in infants as a function of reinforcement schedule. *Child Development 29:* 115–124, 1958.

17. Etzel, B. C., and Gewirtz, J. L. Experimental modification of caretaker-maintained high-rate operant crying in a 6- and a 20-week-old infant (*Infans tyrannotearus*): Extinction of crying with reinforcement of eye

contact and smiling. *Journal of Experimental Child Psychology 5:* 303–317, 1967.

18. Skinner, B. F. Superstition in the pigeon. *Journal of Experimental Psychology 38:* 168–172, 1948.

19. Killeen, P. R. Superstition: A matter of bias, not detectability. *Science: 199,* 88–89, 1978.

20. Silversteen, A. Secondary reinforcement in infants. *Journal of Experimental Child Psychology 13:* 138–144, 1972.

21. Bloom, K. Eye contact as a setting event for infant learning. *Journal of Experimental Child Psychology 17:* 250–263, 1974.

22. Piaget, J. *The Origins of Intelligence in Children,* tr. by Margaret Cook. New York: International Universities Press, 1952.

23. Hunt, J. McV. *Intelligence and Experience.* New York: The Ronald Press Company, 1961.

24. Abravanel, E., Levan-Goldsmidt, E., and Stevenson, M. B. Action initiation: The early phase of infancy. *Child Development 47:* 1032–1044, 1976.

25. Parton, D. A. Learning to imitate in infancy. *Child Development 47:* 14–31, 1976.

26. Meltzoff, A. N., and Moore, M. K. Imitation of facial and manual gestures by human neonates. *Science 198:* 75–78, 1977.

27. Meltzoff, A. N. Personal communication.

28. Bower, T. G. R. *The Perceptual World of the Child.* Cambridge, Mass.: Harvard University Press, 1977.

29. Kagan, J. Do infants think? *Scientific American 226:* 74–82, 1972.

Chapter 6: Delight and Distress

1. Darwin, C. *The Expression of the Emotions in Man and Animals.* New York: Philosophical Library, 1955; Chicago: University of Chicago Press, 1965; first published, London: Murray, 1872.

2. Darwin, C. I.—A biographical sketch of an infant. *Mind: A Quarterly Review of Psychology and Philosophy 2:* 285–294, 1877.

3. Haviland, J. Looking smart: The relationship between affect and intelligence in infancy. In M. Lewis (Ed.), *Origins of Intelligence: Infancy and Early Childhood.* New York: Plenum Press, 1976, pp. 353–377.

4. Young, G., and Décarie, T. G. An ethology-based catalogue of facial/vocal behaviour in infancy. *Animal Behaviour 25:* 95–107, 1977.

5. Watson, J. B. Experimental studies on the growth of the emotions. *The Pedagogical Seminary and Journal of Genetic Psychology 32:* 328–348, 1925.

6. Watson, J. B. *Psychological Care of Infant and Child.* New York: W. W. Norton & Company, 1928.

7. Ekman, P. (Ed.) *Darwin and Facial Expression—A Century of Research in Review.* New York: Academic Press, 1973.

8. Casey, W. S. Personal communication to one of the authors.

9. Bridges, K. M. B. Emotional development in early infancy. *Child Development 3:* 324–341, 1932.

10. Thoman, E. B. Early development of sleeping behaviors in infants. In N. R. Ellis (Ed.), *Aberrant Development in Infancy: Human and Animal Studies.* New York: John Wiley & Sons, 1975.

11. Wolff, P. H. Observations of the early development of smiling. In B. M. Foss (Ed.), *Determinants of Infant Behaviour,* London: Methuen & Company, 1963, Vol. 2, pp. 113–138.

12. Robson, K. S. The role of eye-to-eye contact in maternal-infant attachment. *Journal of Child Psychology and Psychiatry 8:* 13–25, 1967.

13. Brazelton, T. B., Koslowski, B., and Main, M. The origins of reciprocity: The early mother-infant interaction. In M. Lewis and L. A. Rosenblum (Eds.), *The Effect of the Infant on Its Caregiver.* New York: John Wiley & Sons, 1974, pp. 49–76. Brazelton, T. B., Tronick, E., Als, H., and Wise, S. Early mother-infant reciprocity. In *Parent-Infant Interaction.* New York: Associated Scientific Publishers, 1975, pp. 137–154. Tronick, E., Als, H., and Adamson, L. Structure of early face-to-face communicative interactions. In M. Bullowa (Ed.), *Before Speech—The Beginnings of Human Communication.* Cambridge, Eng.: Cambridge University Press, in press.

14. Field, T. M. Effects of early separation, interactive deficits, and experimental manipulations on infant-mother face-to-face interaction. *Child Development 48:* 763–771, 1977.

15. Thoman, E. B., Becker, P. T., and Freese, M. P. Individual patterns of mother-infant interaction. Conference on Application of Observational Ethological Methods to the Study of Mental Retardation, Lake Wilderness, Washington, 1976.

16. Spitz, R. A. *The First Year of Life.* New York: International Universities Press, 1965.

17. Ainsworth, M. D. S. Object relations, dependency, and attachment: A theoretical review of the infant-mother relationship. *Child Development 40:* 969–1025, 1969.

18. Harlow, H. F., Harlow, M. K., and Suomi, S. J. From thought to therapy—Lessons from a primate laboratory. *American Scientist 59:* 538–549, 1971.

19. Bowlby, J. *Attachment and Loss;* Vol. I, *Attachment.* London: Hogarth, 1969.

20. Ainsworth, M. D. S. The development of infant-mother attachment. In B. M. Caldwell and H. N. Ricciuti (Eds.), *Review of Child*

Development Research 3. Chicago: The University of Chicago Press, 1973, pp. 1–94.

21. Rosenblum, L. A., and Youngstein, K. P. Developmental changes in compensatory dyadic response in mother and infant monkeys. In M. Lewis and L. A. Rosenblum (Eds.), *The Effect of the Infant on Its Caregiver*. New York: John Wiley & Sons, 1974.

22. Bell, S. M. The development of the concept of object as related to infant-mother attachment. *Child Development 41:* 291–311, 1970.

23. Landau, R. Extent that the mother represents the social stimulation to which the infant is exposed: Findings from a cross-cultural study. *Developmental Psychology 12:* 399–405, 1976.

24. Lamb, M. E. Father-infant and mother-infant interaction in the first year of life. *Child Development 48:* 167–181, 1977.

25. Bridges, K. M. B. A study of social development in early infancy. *Child Development 4:* 36–52, 1933.

26. Becker, J. M. T. A learning analysis of the development of peer-oriented behavior in nine-month-old infants. *Developmental Psychology 13:* 481–491, 1977.

27. LaBarbera, J. D., Izard, C. E., Vietze, P., and Parisi S. A. Four- and six-month-old infants' visual responses to joy, anger, and neutral expressions. *Child Development 47:* 535–538, 1976.

28. Young-Browne, G., Rosenfeld, H. M., and Horowitz, F. D. Infant discrimination of facial expressions. *Child Development 48:* 555–562, 1977.

Chapter 7: Discovery

1. Rheingold, H. L., and Eckerman, C. O. The infant separates himself from his mother. *Science 168:* 78–83, 1970.

2. Bower, T. G. R. *Development in Infancy*. San Francisco: W. H. Freeman, 1974.

3. Hutt, C. Specific and diversive exploration. In H. W. Reese and L. P. Lipsitt (Eds.), *Advances in Child Development and Behavior 5:* 119–180, 1970.

4. Rheingold, H. L. The effect of environmental stimulation upon social and exploratory behaviour in the human infant. In B. M. Foss (Ed.), *Determinants of Infant Behaviour 1:* London: Methuen, 143–171, 1961.

5. Fenson, L., Kagan, J., Kearsley, R. B., and Zelazo, P. R. The developmental progression of manipulative play in the first two years. *Child Development 47:* 232–236, 1976.

6. Rheingold, H. L. The effect of a strange environment on the behavior of infants. In B. M. Foss (Ed.), *Determinants of Infant Behaviour 4:* London: Methuen, 1969, 137–166.

7. Rheingold, H. L., and Eckerman, C. O. The infant's free entry into a new environment. *Journal of Experimental Child Psychology 8:* 271–283, 1969.

8. Ross, H. S. The influence of novelty and complexity on exploratory behavior in 12-month-old infants. *Journal of Experimental Child Psychology 17:* 436–451, 1974.

9. Schaffer, H. R., and Parry, M. H. Perceptual-motor behaviour in infancy as a function of age and stimulus familiarity. *British Journal of Psychology 60:* 1–9, 1969.

10. Schaffer, H. R., Greenwood, A., and Parry, M. H. The onset of wariness. *Child Development 43:* 165–175, 1972.

11. Rubenstein, J. Concordance of visual and manipulative responsiveness to novel and familiar stimuli: A function of test procedures or of prior experience? *Child Development 47:* 1197–1199, 1976.

12. Rheingold, H. L., and Eckerman, C. O. Fear of the stranger: A critical examination. In H. W. Reese (Ed.), *Advances in Child Development and Behavior 8:* New York: Academic Press, 1973, pp. 185–222.

13. Children's Bureau, U.S. Department of Health, Education, and Welfare, Publication No. 3, *Infant Care.* Washington, D.C.: U.S. Government Printing Office, 1963, reprinted 1969, p. 42.

14. Bronson, G. W. Infants' reactions to unfamiliar persons and novel objects. In *Monographs of the Society for Research in Child Development 37:* 1972, pp. 1–45.

15. Waters, E., Matas, L., and Sroufe, L. A. Infants' reactions to an approaching stranger: Description, validation, and functional significance of wariness. *Child Development 46:* 348–356, 1975.

16. McGhee, P. E. Development of the humor response: A review of the literature. *Psychological Bulletin 76:* 328–348, 1971.

17. Darwin, C. *The Expression of the Emotions in Man and Animals.* New York: Philosophical Library, 1955. (First published 1872.)

18. Washburn, R. W. A study of the smiling and laughing of infants in the first year of life. *Genetic Psychology Monographs 6:* 397–537, 1929.

19. Sroufe, L. A., and Wunsch, J. P. The development of laughter in the first year of life. *Child Development 43:* 1326–1344, 1972.

Chapter 8: Roger and Over

1. Condon, W. S., and Sander, L. W. Neonate movement is synchronized with adult speech: Interactional participation and language acquisition. *Science 183:* 99–101, 1974.

2. Condon, W. S., and Ogston, W. D. Sound film analysis of normal

and pathological behavior patterns. *The Journal of Nervous and Mental Disease 143:* 338–347, 1966.

3. Liberman, A. M., Harris, K. S., Kinney, J. A., and Lane, H. The discrimination of relative onset-time of the components of certain speech and nonspeech patterns. *Journal of Experimental Psychology 61:* 379–388, 1961.

4. Eimas, P. D., Siqueland, E. R., Jusczyk, P., and Vigorito, J. Speech perception in infants. *Science 171:* 303–306, 1971.

5. Butterfield, E. C., and Cairns, G. F. Discussion summary—Infant reception research. In R. L. Schiefelbusch and L. L. Lloyd (Eds.), *Language Perspectives—Acquisition, Retardation, and Intervention.* Baltimore: University Park Press, 1974, pp. 75–102.

6. Hutt, S. J., Hutt, C., Lenard, H. G., v Bernuth, H., and Muntjewerff, W. J. Auditory responsivity in the human neonate. *Nature 218:* 888–890, 1968.

7. Streeter, L. A. Language perception of 2-month-old infants shows effects of both innate mechanisms and experience. *Nature 259:* 39–41, 1976.

8. Eimas, P. D. Speech perception in early infancy. In L. B. Cohen and P. Salapatek (Eds.), *Infant Perception: From Sensation to Cognition;* Vol. II, *Perception of Space, Speech, and Sound.* New York: Academic Press, 1975, pp. 193–231.

9. Moffitt, A. R. Consonant cue perception by twenty- to twenty-four-week-old infants. *Child Development 42:* 717–731, 1971.

10. Morse, P. A. The discrimination of speech and nonspeech stimuli in early infancy. *Journal of Experimental Child Psychology 14:* 477–492, 1972.

11. Graham, F. K., Leavitt, L. A., and Strock, B. D. Precocious cardiac orienting in a human anencephalic infant. *Science 199:* 322–324, 1978.

12. Kuhl, P. K., and Miller, J. D. Speech perception by the chinchilla: Voiced-voiceless distinction in alveolar plosive consonants. *Science 190:* 69–72, 1975.

13. Mattingly, I. G. Speech cues and sign stimuli. *American Scientist 60:* 327–337, 1972.

14. Friedlander, B. Z. Receptive language development in infancy: Issues and problems. *Merrill-Palmer Quarterly 16:* 7–51, 1970.

15. Jones-Molfese, V. Preferences of infants for regular and distorted natural speech stimuli. *Journal of Experimental Child Psychology 23:* 172–179, 1977.

16. Friedlander, B. Z. The effect of speaker identity, voice inflection, vocabulary, and message redundancy on infants' selection of vocal reinforcement. *Journal of Experimental Child Psychology 6:* 443–459, 1968.

17. Bloom, L. Talking, understanding, and thinking. In R. L. Schiefelbusch and L. L. Lloyd (Eds.), *Language Perspectives—Acquisition, Retardation, and Intervention.* Baltimore: University Park Press, 1974, pp. 285–311.

18. Taine, H. A. Taine on the acquisition of language by children. Reports, *Mind: A Quarterly Review of Psychology and Philosophy 2:* 252–259, 1877. Tr. from *Revue Philosophique,* No. 1, Jan. 1876.

19. Darwin C. I.—A biographical sketch of an infant. *Mind: A Quarterly Review of Psychology and Philosophy 2:* 285–294, 1877.

20. Stark, R. E., Rose, S. N., and McLagen, M. Features of infant sounds: The first eight weeks of life. *Journal of Child Language 2:* 205–221, 1975.

21. Cazden, C. B. *Child Language and Education.* New York: Holt, Rinehart and Winston, 1972.

22. Lieberman, P., Crelin, E. S., and Klatt, D. H. Phonetic ability and related anatomy of the newborn and adult human, Neanderthal man, and the chimpanzee. *American Anthropologist 74:* 287–307, 1972.

23. Lieberman, P. On the evolution of language: A unified view. In R. H. Tuttle (Ed.), *Primate Functional Morphological Evolution.* The Hague: Mouton Publishers, 1975, pp. 501–551.

24. Oller, D. K., Wieman, L. A., Doyle, W. J., and Ross, C. Infant babbling and speech. *Journal of Child Language 3:* 1–11, 1976.

25. Trevarthen, C. Project reports: Department of Psychology, University of Edinburgh: Prespeech in communication of infants with adults. *Journal of Child Language 1:* 335–337, 1974.

26. Trevarthen, C. Conversations with a 2-month-old. *New Scientist 62:* 230–235, 1974.

27. Rheingold, H. L., Gewirtz, J. L., and Ross, H. W. Social conditioning of vocalizations in the infant. *Journal of Comparative and Physiological Psychology 52:* 68–73, 1959.

28. Weisberg, P. Social and nonsocial conditioning of infant vocalizations. *Child Development 34:* 377–388, 1963.

29. Todd, G. A., and Palmer, B. Social reinforcement of infant babbling. *Child Development 39:* 591–596, 1968.

30. Bloom, K., and Esposito, A. Social conditioning and its proper control procedures. *Journal of Experimental Child Psychology 19:* 209–222, 1975.

31. Bloom, K. Social elicitation of infant vocal behavior. *Journal of Experimental Child Psychology 20:* 51–58, 1975.

32. McCall, R. B. Smiling and vocalization in infants as indices of perceptual-cognitive processes. *Merrill-Palmer Quarterly 18:* 341–347, 1972.

228 **References**

33. Kagan, J. *Change and Continuity in Infancy.* New York: John Wiley & Sons, 1971.

34. Zelazo, P. R., Kagan, J., and Hartmann, R. Excitement and boredom as determinants of vocalization in infants. *The Journal of Genetic Psychology 126:* 107–117, 1975.

35. Birns, B. The emergence and socialization of sex differences in the earliest years. *Merrill-Palmer Quarterly 22:* 229–254, 1976.

36. Cohen, S. E., and Beckwith, L. Maternal language in infancy. *Developmental Psychology 12:* 371–372, 1976.

37. Tulkin, S. R., and Kagan, J. Mother-child interaction in the first year of life. *Child Development 43:* 31–41, 1972.

38. Snow, C. E. The development of conversation between mothers and babies. *Journal of Child Language 4:* 1–22, 1977.

39. Ferguson, C. A. Baby talk in six languages. *American Anthropology 66:* 103–114. 1964.

Chapter 9: Nature and Nurture

1. Bridger, W. M., and Birns, B. Experience and temperament in human neonates. In G. Newton and S. Levine (Eds.). *Early Experience and Behavior: The Psychobiology of Development.* Springfield, Ill.: Charles C Thomas, 1968.

2. Thomas, A., Chess, S., Birch, H. G., Hertzig, M. E., and Korn, S. *Behavioral Individuality in Early Childhood.* New York: New York University Press, 1963.

3. Thomas, A., Chess S., and Birch, H. G. The origin of personality. *Scientific American 223:* 102–109, 1970.

4. Chess, S. Individuality in children, its importance to the pediatrician. *The Journal of Pediatrics 69:* 676–684, 1966.

5. Flaste, R. Temperament's role—Infants she studies are now grown. *New York Times,* Jan. 31, 1975.

6. Caudill, W., and Weinstein, H. Maternal care and infant behavior in Japan and America. *Psychiatry 32:* 12–43, 1969.

7. Freedman, D. G., and Freedman, N. C. Behavioural differences between Chinese-American and European-American newborns. *Nature 224:* 1227, 1969.

8. Rebelsky, F., and Daniel, P. A. Cross cultural studies of infant intelligence. In M. Lewis (Ed.), *Origins of Intelligence: Infancy and Early Childhood.* New York: Plenum Press, 1976, pp. 279–297.

9. Whiting, B. B. (Ed.). *Six Cultures: Studies in Child Rearing.* New York: John Wiley & Sons, 1963.

10. Leiderman, P. H., Babu, B., Kaglia, J., Kramer, H. C., and Leiderman, G. L. African infant precocity and some social influences during the first year. *Nature 242:* 247–249, 1973.

11. Werner, E. E. Infants around the world—Cross-cultural studies of psychomotor development from birth to two years. *Journal of Cross-Cultural Psychology 3:* 111–134, 1972.

12. Konner, M. Infancy among the Kalahari Desert San. In P. H. Leiderman, S. R. Tulkin, and A. Rosenfeld (Eds.), *Culture and Infancy: Variations in the Human Experience.* New York: Academic Press, 1977, pp. 287–328.

13. Kagan, J., and Klein, R. E. Cross-cultural perspectives on early development. *American Psychologist 28:* 947–961, 1973.

Index

Newborn *(cont'd)*
  orienting reactions, 25
  as research subjects, 27
  responses to social stimulation, 25
  self-consolation, 25–26
  spontaneous activities, 22–23, 33–34
Non-nutritive sucking, 163
Non-rapid-eye-movement sleep, *see*
    NREM sleep
Novelty, responses to, 68, 74–75
  in exploration, 145–47
  wariness of, 147–50, 154
  see also Complexity, responses to
Nowlis, G. H., 48–49
NREM (non-rapid-eye-movement)
    sleep, 28–29, 30–33

Object permanence, 76–77, 100, 101,
    104–105
  and person permanence, 129–30
  test of, 129
Object relations, 125
Orienting reactions, 25
  in attachment, 126
  in exploration, 139
  instrumental conditioning of, 88–89

Pacification
  by continuous stimulation, 39–41
  by maternal interventions, 41–42
  by mother's heartbeat, 38
  by swaddling, 39
Palmomental reflex, 17
Parents, *see* Father; Mother
Parry, M. H., 147–50
Pavlov, I., 78–79, 85
Peiper, A., 50–51
Perception
  categorical, of phonemes, 162, 164
  of collision path, 65–66
  of color, 54–61
  of distance, 66–68
  of rhythm, 10–11
  of speech, 162–67
Permanence, *see* Object permanence;
    Person permanence
Persistence, 193
Personality
  inferred from facial expressions, 109–
    10

  see also Temperament
Person permanence
  and attachment, 129–30
  and object permanence, 129–30
Phonemes
  categorical perception of, 162
  production of, 161–62
  as sign stimuli, 167–68
  voiced, prevoiced, and voiceless, 162
Piaget, J., 48, 79, 98–105, 124, 142
Play
  banging in, 142–43
  compared with exploration, 140
  development of, 101, 142–43
  in infant pairs, 136–37
  symbolic, 142–43
  see also Exploration
Play dialogue, 118
Play face 110
Precocity in undeveloped cultures, 206–
    12
Preferences
  color, 55–59
  for complexity, 68–69
  for faces, 69–72
  food, 1–4, 50–51
  for mothers, versus strangers, 89–90
  speech, 168–72
  taste, 1–4, 47–50
Pregnancy, attitudes toward, 21–22
Premature infants
  classical conditioning of, 81–82
  extra stimulation of, 44–46
  hyperactivity of, 40
Problem solving, 86–87, 105
Proximity behavior
  in bonnet macaques, 126–28
  in human infants, 126–28, 134–36
Pseudoimitation, 101
Psychoanalytic theory of attachment,
    124–26
Puberty
  attraction to infants at, 7
Pupillary reflex
  conditioning of, 84–85

"Quickening" of fetus, 14

Rank, O., 18–19
Rapid-eye-movement sleep, *see* REM